T0330156

Measuring the Global Shadow Economy

Measuring the Global Shadow Economy

The Prevalence of Informal Work and Labour

Colin C. Williams

Professor of Public Policy, School of Management, University of Sheffield, UK

Friedrich Schneider

Professor of Economics and Public Finance, Johannes Kepler University of Linz, Austria

Edward Elgar
PUBLISHING

Cheltenham, UK • Northampton, MA, USA

© Colin C. Williams and Friedrich Schneider 2016

All rights reserved. No part of this publication may be reproduced, stored in a retrieval system or transmitted in any form or by any means, electronic, mechanical or photocopying, recording, or otherwise without the prior permission of the publisher.

Published by
Edward Elgar Publishing Limited
The Lypiatts
15 Lansdown Road
Cheltenham
Glos GL50 2JA
UK

Edward Elgar Publishing, Inc.
William Pratt House
9 Dewey Court
Northampton
Massachusetts 01060
USA

A catalogue record for this book
is available from the British Library

Library of Congress Control Number: 2015950275

This book is available electronically in the **Elgar**online
Economics subject collection
DOI 10.4337/9781784717995

ISBN 978 1 78471 798 8 (cased)
ISBN 978 1 78471 799 5 (eBook)

Typeset by Servis Filmsetting Ltd, Stockport, Cheshire
Printed and bound in Great Britain by TJ International Ltd, Padstow

Contents

Acknowledgements

It takes a long time to write a book. As such, both authors owe a debt of gratitude to their home universities, namely the University of Sheffield and Johannes Kepler University of Linz for making the time available to do so. Without such support, this book would not have been possible. Colin Williams is also grateful to the financial support provided by the European Commission's Framework 7 Industry–Academia Partnerships Programme (IAPP) grant no. 611259, which released further time and resources to enable this book to be written.

Besides this institutional support, there are numerous individuals who have freely given their time in helping us to formulate our ideas on measuring the shadow economy and shadow labour force over the years. In this regard and in alphabetical order, we would like to express our thanks to Kwame Adom, Marijana Baric, Pauline Dibben, Rositsa Dzhekova, Josip Franic, Anjula Gurtoo, Jason Heyes, Usman Ladan, Mark Lansky, Enrico Marcelli, Alvaro Martinez-Perez, Lybuo Mishkov, Olga Onoshchenko, Marina Polak, Abel Polese, Peter Rodgers, Piet Renooy, John Round, Abdoulie Sallah, Arnis Sauka, Joanna Shapland, Muhammad Shehryar, Ruslan Stefanov, Richard White, Jan Windebank and Youssef Youssef. Our sincere apologies to anybody we have forgotten. As always, however, the usual disclaimers apply.

1. Introduction

What methods can be used to measure the varying size and character of the shadow economy across the world? How can the resultant cross-national variations in the prevalence and nature of the shadow economy be explained? And what policy approaches can be used to tackle the shadow economy? This book seeks answers to these questions. Indeed, whenever we as authors give talks on the shadow economy, or listen to others giving talks, one of the first questions asked by audiences not familiar with the subject is whether it is possible to conduct research on work that is not declared to the authorities for tax, social security or labour law purposes. Given that such activities by definition exist in the shadows and are hidden from view, they are correct to question the validity of any measurements of its size or character. Indeed, researching a form of work hidden from the authorities for tax, social security and/or labour law purposes is without doubt a difficult task. Nevertheless, just because something is difficult does not mean that it should not be attempted. Neither does the fact that it is hidden from the authorities mean that it cannot be uncovered. On the one hand, it is wholly possible to expose the extent and character of such work using indirect measurement methods that identify such work in statistical indicators collected for other purposes. On the other hand, and perhaps more contentiously, it can also be at least partially uncovered using surveys. Just because it is hidden from the authorities does not mean that it is necessarily hidden from academics doing research on this topic. Although illegal in the sense that it is not declared to the authorities when it should be, it is often viewed as socially legitimate to engage in such endeavour. The result is that participants will frequently openly discuss in conversation with researchers their engagement in such activity in much the same way as they might discuss participating in voluntary work.

It is not just how this activity can be uncovered, however, that this book addresses. Just as important are the findings these measurement methods produce and what they tell us about the distribution of the shadow economy across the world and its determinants. For much of the twentieth century, the shadow economy was widely perceived as a leftover or residue from some previous mode of production and as steadily disappearing with economic development and the modernization of economies (Lewis, 1959).

What the development of measurement methods that estimate the size of the shadow economy have revealed, however, is that such endeavour does not merely prevail in a few marginal enclaves of the global economy. Rather, and as this book will reveal, it is a persistent and extensive feature of the global economic landscape not only in the developing world but also in the post-socialist transition economies as well as the developed world. It is also a phenomenon that is not solely related to the level of economic development of countries. Many other macro-level conditions also influence the prevalence and nature of the shadow economy.

Understanding the extent and nature of the shadow economy and its determinants, of course, is not simply an 'academic exercise' (in the derogatory sense meaning of little practical use or value). Indeed, quite the opposite is the case. Throughout the world, tackling the shadow economy has moved near the top of policy agendas of governments and supra-national agencies, including the World Bank, International Labour Organization and European Commission. Until now, however, and compared with the amount of scholarship dedicated to measuring its size and character, rather scant attention has been paid by academic commentators to what should be done to tackle the shadow economy. Here, therefore, we wish to start filling this gap by examining the various policy approaches that are available for tackling this sphere in order to more fully understand what might be done to address this extensive and omnipresent sphere.

Before starting to address these issues, however, this introductory chapter first needs to define what we here mean by the shadow economy; second, to explain the reasons why it is important to understand and tackle the shadow economy; and third and finally, to provide an outline of the structure of this book.

DEFINING THE SHADOW ECONOMY

What this book refers to as the 'shadow economy' is known by many other names. Indeed, Table 1.1 lists 44 different adjectives and ten different nouns sometimes used to denote this realm. Analysing the multifarious adjectives used, what becomes quickly apparent is that all describe what is absent, insufficient or missing with regard to work in the shadow economy relative to work in the formal economy. Such endeavour is seen to be for example undeclared, unregulated, unreported, unobserved, irregular, illegitimate and off-the-books.

To denote what is missing or absent, three broad types of definition have been used, namely enterprise-, jobs- and activity-based definitions. Although these three types of definition adopt a different unit of analysis

Table 1.1   Adjectives and nouns used to denote shadow economy

Adjectives			
Bazaar	Black	Cash-in-hand	Clandestine
Concealed	Diverse	Dual	Everyday
Ghetto	Grey	Hidden	Illegal
Illegitimate	Illicit	Informal	Invisible
Irregular	Marginal	Moonlight	Non-observed
Non-official	Occult	Off-the-books	Other
Parallel	Peripheral	Precarious	Second
Shadow	Submerged	Subterranean	System D
Twilight	Undeclared	Underground	Under-the-table
Unexposed	Unobserved	Unofficial	Unorganized
Unrecorded	Unreported	Unregulated	Untaxed
Nouns			
Activity	Economic activity	Economy	Endeavour
Enterprise	Entrepreneurship	Employment	Sector
Sphere	Work		

when defining the shadow economy, what all have in common is that they define the shadow economy in terms of what is absent from, missing or insufficient about enterprises, jobs or activities in the shadow economy relative to enterprises, jobs and activities in the formal economy. That is to say, enterprise-based definitions denote what is missing, absent or insufficient about shadow economy enterprises compared with formal enterprises, jobs-based definitions; what is missing, absent or insufficient about shadow jobs relative to formal jobs and activity-based definitions; what is missing, absent or insufficient about shadow economic activities compared with formal economic activities. Here, we briefly review each type of definition in turn.

The most commonly used enterprise-based definition is that adopted by the 15th International Conference of Labour Statisticians (ICLS) in 1993 (Hussmanns, 2005; ILO, 2011, 2012), which defines enterprises in the shadow economy as 'private unincorporated enterprises that are unregistered or small in terms of the number of employed persons' (ILO, 2012, p. 1). Here, what is meant by each of the terms in this definition is required. By an 'unincorporated' enterprise is meant a production unit that is not constituted as a separate legal entity independent of the individual (or group of individuals) who owns it, and for which no complete set of accounts is kept. An enterprise is deemed to be 'unregistered', meanwhile, when it is not registered under specific forms of national legislation (e.g., factories' or commercial acts, tax or social security laws, professional groups' regulatory acts). The issuing of a trade licence or business permit under local regulations does not qualify as registration. An enterprise is considered 'small', meanwhile, when its size in terms of employment is below a specific threshold (e.g., five employees) determined according to national circumstances (Hussmanns, 2005; ILO, 2011, 2012).

Given the recognition that not all employment in the shadow economy is found in shadow enterprises, and that many employed in the shadow economy work in formal enterprises, a shift has taken place from an enterprise-based to a jobs-based definition of the shadow economy. The most widely used jobs-based definition is that adopted by the 17th ICLS in 2003. This defines jobs in the shadow economy as those jobs lacking basic social or legal protections or employment benefits (ILO, 2011, p. 12). Persons in such jobs include: (a) own-account workers and employers employed in their own shadow enterprises; (b) members of informal producers' cooperatives (not established as legal entities); (c) own-account workers producing goods exclusively for own final use by their household (if considered employed given that the production comprises an important contribution to the total household consumption and is included in the national definition of employment); (d) contributing family workers in formal or shadow enterprises; and (e) employees holding shadow jobs in formal enterprises, shadow enterprises or as paid domestic workers employed by households. As regards (e), employees have shadow jobs if their employment relationship is, in law or in practice, not subject to national labour legislation, income taxation, social protection or entitlement to certain employment benefits (e.g., advance notice of dismissal, severance pay, paid annual or sick leave). The reasons may be the following: non-declaration of the jobs or the employees; casual jobs or jobs of a limited short duration; jobs with hours of work or wages below a specified threshold; employment by unincorporated enterprises or by persons in households; jobs where the employee's place of work is outside the premises of the employer's enterprise; or jobs for which labour regulations are not applied, not enforced or not complied with for any other reason (ILO, 2011, p. 12).

These enterprise- and jobs-based definitions have been most commonly used when studying such endeavour in developing nations. In developed nations, however, enterprise- and/or jobs-based definitions have been less popular. This is because they view enterprises and jobs dichotomously as either shadow or formal. In the developed world nevertheless, there has been growing recognition that much work in the shadow economy is concurrently both. On the one hand, and on enterprises, there is a burgeoning literature that a considerable proportion of shadow work is in formal enterprises that undertake a portion of their work in the shadow economy (Small Business Council, 2004; Williams, 2006a, 2009b, 2010b). On the other hand, and with regard to jobs, there is growing recognition that many formal employees receive from formal employers part of their wage as a declared salary and part cash-in-hand as an undeclared ('envelope') salary (Karpuskiene, 2007; Meriküll and Staehr, 2010; Neef, 2002; Sedlenieks, 2003; Williams, 2009c, 2010a, 2012a, 2012b, 2013c, 2013d, 2014b; Woolfson, 2007; Žabko and Rajevska, 2007). These prominent types of shadow economic activity in developed countries are not included in enterprise-based definitions since this work is in a formal enterprise, and not in jobs-based definitions since the worker is in a formal job (Hussmanns, 2005).

The result is that developed nations have largely adopted activity-based definitions of the shadow economy (Eurofound, 2013; European Commission, 1998, 2007b; Renooy et al., 2004; Sepulveda and Syrett, 2007; Thomas, 1992; Vanderseypen et al., 2013; Williams 2006a; Williams and Windebank, 1995, 1998). The most frequently adopted is the activity-based definition published in 2002 by the Organisation for Economic Co-operation and Development (OECD), International Monetary Fund (IMF), International Labour Organization (ILO) and Interstate Statistical Committee of the Commonwealth of Independent States (CIS STAT) as a supplement to the System of National Accounts (SNA) 1993. This defines 'underground production' (or what is here termed the 'shadow economy') as,

> all legal production activities that are deliberately concealed from public authorities for the following kinds of reasons: to avoid payment of income, value added or other taxes; to avoid payment of social security contributions; to avoid having to meet certain legal standards such as minimum wages, maximum hours, safety or health standards, etc.
>
> (OECD, 2002, p. 139)

Indeed, other activity-based definitions of the shadow economy used in developed nations align closely with this OECD definition. For example, Schneider et al. (2010) similarly define the shadow economy as all market-based legal production of goods and services that are deliberately concealed from public authorities to avoid either payment of taxes, social security contributions or legal labour market standards (e.g., minimum wages, maximum working hours, safety standards). Likewise, although no official definition of the shadow economy exists across the 28 member states of the European Union (EU-28), the most widely used definition is the activity-based definition adopted by the European Commission. This defines the shadow economy as 'any paid activities that are lawful as regards their nature but not declared to the public authorities, taking into account the differences in the regulatory system of Member States' (European Commission, 2007b, p. 2).

There is thus a broad consensus across these activity-based definitions regarding what is included and excluded from the shadow economy. The only absence or insufficiency is that shadow economic activities are not declared to the authorities for tax, social security and/or labour law purposes when they should be declared. If activities possess additional absences or insufficiencies, they tend not to be defined as the shadow economy. For example, if the economic activity is also illegal in terms of the goods and services provided (e.g., illegal drug-trafficking), then these activities are viewed as separate from the shadow economy and defined as 'criminal' activities, while if the economic activity is unpaid, it is defined as belonging to the 'unpaid' sphere rather than the shadow economy.

Of course, and as with any definition, blurred edges exist. Some economic activities are neither reimbursed with monetary income and nor are they unpaid. Rather, they are recompensed in-kind using reciprocal labour or via gifts for the work conducted. In this book, wherever feasible, all economic activities remunerated, either with money or in-kind, are included. As such, barter and the in-kind exchange of services are included since these are often supposed to be declared, albeit usually only above a certain threshold. Indeed, including these activities is particularly important in countries where payment in-kind is a common practice. Here therefore, the shadow economy is viewed as any remunerated activities not declared to the authorities for tax, social security and/or labour law purposes when they should be declared. Wherever feasible to do so, depending on the datasets available, this will be the definition used throughout this book.

WHY STUDY THE SHADOW ECONOMY?

To understand the reasons for studying the shadow economy, it is important and necessary to understand the consequences of its existence for various groups, namely formal businesses, shadow economy enterprises, shadow economy workers, customers of the shadow economy, the wider economy and society, and governments. In the early literature on the shadow economy, the tendency was to highlight solely the negative consequences of the shadow economy (e.g., Castells and Portes, 1989). Since the turn of the millennium, however, a more balanced approach has gradually begun to emerge and there has been a growing recognition that sometimes the shadow economy might have some positive consequences. In this section, therefore, we take each of these groups affected by the shadow economy in turn and review both the negative as well as the positive consequences of the shadow economy for each group. At the outset, however, it needs to be stated that although few attempts have been made to enumerate these negative and positive consequences, the widespread consensus is that the negative consequences far outweigh the positive consequences, and that action is therefore required to reduce the size of the shadow economy.

Formal Businesses

The rationale for tackling the shadow economy so far as formal businesses are concerned is that it results in unfair competition. Shadow economy enterprises have an unfair competitive advantage over formal businesses since they do not necessarily conform to labour laws or health and safety legislation, and they evade taxes and social security payments (Andrews et al., 2011; Bajada and Schneider, 2005; Evans et al., 2006; Grabiner, 2000; Karlinger, 2013; Renooy et al., 2004; Small Business Council, 2004). Indeed, if such shadow enterprises take a significant market share and/or hinder the development and growth of formal businesses, these formal businesses may themselves start to consider whether they should any longer conform to the legal 'rules of the game'. The outcome is that deregulatory cultures may emerge where formal businesses themselves start to operate partially or fully in the shadow economy, and businesses already conducting a portion of their trade in the shadow economy conduct an even greater proportion in the shadows (Gallin, 2001; Grabiner, 2000; Mateman and Renooy, 2001; Small Business Council, 2004; Williams and Windebank, 1998). The outcome is a vicious downward spiral in which ever greater proportions of trade take place in the shadow economy. To prevent this from happening, it is therefore necessary for governments to ensure the 'rule of law' and that businesses operating in the shadow economy are detected and encouraged to move out of the shadow economy.

The consequences of the shadow economy, however, are not universally negative for formal businesses. One positive consequence of the shadow economy is that it acts as an incubator for business start-ups where they can 'test-trade' their business venture in order to see whether it is viable before deciding whether to create a fully formal and legitimate business venture (Williams and Martinez-Perez, 2014a). Indeed, in the UK, for example, some one-fifth of what are now formal enterprises test-traded in the shadow economy before formally registering their business (Williams and Martinez-Perez, 2014c). As Autio and Fu (2015) have shown, some two-thirds of businesses start up without registration in the shadow economy not only in emerging and transition economies (where 0.62 unregistered businesses are created annually for every 100 people compared with 0.37

registered businesses) but also in OECD countries (where 0.62 unregistered businesses compared with 0.43 registered businesses are annually created for every 100 people).

A further advantage of this sphere for formal enterprises is that in contemporary capitalism, flexible production and cost reduction is being achieved by pursuing subcontracting, downsizing and outsourcing arrangements (Castells and Portes, 1989; Davis, 2006; Gallin, 2001; Hudson, 2005; Meagher, 2010; Slavnic, 2010; Taiwo, 2013). The shadow economy is thus increasingly becoming an inherent and integral component of the supply chains of formal businesses because outsourcing and subcontracting to shadow enterprises and workers is cheaper than doing so to formal enterprises (Ketchen et al., 2014). A result is that outsourcing and subcontracting to the shadow economy has thus become a common strategy used by formal enterprises to reduce their production and distribution costs (Castells and Portes, 1989; Meagher, 2010).

Shadow Economy Enterprises

The shadow economy also has consequences for enterprises operating in the shadow economy. Similar to formal businesses, these consequences can be both negative and positive. Starting with the negative consequences, both shadow economy businesses and sole traders working on their own account in the shadow economy find that their opportunities to develop and grow their business are severely constrained for at least five reasons. First, they are often unable to gain access to capital to develop their business since they have no formal accounts (ILO, 2014; Kempson, 1996; Leonard, 1998; Llanes and Barbour, 2007). Second, they cannot advertise their business openly to attract new customers for fear of being detected by the authorities (Williams et al., 2012a). Third, they need to keep their business small in order to stay 'under the radar' of the authorities (Barbour and Llanes, 2013; Polese, 2014; Williams et al., 2012a). Fourth, they cannot secure formal intellectual property rights to process and product innovations (De Beer et al., 2013), and fifth and finally, they lack the same access to business support that is available to formal businesses (ILO, 2002a, 2002b; Karjanen, 2014; Llanes and Barbour, 2007; Williams and Nadin, 2013, 2014).

The shadow economy, however, also has some positive consequences for shadow economy businesses and individuals working on an own-account basis in the shadow economy. First, it provides a source of income that enables them to stay out of poverty and provides them with a means of livelihood when excluded from the formal economy (Williams and Shahid, 2015). Second, it can reduce the barriers to entry into work because the majority of work in the shadow economy is purportedly either labour-intensive production requiring few skills and little start-up capital in developing countries or starts with close social relations in developed nations (Chen, 2012; Williams and Lansky, 2013). Third, the shadow economy provides an exit strategy in contexts where the regulatory burden stifles business development (De Soto, 1989, 2001). Fourth, it provides entrepreneurs with an escape route from corrupt public sector officials who would otherwise demand bribes if one attempted to start up legitimately (Round et al., 2008; Tonoyan et al., 2010) and fifth and finally, the shadow economy arguably provides greater flexibility in where, when and how to work, especially important for women who remain responsible for childcare (Chen, 2012; Snyder, 2004).

Shadow Economy Employees

For those employed in the shadow economy, furthermore, there are similarly both negative and positive consequences. The negative consequences of being employed in waged work in the shadow economy are tenfold. First, such employees do not have access to employment rights such as annual and other leave, sickness pay, redundancy and training (Evans et al., 2006; ILO, 2015; TUC, 2008; Williams and Lansky, 2013). Second, they lack access to a range of other legal rights such as the minimum wage, tax credits and any working hours directives (Dellot, 2012; Renooy et al., 2004; TUC, 2008; Vanderseypen et al., 2013; Williams and Windebank, 1998). Third, they cannot build up rights to the state pension and other contributory benefits, and access occupational pension schemes (Dellot, 2012; Gallin, 2001; ILO, 2002a; Williams and Lansky, 2013). Fourth, they lack access to health and safety standards in the workplace (Evans et al., 2006; Gallin, 2001; ILO, 2002a, 2015; TUC, 2008). Fifth, they have lower job security compared with formal employees (Katungi et al., 2006; Kovács, 2014; Williams, 2001). Sixth, they lack collective bargaining rights (ILO, 2002a, 2014). Seventh, they lose employability due to their lack of evidence of engagement in employment (Barbour and Llanes, 2013; Dellot, 2012). Eighth, they are unable to gain access to credit such as for mortgages or loans if they are shadow employees since they have no evidence of their income (Kempson, 1996; Williams, 2014a). Ninth, they are unable to get an employer's reference (ILO, 2002a; TUC, 2008), and tenth and finally, they suffer a constant fear of detection and risk of prosecution (Grabiner, 2000).

The positive consequences of working in the shadow economy for waged employees meanwhile, are first, that it provides them with a source of income in circumstances when other means of livelihood and/or social protection may not be available to them, and second, it provides them with some flexibility regarding where, when and how they work. On the whole, however, the negative consequences appear to largely outweigh the positive consequences for waged employees in the shadow economy.

Shadow Economy Customers

Another group, sometimes forgotten when considering the consequences of the shadow economy, are the customers who purchase goods and services from this realm. Again, there are both negative and positive consequences. The negative consequences of the shadow economy are first, that such customers find themselves without legal recourse if a poor quality job is undertaken (Eurofound, 2013; Small Business Council, 2004); second, their insurance cover is invalid (Llanes and Barbour, 2007; Small Business Council, 2004); third, they have no guarantees in relation to the quality of the work which is undertaken (Williams et al., 2012a); and fourth, there is no certainty that there has been adherence to health and safety regulations (Dellot, 2012; Williams et al., 2012a). A fifth and final negative consequence is that despite the assumption that goods and services purchased in the shadow economy are cheaper, this might not always be the case. Shadow enterprises operating in various 'bottom of the pyramid' markets are often hugely inefficient and, as such, unlikely to be capable of charging lower prices for the same products (London et al., 2014). Whether this is the case is, of course, open to debate and, similar to many of the other claims regarding the positive and negative consequences of the shadow economy, there is currently little empirical evidence available.

Indeed, turning to the positive consequences for consumers, other commentators have claimed that the shadow economy provides purchasers with more affordable goods and services not only in low-income markets (Ketchen et al., 2014) but also in higher-income economies when payment is made in cash and no receipts change hands (Williams, 2014a; Williams and Martinez-Perez, 2014b; Williams et al., 2012c).

Economies and Societies

There are also consequences for the economies and societies in which work in the shadow economy takes place. The negative consequences for the wider economy and society are first, that because shadow economy enterprises are purportedly low-productivity enterprises and lack the scale to produce efficiently, and the substantial cost advantages they gain by avoiding taxes and regulations more than offsets their low productivity and small scale, they reduce the overall level of productivity in economies and hinder the development of higher-productivity economies, thus hindering overall economic development and growth (La Porta and Schleifer, 2008, 2014; Williams, 2014a). A second negative consequence for the wider economy and society is that the existence of a shadow economy can have knock-on effects on the rule of law and encourage a more casual attitude to the law more widely (Gallin, 2001; Grabiner, 2000; Mateman and Renooy, 2001; Small Business Council, 2004; Williams and Windebank, 1998) and third and finally, shadow economies result in weakened trade union and collective bargaining (Gallin, 2001; TUC, 2008).

Reviewing the possible positive consequences of the shadow economy for wider societies and economies, meanwhile, it has been asserted that the shadow economy first, provides employment and work, even if it is under-employment (Ketchen et al., 2014); second, provides a breeding ground for the micro-enterprise system and test-bed for fledgling businesses; and third and finally, that the income earned in the shadow economy spent in the formal economy boosts demand for formal goods and services and contributes to official economic growth (Schneider and Williams, 2013).

Governments

Finally, and for governments, the consequences of the shadow economy are again both negative and positive. The negative consequences are four-fold. First, and the principal focus for most governments is that the shadow economy causes a loss of revenue for the state in terms of non-payment of direct and indirect taxes (Bajada and Schneider, 2005; Evans et al., 2006; Grabiner, 2000; Müller and Miggelbrink, 2014; Vanderseypen et al., 2013; Williams and Windebank, 1998). Second, the shadow economy has knock-on effects on efforts to forge social cohesion at a societal level by reducing the money available to governments to pursue social integration and mobility initiatives (Andrews et al., 2011; Eurofound, 2013; Vanderseypen et al., 2013). Third, it results in a loss of regulatory control over the quality of jobs and services provided in the economy (ILO, 2013; Vanderseypen et al., 2013; Williams and Lansky, 2013). Fourth and finally, if a significant segment of the population is routinely engaged in such activity, it may result in a more casual attitude towards the law more widely (Andrews et al., 2011; Dong et al., 2012; Karjanen, 2014; Morris and Polese, 2014; Ojo et al., 2013; Sasunkevich, 2014).

The positive consequences for governments, at least in the eyes of some commentators, are first, that it acts as a brake on governments introducing burdensome regulatory regimes because if they do, then businesses will decamp into the shadow economy in order to avoid the burdensome costs and regulations involved (De Soto, 1989, 2001). A second positive consequence of the shadow economy for governments is that any 'on the job' training in shadow enterprises alleviates pressure on the state and its agencies to provide training during times of reduced public spending (Williams, 2014a).

In sum, there are multifarious rationales for studying the shadow economy due to its consequences for formal businesses, shadow economy enterprises, shadow economy employees, customers of the shadow economy, the wider economy and society, and governments. Although most of these consequences have not been enumerated so as to measure the actual impacts of the shadow economy, there is little doubt that the shadow economy is not some minor and unimportant realm in terms of its consequences. Neither, moreover, is there much doubt that if one was to enumerate these consequences, that the negative consequences would outweigh the positive consequences. Therefore, in sum, what can be stated with certainty is not only that the shadow economy is an important feature of the contemporary global economic landscape but also that it has an overall deleterious effect on the lives of millions of people. Given this, we here turn our attention to the structure of this book, which seeks to understand not only how the shadow economy is measured and the findings regarding its extent, nature and determinants, but also what might be done to tackle the shadow economy.

STRUCTURE OF THE BOOK

This book is divided into four parts. In Part I, we review the measurement methods that have been used to evaluate the extent and nature of the shadow economy and shadow labour force. To do this, Chapter 2 provides an overview of the range of indirect measurement methods that have been employed to measure the shadow economy. This provides a comprehensive review of the different indirect methods, including a detailed outline of the methodology underpinning the indirect measurement method most widely used to estimate the size of the shadow economy, namely the MIMIC method developed by one of the authors, namely Friedrich Schneider. This is then followed in Chapter 3 by a review of how direct survey methods have sought to understand the magnitude and character of the shadow labour force. This provides a comprehensive review of the different direct survey methods that can and have been used to measure the shadow labour force and how the results regarding participation vary according to the different methods used. The outcome will be a comprehensive review of the different measurement methods available for estimating the prevalence and nature of the shadow economy and shadow labour force.

With this understanding of the measurement methods in hand, Part II of the book then turns its attention to reviewing the findings of the MIMIC indirect measurement method that has been used to evaluate the size and character of the shadow economy across the world. To do this, Chapter 4 reviews the results of applying the MIMIC method to understanding the prevalence of the shadow economy in 162 developing and transition economies over the period from 1999 until 2007. Chapter 5 then reviews the results of applying the MIMIC method to understanding the size of the shadow economy across OECD countries as well as the various country-level determinants of the shadow economy across these OECD nations.

Part III then turns attention to examining the results of using direct survey methods to measure the size and nature of the shadow labour force across the globe. Chapter 6 reviews the findings regarding the size and nature of the shadow labour force in developing and transition economies using International Labour Organization data, as well as the country-level determinants that influence the cross-national variations in the size and nature of the shadow labour force across these developing and transition economies. Chapter 7 then examines the results regarding the extent and character of the shadow labour force in developed countries using the 2007 Eurobarometer survey of participation in the shadow labour force across 27 European countries. This again also explores the country-level determinants of the cross-national variations in the prevalence and nature of the shadow labour force.

Having provided this review of the cross-national variations in the shadow economy and shadow labour force using both indirect and direct measurement methods, Part IV then turns its attention to how the shadow economy and shadow labour force can be tackled. To do this Chapter 8 provides a conceptual framework for understanding the range of potential policy approaches available for tackling the shadow economy and shadow labour force and, following this, reveals how the evidence available suggests that most governments across the world use only a narrow range of policy measures when doing so and not necessarily measures that tackle the determinants of the shadow economy and shadow labour force. The result in Chapter 9 is the presentation of a potential way forward for governments seeking to tackle in a more effective manner the shadow economy and shadow labour market across the world. This chapter argues that rather than focus on measures to cure the problem once it has occurred, a more preventative approach is required that deals with the determinants of the shadow economy and shadow labour force. This, as will be shown, requires some fresh thinking and the adoption of a much wider range of policy measures than are currently used.

In the concluding Chapter 10, the findings of the preceding chapters are then synthesized and conclusions drawn about the way forward both for measuring the shadow economy and shadow labour force as well as for tackling this sphere. On the one hand, this will reveal the need for the longstanding division between those using indirect and direct measurement methods to be transcended and for recognition that it is necessary to use both indirect and direct methods if the size and nature of the shadow economy and shadow labour force is to be more comprehensively understood. On the other hand, it will reveal the need for a serious rethinking regarding the determinants of the shadow economy and shadow labour force and how they are to be tackled. In doing so, we hope that this book will contribute significantly to the advancement of understanding not only regarding the measurement and understanding of the shadow economy but also, perhaps more importantly, what needs to be done to tackle this persistent and extensive sphere that remains omnipresent across the global economic landscape.

PART I

Measurement methods

2. Measuring the shadow economy: a review of indirect methods

Estimating the size of a shadow economy is a difficult and challenging task. When measuring the shadow economy, two contrasting methods are used. On the one hand, there are direct survey methods. These are microeconomic approaches that largely use surveys. The main disadvantages of this method are the flaws of all surveys. For example, the average precision and results depend greatly on the respondents' willingness to cooperate, it is difficult to assess the amount of shadow work from a direct questionnaire, most interviewees hesitate to confess to fraudulent behaviour and responses are of uncertain reliability, which makes it difficult to calculate a true estimate (in monetary terms) of the extent of the shadow economy. On the whole, moreover, these surveys capture the shadow labour activities in households but rarely in or between firms and do not provide value-added figures. However, they have one considerable advantage; they provide detailed information about the structure of the shadow economy, as well as the socio-economic characteristics and motives of those who work in the shadow economy, even if the results are very sensitive to the way the survey is designed and the questionnaire is formulated (see Mogensen, 1985; Mogensen et al., 1995; Pedersen, 2003).

On the other hand, indirect measurement methods, which are also called indicator approaches, are widely used in order to overcome these shortcomings. In this chapter, we give a short but comprehensive overview of these approaches for estimating the size of the shadow economy. To do this, we provide a brief review of first, the approach that seeks to measure the discrepancy between national expenditure and income statistics; second, the approach that measures the discrepancy between the official and actual labour force; third, the transactions approach; fourth, the currency demand approach; fifth, the physical input (electricity consumption) method; and sixth, and in more detail, the most popular method – the model approach – which will be employed in Part II of this book to measure the size of the shadow economy. Seventh, we provide an analysis of the contrasting estimates of the size of the shadow economy in Germany using these different measurement methods before drawing some conclusions regarding their usage.

THE DISCREPANCY BETWEEN NATIONAL EXPENDITURE AND INCOME STATISTICS

A first indirect measurement method, or indicator approach, evaluates the differences in expenditure and income statistics. In national accounting, the income measure of gross national product (GNP) should be equal to the expenditure measure of GNP. Thus, if an independent estimate of the expenditure side of the national accounts is available, the gap between the expenditure measure and the income measure can be used as an indicator of the extent of the shadow economy. Since national accounts statisticians are anxious to minimize this discrepancy, the initial discrepancy or first estimate, rather than the published discrepancy, should be employed as an estimate of the shadow economy. If all the components of the expenditure side are measured without error, then this approach would indeed yield a good estimate of the size of the shadow economy. Unfortunately, however, this is not the case. Instead, the discrepancy reflects all omissions and errors everywhere in the national accounts statistics as well as the shadow economy. These estimates may therefore be crude and of questionable reliability.

Nevertheless, this approach has been used both at the aggregate national level as well as through detailed microeconomic studies of different types of individuals or households. On the one hand, therefore, aggregate level studies analyse the discrepancy between national expenditure and income to estimate the size of the shadow economy. Such studies have been conducted in Austria (Franz, 1983), Canada (Morissette, 2014), Germany (for example, Del Boca, 1981; Langfeldt, 1984; Petersen, 1982), Sweden (for example, Apel, 1994), the UK (Macafee, 1980; O'Higgins, 1989; Smith, 1985) and the US (for example, Macafee, 1980; Paglin, 1994; Park, 1979). On the other hand, there are studies of income/expenditure discrepancies at the household level. These use household income and expenditure data to estimate the degree of income under-reporting. In the UK, for example, this has been analysed using the Family Expenditure Survey (FES) (Dilnot and Morris, 1981; Macafee, 1980; O'Higgins, 1989). Although this method has advantages over other indirect monetary methods, not least its reliance on relatively direct and statistically representative survey data, its problems remain manifold (Thomas, 1988, 1992; Smith, 1986). For the discrepancy to represent a reasonable measure of the magnitude of the shadow economy, one has to make a number of assumptions about the accuracy of the income and expenditure data.

On the expenditure side, estimates depend upon the accurate declaration of expenditure. Mattera (1985) argues that this is naive and that for most people, spending is either over- or underestimated during a survey because few people keep expenditure records, unlike income, which for employees comes in regular recorded uniform instalments. On the income side, meanwhile, these studies are unable to decipher whether the income derives from criminal or shadow work, or even whether it derives from wealth accumulated earlier such as savings. In addition, there are problems of non-response as well as under-reporting (Thomas, 1992). Consequently, the accuracy of this method is doubtful. Weck-Hannemann and Frey (1985) clearly display this when reporting that the national income in Switzerland is larger than expenditure. As such, the Swiss shadow economy must be negative. This is nonsensical and shows that the discrepancy does not display the level of the shadow economy but must be due to other factors.

THE DISCREPANCY BETWEEN THE OFFICIAL AND ACTUAL LABOUR FORCE

The methods that use formal labour force statistics to identify traces of the shadow economy are of several varieties. A first crude method simply views a decline in the employment participation rate in the official economy as an indication of increased activity in the shadow economy. If total labour force participation is assumed to be constant, then a decreasing employment participation rate can be seen as an indicator of an increase in the shadow economy. Such studies have been used in Italy (Contini, 1981; Del Boca, 1981) and the United States (O'Neill, 1983), and also cross-nationally (Williams, 2009a, 2013b; Williams and Lansky, 2013; Rodgers and Williams, 2012). The weakness of this method is that differences in the employment participation rate may also have other causes. There is also the fact that people can work in the shadow economy and have a job in the official economy. Therefore such an estimate can be viewed as providing a very weak indicator of the size and development of the shadow economy.

The second method examines unaccountable increases in the numbers in various types of employment (for example, self-employment, second-job holding) as a proxy indicator of the size of the shadow economy (for example, Crnkovic-Pozaic, 1999; Del Boca and Forte, 1982; Helberger and Schwarze, 1986). However, the notion that shadow work prevails in these categories of employment is an assumption, rather than a finding, and one has no way of knowing the degree to which the shadow economy, rather than other factors, has led to this increase. The third technique using labour force statistics seeks discrepancies in the results of different official surveys, such as the population census and firm surveys (for example, Flaming et al., 2005; Lobo, 1990; Mattera, 1985; US Congress Joint Economic Committee, 1983). Again, whether the variations identified are purely due to the shadow economy, or whether other survey design issues or factors are involved, is difficult to discern. A fourth popular application of discrepancy methods is to compare the findings of labour force surveys (LFS) with the recorded labour demand (for example, based on company declarations to tax or social security authorities or national statistical offices). However, the problem with this approach again stems from its use of different sources of information, which may use different definitions, classifications and periods of measurement. Another shortcoming is that such discrepancy methods exclude certain sectors (for example, private households acting as employers or agriculture) that may be particularly relevant for shadow work.

THE TRANSACTIONS APPROACH

Another approach that examines transactions has been most fully developed by Feige (1996) and applied in for example the Netherlands (Boeschoten and Fase, 1984) and Germany (Langfeldt, 1984). It is based upon the assumption that there is a constant relation over time between the volume of transactions and official GNP, as summarized by the well-known Fisher quantity equation, or $M*V = p*T$ (with M money, V velocity, p prices and T total transactions). Assumptions also have to be made about the velocity of money and about the relationship between the value of total transactions $p*T$ and total (official + unofficial) nominal GNP. Relating total nominal GNP to total transactions, the GNP of the shadow economy can be calculated by subtracting the official GNP from total nominal GNP.

However, to derive figures for the size of the shadow economy, one must also assume a base year in which there is no shadow economy and therefore the ratio of $p*T$ to total nominal (official = total) GNP was 'normal' and would have been constant over time if there had been no shadow economy. To obtain reliable shadow economy estimates, precise figures of the total volume of transactions should be available. This is particularly difficult for cash transactions because they depend, among other factors, on the durability of bank notes in terms of the quality of the paper on which they are printed. Furthermore, the assumption is made that all variations in the ratio between the total value of transactions and the officially measured GNP are due to the shadow economy. This means that a considerable amount of data is required in order to eliminate financial transactions from 'pure' cross payments, which are legal and have nothing to do with the shadow economy. In general, although this approach is theoretically attractive, the empirical requirements necessary to obtain reliable estimates are so difficult to fulfil that its application can lead to doubtful results. It is also difficult to differentiate shadow economy transactions from criminal transactions. The result is that this approach has been subjected to widespread criticism (Boeschoten and Fase, 1984; Dallago, 1990; Frey and Pommerehne, 1984; Giles, 1999a; Kirchgässner, 1984; Tanzi, 1982a,1982b, 1986; Thomas, 1986, 1992, 1999).

THE CURRENCY DEMAND APPROACH

The currency demand approach was first used by Cagan (1958), who considered the correlation between currency demand and tax pressure (as one cause of the shadow economy) for the United States over the period 1919 to 1955. Two decades later, Gutmann (1977) used the same approach but without any statistical procedures. Cagan's approach was further developed by Tanzi (1980, 1983), who estimated a currency demand function for the United States for the period 1929 to 1980 in order to calculate the size of the shadow economy. His approach assumes that shadow (or hidden) transactions are undertaken in the form of cash payments, so as to leave no observable traces for the authorities. An increase in the size of the shadow economy will therefore increase the demand for currency. To isolate the resulting excess demand for currency, an equation for currency demand is estimated over time. All conventional possible factors, such as the development of income, payment habits, interest rates, credit and other debit cards as a substitute for cash and so on, are controlled for. Additionally, such variables as the direct and indirect tax burden, government regulation, state institutions and tax morale, which are assumed to be the major factors causing people to work in the shadow economy, are included in the estimation equation. The basic regression equation for the currency demand, proposed by Tanzi (1983), is the following:

$$ln\,(C\,/\,M_2)_t = \beta_0 + \beta_1\,ln\,(1 + TW)_t + \beta_2\,ln\,(WS\,/\,Y)_t + \beta_3\,ln\,R_t$$

$$+ \beta_4\,ln\,(Y\,/\,N)_t + u_t,$$

with $\beta_1 > 0$, $\beta_2 > 0$, $\beta_3 < 0$, $\beta_4 > 0$, where ln denotes natural logarithms, C/M_2 is the ratio of cash holdings to current and deposit accounts, TW is a weighted average tax rate (to proxy changes in the size of the shadow economy), WS/Y is a proportion of wages and salaries in national income (to capture changing payment and money holding patterns), R is the interest paid on savings deposits (to capture the opportunity cost of holding cash) and Y/N is the per capita income. Any 'excess' increase in currency, or the amount unexplained by conventional or normal factors is then attributed to the rising tax burden and other reasons leading people to work in the shadow economy. Figures for the size and development of the shadow economy can be calculated in a first step by comparing the difference between the development of currency when the direct and indirect tax burden and government regulation are held at lowest values, and the development of currency with the current (higher) burden of taxation and government regulation. Assuming in a second step the same income velocity for currency used in the shadow economy as for legal *M1* in the official economy, the size of the shadow can be computed and compared to the official gross domestic product (GDP). This currency demand equation has been criticized by Thomas (1999), and these criticisms taken into account in the work of Giles (1999a, 1999b) and Bhattacharyya (1999) who both use more modern econometric techniques.

This is one of the most commonly used approaches. It has been applied to many countries all over the world (see Johnson et al., 1998a; Karmann, 1986, 1990; Schneider, 1997, 1998, 2011; Schneider and Williams, 2013). Nevertheless, it has also been subject to widespread criticism (Ahumada et al., 2004; Feige, 1986; Pozo, 1996; Pedersen, 2003; Schneider and Williams, 2013; Thomas, 1992, 1999). The most commonly raised objections to this method are sevenfold. First, not all transactions in the shadow economy are paid in cash. Isachsen and Strom (1985) using the survey method, find that in Norway in 1980, roughly 80 per cent of all transactions in the shadow economy were paid in cash. The size of the total shadow economy (including barter) may thus be even larger than previously estimated.

Second, most studies consider only one particular factor, the tax burden, as a cause of the shadow economy. Others, such as the impact of regulation, taxpayers' attitudes toward the state and tax morale, are not considered. This is because reliable data is not available for most countries. If, as seems likely, these other factors also have an impact on the extent of the shadow economy, it might again be higher than reported in most studies. One (weak) justification for the use of only the tax variable, of course, is that this variable has by far the strongest impact on the size of the shadow economy. This is debatable. Although Pommerehne and Schneider (1985) show in the USA that the tax variable has a dominating influence and contributes roughly 60–70 per cent to the size of the shadow economy, a study by Frey and Weck-Hannemann (1984) shows that 'tax immorality' has a quantitatively larger and statistically stronger influence than the direct tax share (see also Zilberfarb, 1986).

Third, and as discussed by Garcia (1978), Park (1979) and Feige (1996), increases in currency demand deposits are largely due to a slowdown in demand deposits rather than to an increase in currency caused by activities in the shadow economy, at least in the case of the United States.

Fourth, Blades (1982) and Feige (1986, 1996) criticize Tanzi's studies on the grounds that the US dollar is used as an international currency and that Tanzi should have considered (and controlled for) the presence of US dollars, which are used as an international currency and held in cash abroad. Another study by Tanzi (1982a, pp. 110–13) explicitly deals with this criticism. A very careful investigation of the amount of US dollars used abroad and US currency used in the shadow economy and for 'classical' criminal activities has been also undertaken by Rogoff (1998), who concludes that large denomination bills are the major driving force for the growth of the shadow economy and classical crime activities, due largely to reduced transaction costs. In addition, Frey and Pommerehne (1984) and Thomas (1986, 1992, 1999) claim that Tanzi's parameter estimates are not very stable. However, in studies of European countries, Kirchgässner (1983, 1984) and Schneider (1986) conclude that the estimation results for Germany, Denmark, Norway and Sweden are quite robust when using the currency demand method. Hill and Kabir (1996, p. 1553) find for Canada that the rise of the shadow economy varies with respect to the tax variable used; they conclude 'when the theoretically best tax rates are selected and a range of plausible velocity values is used, this method estimates underground economic growth between 1964 and 1995 at between 3 per cent and 11 per cent of GDP'.

Fifth, most studies assume the same velocity of money in the formal and shadow economies. As argued by Hill and Kabir (1996) for Canada and by Klovland (1984) for the Scandinavian countries, there is considerable uncertainty about the velocity of money in the formal economy, and the velocity of money in the shadow economy is even more difficult to estimate. Without knowledge about the velocity of currency in the shadow economy, one has to accept the assumption of an equal velocity of money in both sectors.

Sixth, Ahumada et al. (2004) show that the currency approach together with the assumption of equal income velocity of money in the formal and shadow economies is only correct if the income elasticity is one. And seventh and finally, the assumption of no shadow economy in a base year is open to criticism. Relaxing this assumption would again imply an upward adjustment of the size of the shadow economy.

There is also a question regarding how the shadow economy is defined here since it is viewed as including all cash transactions. Although this has some overlap with the shadow economy as defined in this book, it is important to realise that this method also includes many criminal activities and also omits shadow activities where non-cash transactions are involved.

THE PHYSICAL INPUT (ELECTRICITY CONSUMPTION) METHOD

In recent decades, a number of commentators have used physical inputs to measure the size of the shadow economy. By far the most popular of these physical input methods is that which examines electricity consumption as a proxy indicator of the size of the shadow economy. In this regard, two electricity consumption methods are available, namely the Kaufmann–Kaliberda method and the Lackó method. Here, each is considered in turn.

The Kaufmann–Kaliberda Method

To measure overall (official and unofficial) economic activity in an economy, Kaufmann and Kaliberda (1996) assume that electric-power consumption is regarded as the single best physical indicator of overall (or official plus unofficial) economic activity. Overall economic activity and electricity consumption have been empirically observed throughout the world to move in lockstep with an electricity-to-GDP elasticity usually close to one. This means that the growth of total electricity consumption is an indicator for growth of overall (official and unofficial) GDP. By having this proxy measurement for the overall economy and then subtracting from this overall measure the estimates of official GDP, Kaufmann and Kaliberda (1996) derive an estimate of unofficial GDP. This method is very simple and appealing. Indeed, it has been used by Lizzeri (1979), Del Boca and Forte (1982) prior to Kaufmann and Kaliberda, and then was used later by Portes (1996) and Johnson et al. (1997). However, it can also be criticized on various grounds. First, not all shadow economy activities require a considerable amount of electricity (for example, personal services), and other energy sources can be used (for example, gas, oil and coal). Only a part of the shadow economy will be indicated. Second, over time, there has been considerable technical progress so that both the production and use of electricity are more efficient than in the past, and this will apply in both official and unofficial uses. And third and finally, there may be considerable differences or changes in the elasticity of electricity/GDP across countries and over time. Johnson et al. (1997), however, make an attempt to adjust for changes in the elasticity of electricity/GDP.

The Lackó Method

Another variant of this approach is the method developed by Lackó (1998, 1999, 2000a, 2000b) who assumes that a certain part of the shadow economy is associated with the household consumption of electricity. This part comprises the so-called household production, do-it-yourself activities, and other non-registered production and services. Lackó further assumes that in countries where the portion of the shadow economy associated with the household electricity consumption is high, the rest of the shadow economy (or the part Lackó cannot measure) will also be high. Lackó (1996, pp.19 ff.) assumes that in each country a part of the household consumption of electricity is used in the shadow economy. Lackó's approach (1998, p.133) can be described by the following two equations:

$$\ln E_i = \alpha_1 \ln C_i + \alpha_2 \ln PR_i + \alpha_3 G_i + \alpha_4 Q_i + \alpha_5 H_i + u_i,$$

$$\text{with } \alpha_1 > 0, \alpha_2 < 0, \alpha_3 > 0, \alpha_4 < 0, \alpha_5 > 0 \text{ and}$$

$$H_i = \beta_1 T_i + \beta_2 (S_i - T_i) + \beta_3 D_i \text{ with } \beta_1 > 0, \beta_2 < 0, \beta_3 > 0$$

where i indicates the number assigned to the country,
E_i is per capita household electricity consumption in country i,
C_i is per capita real consumption of households without the consumption of electricity in country i in US dollars (at purchasing power parity),
PR_i is the real price of consumption of 1 kWh of residential electricity in US dollars (at purchasing power parity),
G_i is the relative frequency of months with the need of heating in houses in country i,
Q_i is the ratio of energy sources other than electricity energy to all energy sources in household energy consumption,
H_i is the per capita output of the hidden economy,
T_i is the ratio of the sum of paid personal income, corporate profit and taxes on goods and services to GDP,
S_i is the ratio of public social welfare expenditures to GDP, and
D_i is the sum on number of dependants over 14 years and of inactive earners, both per 100 active earners.

In a cross-national study, she estimates the first equation substituting for H_i with the second equation. For the calculation of the actual size (value added) of the shadow economy, Lackó further must know how much GDP is produced by one unit of electricity in the shadow economy of each country. Since these data are not known, she takes the result of one of the known shadow economy estimates calculated for a market economy with another approach for the early 1990s, and applies this to the other countries. Lackó used the shadow economy of the United States as such a base, the shadow economy value of 10.5 per cent of GDP taken from Morris

(1993) and calculated the size of the shadow economy for other countries. Lackó's method is open to criticism. First, not all shadow economy activities require a considerable amount of electricity and other energy sources can be used. Second, shadow economy activities do not take place only in the household sector. Third, it is doubtful whether the ratio of social welfare expenditures can be used as the explanatory factor for the shadow economy, especially in transition and developing countries. And fourth, it is questionable which is the most reliable base-value of the shadow economy that is used to calculate the shadow economy for other countries, especially for transition and developing countries. Furthermore, both of these electricity consumption approaches rely on a broad definition of the shadow economy because they measure all (illegal) activities that require electric power.

THE MODEL APPROACH

General Remarks

All the methods described so far consider just one indicator to capture the effects of the shadow economy. However, shadow economy effects show up simultaneously in the production, labour and money markets. An even more important critique is that the causes that determine the size of the shadow economy are taken into account only in some of the monetary approach studies that usually consider one cause, the burden of taxation. The model approach explicitly considers multiple causes of the existence and growth of the shadow economy (Dell'Anno, 2003; Dell'Anno and Schneider, 2004; Giles, 1997a, 1997b, 1999a, 1999b, 1999c; Giles and Tedds, 2002; Giles et al., 2002; Johnson et al., 1998a, 1998b; Pozo, 1996; Schneider, 2003, 2005, 2011; Thomas, 1992), as well as the multiple effects of the shadow economy over time. The empirical method used is quite different from those used so far. It is based on the statistical theory of unobserved variables, which considers multiple causes and multiple indicators (MIMIC) of the phenomenon to be measured.

This model approach has been commonly used. Aigner et al. (1988, p. 233) apply this approach in the United States and Karmann (1986, 1990) in Germany. The pioneers of this model approach are Weck-Hannemann (1983) and Frey and Weck-Hannemann (1984), who applied this approach to cross-section data on 24 OECD countries for various years. They developed the concept of 'soft modelling' (Frey et al., 1982; Frey and Weck (1983a, 1983b), an approach that has been used to provide a ranking of the relative size of the shadow economy in different countries. One paper dealing extensively with the MIMIC approach, its development and its weaknesses is Dell'Anno (2003) as well as the excellent study by Giles and Tedds (2002).

As the size of the shadow economy is an unknown (hidden) figure, a latent estimator approach using the MIMIC (that is, multiple indicators, multiple causes estimation) procedure is applied. This method is based on the statistical theory of unobserved variables. The statistical idea behind such a model is to compare a sample covariance matrix, that is, a covariance matrix of observable variables, with the parametric structure imposed on this matrix by a hypothesized model. Estimation of a MIMIC model with a latent variable can be done by means of a computer program for the analysis of covariance structures, such as LISREL (Linear Structural Relations). A useful overview of the LISREL software package in an economics journal is Cziraky (2004).

Using covariance information among the observable variables, the unobservable variable is in the first step linked to observable variables in a factor analytical model, also called a measurement model. Second, the relationships between the unobservable variable and observable variables are specified through a structural model. Therefore, a MIMIC model is the simultaneous specification of a factor and a structural model. In this sense, the MIMIC model tests the consistency of a 'structural' theory through data and is thus a confirmatory, rather than an exploratory technique. An economic theory is thus tested examining the consistency of actual data with the hypothesized relationships between the unobservable (latent) variable or factor and the observable (measurable) variables. On the contrary, in an exploratory factor analysis, a model is not specified in advance. That is to say, beyond the specification of the number of latent variables (factors) and observed variables, the researcher does not specify any structure of the model. This means that one assumes that all factors are correlated, all observable variables are directly influenced by all factors, and all measurement errors are uncorrelated with each other. In practice, however, the distinction between a confirmatory and an exploratory factor analysis is less strong. Facing poorly fitting models, researchers using the MIMIC model often modify their models in an exploratory way in order to improve the fit. Thus, most applications fall between the two extreme cases of exploratory (non-specified model structure) and confirmatory (ex-ante specified model structure) factor analysis (Long, 1983a, pp. 11–17).

In general, a confirmatory factor analysis has two goals: (a) to estimate parameters such as coefficients and variances; and (b) to assess the fit of the model. For the analysis of shadow economy activities these two goals mean (a) to estimate the relationships between a set of observable variables, divided into causes and indicators, and the shadow economy activity (unobservable variable); and (b) to test if the researcher's theory or the derived hypotheses as a whole fit the data. MIMIC models are, compared to regression models, rarely used by economists, which might be due to an under-evaluation of their capabilities with respect to their potential contribution to economic research.

A Detailed Description of the MIMIC Model

The idea of the MIMIC model application is to examine the relationships between the latent variable size of shadow economy activities and observable variables in terms of the relationships among a set of observable variables by using their covariance information. The observable variables are divided into causes and indicators of the latent variable (see Figure 2.1). The key benefits of the MIMIC model are that it allows modelling shadow economy activities as an unobservable (latent) variable and that it takes into account its multiple determinants (causes) and multiple effects (indicators). A factor-analytic approach is used to measure the size of shadow economy activities as an unobserved variable over time. The unknown coefficients are estimated in a set of structural equations, as the 'unobserved' variable – that is, the size of the shadow economy – cannot be measured directly. Formally, the MIMIC model consists of two parts: the structural equation model and the measurement model.

In the measurement model, the unobservable variable η_t determines a p vector $y'_t = (y_{1t}, y_{2t}, \ldots, y_{pt})'$ of indicators, that is, observable variables that reflect the shadow economy activities, subject to a p vector of random error terms $\varepsilon'_t = (\varepsilon_{1t}, \varepsilon_{2t}, \ldots, \varepsilon_{pt})'$. The unobservable variable η_t is a scalar and λ is a p column vector of parameters that relates y_t to η_t. The measurement equation is given by:

CAUSES   INDICATORS

Figure 2.1   The MIMIC model

$$y_t = \lambda \eta_t + \varepsilon_t \qquad (2.1)$$

The structural model determines the unobservable variable η_t by a set of exogenous causes $x'_t = (x_{1t}, x_{2t}, \ldots, x_{qt})'$ that may be useful in predicting its movement and size, subject to a structural disturbance error term ζ_t. The structural equation is given by:

$$\eta_t = \gamma' x_t + \zeta_t \qquad (2.2)$$

where γ' is a q row vector of structural parameters (that is, without loss of generality, all variables are taken as standardized deviations from their means). In equations (2.1) and (2.2) it is assumed that ζ_t and the elements of ε_t are normally, independently and identically distributed, the variance of the structural disturbance term ζ_t is denoted by ψ, and $\Theta_\varepsilon = E(\varepsilon_t \varepsilon_t')$ is the $(p \times p)$ covariance matrix of the measurement errors. In the standard MIMIC model the measurement errors are assumed to be independent of each other, but this restriction could be relaxed (Stapleton, 1978, p. 53). Figure 2.1 shows the path diagram of the MIMIC model.

The MIMIC model of shadow economy activities estimated in this paper uses three indicators and nine causes. Hence, within this model, equations (2.1) and (2.2) are specified as follows:

$$\begin{bmatrix} y_{1t} \\ y_{2t} \\ y_{3t} \end{bmatrix} = \begin{bmatrix} \lambda_1 \\ \lambda_2 \\ \lambda_3 \end{bmatrix} \cdot \eta_t + \begin{bmatrix} \varepsilon_{1t} \\ \varepsilon_{2t} \\ \varepsilon_{3t} \end{bmatrix} \qquad (2.3)$$

$$\eta_t = [\gamma_1 \gamma_2 \gamma_3 \gamma_4 \gamma_5 \gamma_6 \gamma_7 \gamma_8 \gamma_9] \cdot \begin{bmatrix} X_{1t} \\ X_{2t} \\ X_{3t} \\ X_{4t} \\ X_{5t} \\ X_{6t} \\ X_{7t} \\ X_{8t} \\ X_{9t} \end{bmatrix} + \zeta t \qquad (2.4)$$

Substituting (2.1) into (2.2) yields a reduced form equation that expresses the relationships between the observed causes and indicators, that is, between x_t and y_t. This is shown in equation (2.5):

$$y_t = \Pi x_t + z_t \tag{2.5}$$

where: $\Pi = \lambda\gamma'$ is a 3×9 reduced form coefficient matrix and $z_t = \lambda\zeta_t + \varepsilon_t$ is a reduced form vector of a linear transformation of disturbances that has a (3×3) reduced form covariance matrix Ω given as:

$$\Omega = \mathrm{Cov}(z_t) = E[(\lambda\zeta_t + \varepsilon_t)(\lambda\zeta_t + \varepsilon_t)'] = \lambda\psi\lambda' + \Theta_\varepsilon \tag{2.6}$$

In equation (2.6), $\psi = \mathrm{Var}(\zeta_t)$ and $\Theta_\varepsilon = E(\varepsilon_t\varepsilon_t')$ is the measurement error's covariance matrix.

In general, estimation of a MIMIC model uses covariance information of sample data to derive estimates of population parameters. Instead of minimizing the distance between observed and predicted individual values, as in standard econometrics, the MIMIC model minimizes the distance between an observed (sample) covariance matrix and the covariance matrix predicted by the model the researcher imposes on the data. The idea behind that approach is that the covariance matrix of the observed variables is a function of a set of model parameters:

$$\Sigma = \Sigma(\theta) \tag{2.7}$$

where Σ is the population covariance matrix of the observed variables, θ is a vector that contains the parameters of the model and $\Sigma(\theta)$ is the covariance matrix as a function of θ, implying that each element of the covariance matrix is a function of one or more model parameters. If the hypothesized model is correct and the parameters are known, the population covariance matrix would be exactly reproduced, that is, Σ will equal $\Sigma(\theta)$. In practice, however, one does not know either the population variances and covariances or the parameters, but instead uses the sample covariance matrix and sample estimates of the unknown parameters for estimation (Bollen, 1989, p. 256).

Estimation is thus performed by finding values for $\hat{\theta} = f(\hat{\lambda},\hat{\gamma},\hat{\psi},\hat{\Phi},\hat{\Theta}_\varepsilon)$ producing an estimate of the models covariance matrix $\hat{\Sigma}$ that most closely corresponds to the sample covariance matrix S. During this estimation procedure, all possible matrices that meet the imposed restrictions are considered. If an estimate Σ^* of $\hat{\Sigma}$ is close to S, one might conclude that θ^* is a reasonable estimate of the model's parameters. Hence, estimation of a MIMIC model is reduced to the problem of measuring how close Σ^* is to S and if this estimate is the most accurate, that is, if it is the best estimate given the set of all possible estimates that meet the imposed restrictions (Long, 1983b, pp. 42–5). The covariance equation of the MIMIC model can be derived and has the following functional form:

$$\hat{\Sigma} = \left[\begin{array}{c|c} \hat{\lambda}(\hat{\gamma}'\hat{\Phi}\hat{\gamma} + \hat{\psi})\hat{\lambda}' + \hat{\Theta}_\varepsilon & \hat{\lambda}\hat{\gamma}'\hat{\Phi} \\ \hline \hat{\Phi}\hat{\gamma}\hat{\lambda}' & \hat{\Phi} \end{array} \right] \qquad (2.8)$$

The function measuring how close a given Σ^* is to the sample covariance matrix S is called the fitting function $F(S; \Sigma^*)$. The θ^* of all possible θ^* that meets the imposed constraints on λ, γ, Φ, ψ and Θ_ε and minimizes the fitting function, given the sample covariance matrix S, is the sample estimate $\hat{\theta}$ of the population parameters. This means that if one set of estimates θ_1^* produces the matrix Σ_1^* and a second set θ_2^* produces the matrix Σ_2^* and if $F(S; \Sigma_1^*) < F(S; \Sigma_2^*)$, Σ_1^* is then considered to be closer to S than Σ_2^* (Long, 1983a, p. 56).

The most widely used fitting function is the maximum likelihood (ML) function. Of course, other estimation procedures such as unweighted least squares (ULS) and generalized least squares (GLS) are also available. ULS has the advantage that it is easier to compute and leads to a consistent estimator without the assumption that the observed variables have a particular distribution. Important disadvantages of ULS are, however, that ULS does not lead to the asymptotically most efficient estimator of θ and that F_{ULS} is not scale invariant. The GLS estimator has similar statistical properties like the ML estimator but the significance tests are no longer accurate if the distribution of the observed variables has very 'fat' or 'thin' tails. Moreover, F_{GLS} accepts the wrong model more often than ML and parameter estimates tend to suffer when using F_{GLS}. Thus, ML seems to be superior (see, for example, Bollen, 1989, pp. 111–15; Olssen et al., 1999, 2000; Jöreskog and Sörbom, 2001, pp. 20–24). Hence, under the assumption that $\Sigma(\theta)$ and S are positive definite, that is, non-singular, and S has a Wishart distribution, the following fitting function is minimized:

$$F_{ML} = \log|\Sigma(\theta)| + tr[S\Sigma^{-1}(\theta)] - \log|S| - (p + q) \qquad (2.9)$$

where $\log| \ |$ is the log of the determinant of the respective matrix and $(p + q)$ is the number of observed variables. In general, no closed form or explicit solution for the structural parameters that minimize F_{ML} exists. Hence, the values of λ, γ, Φ, ψ and Θ_ε that minimize the fitting function are estimated applying iterative numerical procedures (see Bollen, 1989, Appendix 4C). The ML estimator is widely used because of its desirable properties (see Bollen, 1989, pp. 107–23):

First, the ML estimator is asymptotically unbiased.
Second, the ML estimator is consistent, that is plim $\hat{\theta} = \theta$ ($\hat{\theta}$ is the ML estimator and θ is the population parameter).

Third, the ML estimator is asymptotically efficient, that is, among all consistent estimators no other has a smaller asymptotic variance.

Fourth, the ML estimator is asymptotically normally distributed, meaning that the ratio of the estimated parameter and its standard error approximate a z- distribution in large samples.

Fifth, a final important characteristic of the ML estimator is scale invariance (Swaminathan and Algina, 1978). The scale invariance property implies that changes in the measurement unit of one or more of the observed variables do not change the value of the fitting function. This means that $\hat{\lambda}$, $\hat{\gamma}$, $\hat{\Phi}$, $\hat{\psi}$ and $\hat{\theta}_{\varepsilon}$ are the same for any change of scale.

It is widely accepted by most scholars who estimate the size and development of shadow economic activities using the MIMIC model or more general structural equation models (SEMs) with more than one unobservable variable, that such an empirical exercise is a 'minefield', regardless of which method is used. For example, in evaluating the currently available shadow economy estimates of different scholars, one should keep in mind that there is no best or commonly accepted method. Each approach has its strengths and weaknesses and can provide specific insights and results. Although SEM/MIMIC model applications in economics are 'accompanied' by criticisms, they are increasingly used for estimating the shadow economy and other informal economic activities.

In comparison with other statistical methods, SEMs/MIMIC models offer several advantages for the estimation of shadow economic activities. According to Giles and Tedds (2002), the MIMIC approach is a wider approach than most other competing methods, since it allows one to take multiple indicator and causal variables into consideration at the same time. Moreover, it is quite flexible, allowing one to vary the choice of causal and indicator variables according to the particular features of the shadow economic activity studied, the period in question and the availability of data. SEMs/MIMIC models lead to a formal estimation and to testing procedures, such as those based on the method of maximum likelihood. These procedures are well-known and are generally 'optimal', if the sample is sufficiently large (Giles and Tedds, 2002). Schneider and Enste (2000b) emphasize that these models lead to some progress in estimation techniques for the size and development of the shadow economy, because this methodology allows a wide flexibility in its application. Therefore, they consider it potentially superior to other estimation methods. Cassar (2001) argues that, when compared to other methods, SEMs/MIMIC models do not need restrictive assumptions to operate. Analogously, Thomas (1992, p. 168) argues that the only real constraint of this approach is not in its conceptual structure, but the choice of variables. These positive aspects of the SEM approach in general and the MIMIC model in particular do not only apply in its application to the shadow economy, but to all informal economic activities. This means again, that the MIMIC procedure relies on a broad definition of the shadow economy.

Criticism of the MIMIC Model

Of course this method has its disadvantages or limitations too, which are identified in the literature. The three most important points of criticism focus on the model's implementations, the sample used and the reliability of the estimates:

1. The most common objection to estimating shadow economic activities using SEMs concerns the meaning of the latent variable (for example, Helberger and Knepel, 1988; Dell'Anno, 2003). The confirmatory rather than exploratory nature of this approach means that one is more likely to determine whether a certain model is valid than to 'find' a suitable model. Therefore, it is possible that the specified model includes potential definitions or informal economic activities other than the one studied. For example, it is difficult for a researcher to ensure that traditional crime activities such as drug-dealing are completely excluded from the analysis of the shadow economy. This criticism, which is probably the most common in the literature, remains difficult to overcome as it goes back to the theoretical assumptions behind the choice of variables and empirical limitations on data availability.
2. Helberger and Knepel (1988) argue that SEM/MIMIC model estimations lead to unstable coefficients with respect to changes of the sample size and alternative model specifications. Dell'Anno (2003) shows, however, that instability disappears asymptotically as the sample size increases. Another issue is the application of SEMs to time series data because only simple analytical tools such as q- and stemleaf plots are available to analyse the properties of the residuals (Dell'Anno 2003). Particularly critical are the assumptions $E(\varsigma_{ik}^2) = Var(\varsigma_i)$ for all k (homoscedasticity assumption) and $Cov(\Sigma_{ik}, \Sigma_{il}) = 0$ for all $k \neq l$ (no autocorrelation in the error terms). Unfortunately, corrections for autocorrelated and heteroscedastic error terms have not yet received sufficient attention in models with unobservable variables (Bollen, 1989, p. 58). An interesting exception is Folmer and Karmann (1992).
3. Criticism is also related to the benchmarking procedure used to derive 'real world' figures of shadow economic activities (Breusch, 2005a, 2005b). As the latent variable and its unit of measurement are not

observed, SEMs just provide a set of estimated coefficients from which one can calculate an index that shows the dynamics of the unobservable variable. Application of the so-called calibration or benchmarking procedure, regardless of which one is used, requires experimentation and a comparison of the calibrated values in a wide academic debate. Unfortunately, at this stage of research on the application of the SEM/MIMIC approach in economics it is not clear which benchmarking method is the best or the most reliable (see Dell'Anno and Schneider, 2009 for a detailed discussion on different benchmarking procedures).

The economic literature using SEMs is well aware of these limitations. Consequently, it acknowledges that it is not an easy task to apply this methodology to an economic dataset, but also argues that this does not mean one should abandon the SEM approach. On the contrary, following an interdisciplinary approach to economics, SEMs are valuable tools for economic analysis, particularly when studying the shadow economy. However, the mentioned objections should be considered as an incentive for further (economic) research in this field rather than as a suggestion to abandon this method. Again, going back to the definition of the shadow economy, the MIMIC estimation provides upper-bound macro value-added figures, including mostly legally bought material.

EVALUATING THE RESULTS OF USING VARIOUS INDIRECT MEASUREMENT METHODS: A CASE STUDY OF GERMANY

Different estimation methods produce sometimes radically varying results regarding the size of the shadow economy. To see this, we here use a case study of Germany to reveal how the size of the shadow economy varies according to the measurement methods used. Table 2.1 reports the results of the size of the German shadow economy using different measurement methods. The oldest estimate uses the direct survey method of the Institut für Demoskopie (IfD) in Allensbach (Germany) and shows that the shadow economy was 3.6 per cent of official GDP in 1974. In a later study, Feld and Larsen (2005, 2009) report the results of direct surveys for the years 2001 to 2006. Using the officially paid wage rate, they conclude that the shadow economy was 4.1 per cent of GDP in 2001, 3.1 per cent in 2004, 3.6 per cent in 2005 and 2.5 per cent in 2006. Using the much lower shadow economy wage rate, these estimates shrink, however, to 1.3 per cent in 2001 and 1.0 per cent in 2004, respectively.

It is well-known, however, that the survey method produces lower-bound

Table 2.1   The size of the shadow economy in Germany according to different methods (in percentage of official GDP)

Method/Source	Shadow economy (as percentage of official GDP) in:							
	1970	1975	1980	1985	1990	1995	2000	2005
Survey								
IfD Allensbach (1975)	–	3.6[1]	–	–	–	–	–	–
Feld and Larsen (2005)	–	–	–	–	–	–	4.1[2]	3.1[2]
	–	–	–	–	–	–	1.3[3]	1.0[3]
Income/expenditure discrepancies								
Lippert and Walker (1997)	11.0	10.2	13.4	–	–	–	–	–
Official/actual employment discrepancies								
Langfeldt (1984)	23.0	38.5	34.0	–	–	–	–	–
Physical input method								
Feld and Larsen (2005)	–	–	–	14.5	14.6	–	–	–
Transactions approach	17.2	22.3	29.3	31.4	–	–	–	–
Currency demand approach								
Kirchgässner (1983)	3.1	6.0	10.3	–	–	–	–	–
Langfeldt (1984)	12.1	11.8	12.6	–	–	–	–	–
Schneider and Enste (2000a)	4.5	7.8	9.2	11.3	11.8	12.5	14.7	–
Latent ((DY)MIMIC) approach								
Frey and Weck (1983a, 1983b)	5.8	6.1	8.2	–	–	–	–	–
								–
Pickhardt and Sardà Pons (2006)	–	–	9.4	10.1	11.4	15.1	16.3	
Schneider (2005, 2007)	4.2	5.8	10.8	11.2	12.2	13.9	16.0	15.4
Soft modelling								
Weck-Hannemann (1983)	–	8.3	–	–	–	–	–	–

Notes:
1 1974.
2 2001 and 2004; calculated using wages in the official economy.
3 2001 and 2004; calculated using actual 'black' hourly wages paid.

estimates of the size of the shadow economy or what some might view as underestimates of its size. Other more indirect measurement methods, however, produce higher estimates of its size. Using the discrepancy method and applying national income statistics for example, Lippert and Walker (1997) estimate the size of the German shadow economy from 1970 to 1980 as being between 11.0 per cent and 13.4 per cent of official GDP. Using the discrepancy method applying official and actual employment, meanwhile, Langfeldt (1984) produces much higher estimates for 1970 to 1980, ranging from 23.0 per cent to 38.5 per cent. Applying the physical input method (electricity approach) furthermore, Feld and Larsen (2005) produce results of 14.5 per cent for the year 1985 and 14.6 per cent for 1990. The monetary transaction method developed by Feige calculates the shadow economy to be of about 30 per cent between 1980 and 1985. These are the highest estimates. Switching to the currency demand approach, first used by Kirchgässner (1983, 1984), his study provides values of 3.1 per cent in 1970 and 10.3 per cent in 1980. Kirchgässner's values are quite similar to those obtained by Schneider and Enste (2000a), who also use the currency demand approach to estimate the size of the shadow economy, which are 4.5 per cent in 1970 and 14.7 per cent in 2000. Using the MIMIC estimation procedure, which was first applied by Frey and Weck (1983a, 1983b), the results are quite similar to those from the currency demand approach, which is perhaps not surprising since the calibration start-values have been used from the currency demand approach in order to transform the relative estimates of the MIMIC approach. Frey and Weck (1983a, 1983b) calculate a shadow economy in Germany in 1970 of 5.8 per cent, which increases to 8.2 per cent in 1980. Pickhardt and Sardà Pons (2006), whose sample used for the MIMIC estimations started a bit later, produce a value of 9.4 per cent in 1980, which increases to 16.3 per cent in the year 2000. These are quite similar values to Schneider (2005, 2007). Finally, using the soft modelling variant of the MIMIC approach, Weck-Hannemann (1983) gets a value of 8.3 per cent of GDP in 1975.

As Table 2.1 reveals, therefore, different estimation procedures produce different results. It is safe to say that the figures produced by the transactions and discrepancy approaches are unrealistically large. A size of the shadow economy of almost one third of official GDP in the mid-1980s is most likely to be an overestimate. The figures obtained using the currency demand and the hidden (latent, MIMIC) approaches are, on the other hand, relatively close together and much lower than those produced by the discrepancy or transactions approach. The estimates from the MIMIC approach can be regarded as the most reasonable estimates of the size of the shadow economy and the survey model is likely to produce too low estimates for the reasons already discussed.

Table 2.2   A comparison of the size of the German shadow economy using the survey and the MIMIC method, year 2006

Various kinds of shadow economy activities/values	Shadow economy as % of official GDP	Shadow economy in bill. Euro	% share of the overall shadow economy
Shadow activities from labour	5.0–6.0	117–140	33–40
(hours worked, *survey results*)	3.0–4.0	70–90	20–25
+ Material (used)	4.0–5.0	90–117	25–33
+ Illegal activities (goods and services)	1.0–2.0	23–45	7–13
+ already in the official GDP included illegal activities			
Sum (1) to (4)	13.0–17.0	300–92	85–111
Overall (total) shadow economy (estimated by the MIMIC and calibrated by the currency demand procedure)	15.0	340	100

Source: Enste and Schneider (2006) and own calculations

Finally, in Table 2.2, a comparison of the size of the German shadow economy using the survey and the MIMIC method for the year 2006 is undertaken. As we see, the difference between the estimates of the macro-method (here the MIMIC estimation procedure) and the results from the survey method is quite large. In Table 2.2 an attempt is undertaken to demonstrate the major difference between these two estimation methods. The first line of Table 2.2 clearly shows shadow economy activities from labour (hours worked, survey results). They range from 5.0 per cent to 6.0 per cent in the year 2006. If one adds to this used material, illegal activities and those that are already included in the official GDP, one gets a value between 13.0 per cent and 17.0 per cent of GDP, which comes very close to the 15.0 per cent of the MIMIC estimation results. Hence, one realizes that the macro-results of course include the used materials and illegal activities, so that it is not amazing to find much larger results.

CONCLUSIONS

In this chapter, the indirect measurement methods used to evaluate the size of the shadow economy have been evaluated and a case study of Germany provided in order to show the different results produced using various measurement methods. This has revealed that the different measurement methods produce very different results for the size of the shadow economy. Here, therefore, we first summarize our findings about the indirect measurement methods used to estimate the size and development of the shadow economy and raise some critical remarks.

Starting with the discrepancy method, the difficulty is that often a combination of 'rough' estimations and unclear assumptions are made, and the calculation method is often not clear with the documentation and procedure often not made public (see Thomas, 1992). The monetary and/or electricity methods, meanwhile, result in some very high estimates and only macro-estimates are available. Moreover, a breakdown by sector or industry is not possible, and there are great difficulties confronted when attempting to convert millions of kWh into a value-added figure when using the electricity method (see Schneider and Williams, 2013; Thomas, 1992). The MIMIC (latent) method, furthermore, has several critical issues associated with it. These include: only relative coefficients, no absolute values, are obtained; the estimations are quite often highly sensitive with respect to changes in the data and specifications; there are difficulties in differentiating between the selection of causes and indicators, and the calibration procedure and starting values used have a significant influence on the results obtained, as can be seen by comparing Breusch (2005a, 2005b) and Schneider and Williams (2013).

The direct survey method, meanwhile, which will be addressed in more detail in the next chapter, has the disadvantage that quite often only households are considered and firms are, at least partly, left out, that non-responses and/or incorrect responses are given and that results of the financial volume of 'black' hours worked or participation rates, and not of value added, are obtained, as can be seen by comparing Feld and Larsen (2005, 2008, 2009) and Kazemier (2006).

3. Measuring the shadow labour force: a review of direct survey methods

Although many use indirect methods to evaluate the size of the shadow economy, an increasing number of scholars are employing direct surveys, not least because there has been a desire to understand the nature of work in the shadow economy, the characteristics of the shadow labour force and motives of participants. Those advocating direct methods criticize the indirect methods for providing very little information regarding the structure of the shadow economy. They argue that indirect methods possess some very crude assumptions concerning its nature that are far from proven (Thomas, 1992; Williams, 2004a; Williams and Windebank, 1998, 1999, 2001, 2003). In previous decades when little empirical data was available, such methods might have played an important role in highlighting the existence of the shadow economy. Today nevertheless, the growing number of direct surveys means that indirect methods are no longer perhaps as necessary as was previously the case (Williams, 2006a).

However, the major criticism of direct survey methods is that they naively assume that people will reveal to them their participation in the shadow economy, or even know about it. On the one hand, purchasers may not even know if the work is in the shadow economy and on the other hand, sellers will be reticent about disclosing the extent of their shadow work. The former point might well be valid. However, it is not necessarily the case that those supplying work in the shadow economy will be untruthful in their dealings with researchers. As Bàculo (2001, p. 2) states regarding her face-to-face interviews, 'they were curious and flattered that university researchers were interested in their problems' and were more than willing to share their experiences. Pahl (1984) similarly found that when comparing the results from individuals as suppliers and purchasers, the same level of shadow work was discovered. The implication therefore is that individuals are not secretive about their shadow activities.

Similar conclusions are reached about the openness of research participants in Canada (Fortin et al., 1996) and the UK (Leonard, 1994; MacDonald, 1994; Williams, 2004a). As MacDonald (1994) reveals in his study of the unemployed in a UK deprived region, 'fiddly work' was not a sensitive subject to participants. They happily talked about it in the same breath as discussing, for instance, their experiences of starting up in self-employment or of voluntary work. This willingness of people to talk openly about their shadow labour was also found in Belfast (Leonard, 1994). Indeed, neither are there any grounds for assuming that businesses will not report their participation in the shadow economy. In one of the few direct surveys that interviews businesses about the extent of their shadow labour, the 2002 EBRD/World Bank Business Environment and Enterprise Performance Survey implemented in 26 countries of East-Central Europe and the Commonwealth of Independent States (CIS), Fries et al. (2003) identify that it is wholly possible to collect such data. There have also been several qualitative surveys that again reveal the willingness of both employers and employees to openly talk about their participation in the shadow economy (for example, Jones et al., 2004; Ram et al., 2001, 2002a, 2002b, 2003, 2007). This is perhaps because although shadow labour is illegal in terms of the laws and regulations of formal institutions, it is seen as legitimate endeavour from the perspective of informal institutions, namely the norms, values and beliefs of the population (Webb et al., 2009). Consequently, it is openly discussed, which makes reliable data collection possible using direct survey methods.

As such, direct surveys have been conducted in Belgium (Kesteloot and Meert, 1999), Canada (Fortin et al., 1996), Denmark (Mogensen et. al., 1995; Pedersen, 2003), Germany (Buehn, 2012; Feld and Larsen, 2005, 2008, 2009, 2012; Feld et al., 2007), Italy (Bàculo, 2001), Norway (Isachsen and Strom, 1985), the Netherlands (van Eck and Kazemier, 1988; Renooy, 1990), the UK (for example, Brill, 2011; Leonard, 1994; Pahl, 1984; Williams, 2004a, 2006a; Williams and Windebank, 2003; Williams et al., 2012a), Sweden (Jönsson, 2001) and the USA (Jensen et al., 1995; Nelson and Smith, 1999). There have also been cross-national direct surveys of participation in the shadow economy that use the same definition and survey methodology in all member states of the European Union (European Commission, 2007a, 2014). Here therefore, the direct survey methods available are reviewed by, first, analysing some key variations in their design and, second, reporting the results of a Netherlands study that sought to evaluate the pros and cons of different direct survey methods.

VARIATIONS IN THE DESIGN OF DIRECT SURVEYS

To review the key variations in the design of direct surveys, we here discuss the variations in, first, the unit of analysis examined; second, the data collection methodology used; third, a range of questionnaire design issues;

fourth, the sample size; fifth, the sampled populations; and sixth and finally, the sampling method used.

Unit of Analysis

Researchers can take either the enterprise or the household as the unit of analysis when conducting direct surveys. Most studies take the household as the unit of analysis and request information from participants as both purchasers and suppliers of work in the shadow economy (for example, European Commission, 2014; Leonard, 1994; Pahl, 1984; Warde, 1990; Williams, 2004a; Williams and Round, 2009). The advantage is that these survey home-based businesses, which constitute more than one-third of all businesses (Mason et al., 2008). They also often analyse shadow labour as part of the wider coping strategies used by households in their daily lives that makes it easier for participants to talk about their work in the shadow economy. Fewer have used the enterprise as a unit of analysis (for exceptions, see Fries et al., 2003; Ram et al., 2001, 2002a, 2002b, 2003; Williams, 2006c, 2006d; Williams et al., 2012a). When they do, they often confine questions to either the impacts that the shadow economy has had on the enterprises of the participants or their perceptions of the size of the shadow economy in their sector (Meriküll et al., 2013; Putniņš and Sauka, 2015; Sauka and Putniņš, 2011). They do not generally ask enterprises about the proportion of their transactions or turnover that is in the shadow economy.

Data Collection Methodology

Data can be collected about participants' shadow labour through either mail-shot questionnaires (for example, Fortin et al., 1996), internet surveys (Kazemier, 2014), telephone interviews (for example, Bajada, 2011; Jönsson, 2001) or face-to-face interviews of the unstructured (for example, Bàculo, 2001; Howe, 1988) or structured variety (for example, Pahl, 1984; Williams, 2004a) using either mostly open- or closed-ended questions. Most direct surveys use face-to-face interviews (for example Leonard, 1994; Pahl, 1984). Until now, besides some experimental work in the Netherlands (Kazemier, 2014), online surveys are relatively unde-veloped in this field of enquiry. Neither has 'big data' been used, such as from social media sites or eBay. Here, therefore, we provide a brief review of the alternative methods available for collecting data on shadow labour and, following this, provide a review of a limited number of studies that have sought to provide a comparative evaluation of these different methods.

Mail-shot questionnaires

Postal surveys are relatively cheaper than in-home face-to-face surveys and self-completion methods yield higher reporting levels of socially undesirable behaviour and attitudes than interviewer-administered methods. This is because the presence of the interviewer in the latter may encourage participants to provide socially desirable answers to sensitive questions. Self-completion methods might therefore be expected to identify actors in the shadow economy at a higher rate than interviewer-administered methods. However, postal surveys have a number of shortcomings. They yield somewhat lower response rates than face-to-face surveys and are susceptible to high levels of non-response bias, which are hard to mitigate. Even if monetary incentives are used to increase the response rate, there remains little or no incentive for participants to report activities in the shadow economy. Postal surveys are also susceptible to respondent selection bias because the researcher is reliant on participants adhering to rules about which household member should complete the survey. They are also unsuitable for participants who have difficulty reading, and are very poorly suited to long and complex questionnaires. Overall, therefore, the risk of non-response bias and constraints on questionnaire design outweigh the potential advantages of a postal survey approach when seeking to evaluate the shadow labour force.

Telephone interviews

In terms of interviewer-administered methods, telephone interviewing is one approach that has been used. Telephone surveys provide a lower-cost method of obtaining general population samples than face-to-face surveys. However, telephone surveys have a number of disadvantages relative to face-to-face surveys, both generally and in relation to studying shadow labour in particular. First, there is no satisfactory population list of individuals or households in many countries that includes telephone numbers. As a result, telephone surveys of the general population tend to use variants of an approach loosely termed random digit dialling (RDD), whereby samples of telephone numbers are generated either from all possible numbers or using a 'list-assisted' approach such as from directories. These methods are usually based on residential landline numbers only and therefore exclude the population of 'mobile-only' households, which in the UK, for example, accounts for some 15 per cent of households. Critically, these households differ significantly in profile from households with access to a fixed line in important respects for this study, notably in relation to age and social class. For example, a quarter (26 per cent) of 25–34-year-olds in the UK are mobile-only compared with 6 per cent of 55–64s, 5 per cent of 65–74 year-olds and 1 per cent of those aged 75 and over (Ofcom,

2012). Although weighting can remove the bias caused by the omission of mobile-only respondents in fixed-line surveys, the differences in behaviour between the mobile-only and landline populations cannot be controlled by weighting. The inclusion of mobile phone numbers in the sampling frame can be used to address this coverage issue, but this increases costs significantly and results in lower cooperation rates. Both probability and quota sampling methods can be used as a basis for respondent selection, but achievable response rates for probability-based surveys (typically 25–35 per cent) are around half those achievable for equivalent face-to-face surveys, and lower still if a dual frame approach is used. As a result, the benefits of using probability rather than quota sampling in telephone surveys are questionable. Indeed, these coverage and response rate issues explain the decline in use of this method in social surveys in recent years. Moreover, while computer-aided telephone interview (CATI) surveys can handle complex questionnaire structures, they are unsuitable for interviews longer than 25–30 minutes. In this respect, they offer less flexibility than a bespoke face-to-face approach.

In addition to these generic shortcomings, telephone surveys have weaknesses relative to other data collection methods when asking sensitive questions. While it is possible to ask sensitive questions in telephone surveys, the fact that the interviewer must read out both questions and responses is likely to increase the risk that participants will give socially desirable answers. In contrast, face-to-face surveys can use self-completion and 'concealed response' techniques (whereby responses are numbered/lettered and randomly ordered on a show card and respondents only give their response as a number/letter) as a means of eliciting honest responses to sensitive questions. Indeed, Pedersen (2003) found that a pilot telephone survey in Germany yielded an unrealistically low incidence of shadow economy activities, and that, when the pilot was rerun using a face-to-face approach, respondents were more likely to divulge shadow economy activities. The researchers hypothesized that this might be because the face-to-face environment was more conducive to establishing the level of trust in the interviewer necessary for the participant to volunteer this information.

Internet surveys
Online access panels provide a very low cost method of identifying low prevalence groups in the population, and offer the same benefits as postal surveys in terms of their relative anonymity. Unlike postal surveys, complex questionnaire structures are possible because the questionnaire is computer-assisted, although single topic interview lengths beyond 15–20 minutes are not recommended. Like postal surveys, online surveys are unsuitable for respondents who have difficulty reading. However, the

main disadvantages of using an online panel as a sampling frame are that (a) coverage is restricted to the online population and (b) panellists tend to be unrepresentative of the population, even if they have the same demographic profile.

Multiple methods are used for recruitment to online panels, with controls put in place to boost representation of under-represented population groups. Nonetheless some groups (notably the youngest and oldest age groups) are heavily under-represented and significant concerns remain about the representativeness of those joining panels. Online panels are also heavily used, resulting in low response rates and low levels of respondent engagement. This can lead to a tendency for some panellists to use short-cuts such as 'straight-lining' (that is, selecting the same response option for a set of items, particularly in batteries of attitude statements, rather than discriminating between individual statements, as a means of 'speeding' through the interview) when responding. While quality control measures can be put in place to identify and remove offenders, these issues remain an ongoing concern for online access panels.

Face-to-face interviews
Face-to-face approaches can include street interviewing, although these generally do not provide sufficiently robust and representative samples. Here, therefore, this option is not discussed further. In-home (household) data collection provides a high-quality design option for most survey work and offers specific benefits when studying the shadow economy. The availability of a comprehensive sampling frame of residential addresses in many countries means that in-home surveys provide full coverage of the population that lives in private residential accommodation. In-home surveys permit longer interviews than other data collection methods (at least in bespoke surveys) and can handle complex questionnaire structures with the use of computer-aided personal interviewing (CAPI). While the presence of an interviewer can deter honest responses to sensitive questions, self-completion and 'concealed response' techniques can be used to mitigate this problem.

In-home surveys also provide the opportunity to ask respondents to access documentary evidence to verify information, although this relies on participants being able and willing to access the information in advance of the interview, or to retrieve it quickly during the interview itself, and is not always practical or cost-effective.

The main disadvantage of in-home interviews is that they are expensive and can take a long time to complete, although an omnibus approach can eliminate both of these disadvantages, particularly when the incidence of the target population is very low. Overall, an in-home approach has been the most widely used direct survey approach adopted when studying shadow labour.

Comparative evaluation of data collection techniques

One study compares the impacts of various data collection techniques used during 1983 and 1984 in the Netherlands. Kazemier and van Eck (1992) compare the outcomes of several data collection methodologies (face-to-face, mail and telephone) and gradual and direct approaches (considered below). Among the different variants tested, the face-to-face data collection method combined with a gradual approach produced the highest levels of participation in shadow labour of all direct survey methods. Isachsen and Strom (1989), however, identify that in Norway, survey participants were almost twice as likely to admit participation in shadow labour when they responded to an anonymous mail-in written questionnaire as when they participated in a face-to-face interview. There is thus no clear-cut conclusion that can be reached from the experiments with different data collection techniques so far conducted, about which is most effective to use. Nonetheless, the tendency has been for most data collection to adopt an in-home face-to-face data collection technique. This will be returned to below.

Questionnaire Design Issues

Defining the shadow economy

A first issue regarding questionnaire design is whether to explicitly communicate to the participant what is meant by the shadow economy. Conventionally, few direct surveys did so. The resultant problem was that one had no way of knowing whether participants were defining their work in the shadow economy in the same way, or in the manner intended by the researchers. Following in the path of Pedersen (1998, 2003), recent studies, notably the cross-national surveys of undeclared work in the member states of the European Union (European Commission, 2007a, 2014), have included an explicit definition of the shadow economy, which they communicate to participants during the interview.

The reference period

In most surveys, questions about participation in the shadow economy use a time limit. The most common is the past 12 months (for example, European Commission, 2014; Williams and Windebank, 2001). This is in line with standard survey research practice, which seeks to maximize recall while controlling for potential seasonal effects. Importantly, it also enables comparison of results over time if the study is repeated at a later

point in time. Some also ask questions about shadow work without impos-
ing a time limit, which obviously leads to higher results. Hanousek and
Palda (2003), meanwhile, ask about engagement in shadow activities in
three different reference years (2000, 1999, 1995) so as to try to obtain
longitudinal data.

Direct versus gradual approach

Given that activity in the shadow economy is a sensitive topic because it
is by definition illegal (even if socially legitimate), direct survey methods
use a range of techniques in their survey design to elicit such information.
In early surveys, this involved a household work practices approach. A
range of everyday tasks was listed and then participants were asked about
the form of work last used to get each task completed, and following
this, whether they had undertaken any of these tasks for others and if so,
whether they had been paid cash-in-hand for doing so (for example, Pahl,
1984; Williams, 2004a). In recent years, however, another type of gradual
approach has come to the fore. This firstly asks respondents about less
sensitive issues (for example, general opinions on the shadow economy),
then turns to asking them about instances where they have purchased work
in the shadow economy before addressing whether they have supplied
work in the shadow economy (European Commission, 2007a, 2014). In
a study comparing the impacts of using gradual approaches versus direct
approaches in the Netherlands, Kazemier and van Eck (1992) find that the
gradual approach produced much higher rates of participation in shadow
work than the direct approach during structured face-to-face interviews,
but not in the case of mail and telephone surveys. Indeed, the lengthier the
set of 'priming' questions, the higher the eventual rates of participation in
the shadow economy. Pedersen (1998, 2003) who used lengthier priming
questions elicited higher response rates than the Eurobarometer survey
(European Commission, 2007a) that used a shorter lead-in prior to asking
questions about participation in the shadow economy.

Supply- and/or demand-side

Household surveys mostly ask about both the demand and supply side
(European Commission, 2007a, 2014; Fortin et al., 1996; Isachsen et al.,
1982; Lemieux et al., 1994; Williams, 2004a), although some examine
respondents only as purchasers (for example, McCrohan et al., 1991;
Smith, 1985). Surveys using businesses as the unit of analysis, however,
have so far largely avoided asking questions of whether businesses engage
in off-the-books transactions (Williams, 2006b). Instead, business surveys
have tended to explore only the impacts of the shadow economy on the
business under investigation (for example, World Bank, 2014).

Relationship between purchasers and sellers

In recent decades, investigations have taken place on the relationship between the clients and providers of shadow labour. This arises out of recognition in qualitative studies that a large proportion of shadow labour is by and for kin, friends and neighbours (Cornuel and Duriez, 1985; Jensen et al., 1995). This then resulted in some national surveys investigating the relationship between the buyers and sellers of shadow work (Persson and Malmer, 2006; Williams, 2004a) and eventually its inclusion in cross-national comparative surveys (European Commission, 2007a, 2014). When combined with their reasons for engaging in such work both as customers and suppliers, the social relations and motives underpinning the heterogeneous forms of shadow labour can be unpacked (European Commission, 2007a, 2014; Howe, 1990; Williams, 2004a).

Encouraging honest reporting/minimizing social desirability bias

Minimizing the risk of social desirability bias is a key challenge for studies of shadow labour. An example is that participants may assert that the shadow work was conducted for closer social relations and perhaps for redistributive reasons and/or to help them out. This is because shadow work conducted by individuals for other households tends to be deemed more socially acceptable than work conducted by firms or work conducted by individuals for firms (see Williams, 2014a). Several strategies can be used, however, to reduce such social desirability bias in responses. A first tactic is to use an omnibus survey whose key advantage is that participants are recruited on the basis of a general mixed-topic interview, and therefore the survey subject does not need to be flagged up to respondents, and will simply follow a previous section in the questionnaire with an appropriate lead-in. A second tactic relates to question ordering, putting more sensitive questions later after a rapport with the interviewer has been built up. A third strategy is to use self-completion/concealed response techniques where respondents report a coded letter or number to indicate their response. A fourth approach is to use 'face-saving' techniques. The Rockwool and Eurobarometer questionnaires frame questions as non-judgementally as possible – for example, by stating that this type of activity is relatively common/within social norms – thus helping to 'legitimize' admission to certain behaviours. Other typical 'face-saving' techniques are to acknowledge in the question wording that we do not all always behave as we feel we should. A fifth and final approach is to give repeated reassurances of anonymity to remind respondents of the commitment to confidentiality. In practice, of course, a mix of all these measures can be used in the same questionnaire.

Using appropriate terminology

It is important to communicate concepts to research participants in a way that is clear and unambiguous. This requires the avoidance of overly complex terminologies that can act as a barrier to engagement, as well as lead to inaccurate measures and high levels of 'don't know' responses. Cognitive testing and question assessment helps identify any words, phrases and concepts that are subject to misunderstanding or misinterpretation, and helps ensure the question wording is suitable across all audiences. A first step therefore, is to examine questions by considering specific criteria (such as clarity, assumptions, instructions, knowledge/recall, task difficulty, sensitivity and social desirability bias) in order to decide whether the question exhibits features that are likely to cause problems.

A second step is then to engage in cognitive testing. Cognitive testing is used as a question development tool to understand the thought processes that a respondent uses in trying to answer a survey question. The aim is to see whether the respondent understands both the question as a whole and any key specific words and phrases it might contain, what sort of information the participant needs to retrieve in order to answer the question, and what decision processes the respondent uses in coming to an answer. The technique enables the wording and format of survey questions to be fine-tuned, with a view to ensuring that participants understand the questions, interpret them in the same way and are able to answer them without ambiguity. In cognitive pilot tests, therefore, a number of cognitive techniques such as concurrent and retrospective thinking aloud, verbal probing, observation and paraphrasing are used. The researcher observes the respondent to identify and note areas of apparent doubt, misunderstanding or incomprehension. In this way, the researcher is able to witness not only the verbal communication that takes place, but also the non-verbal reactions of the respondent. This allows instances where the respondent feels uncomfortable answering a question to be identified, and to assess what can be done to alleviate the sensitivity of the question and/or provide added reassurance.

Validating responses

To ensure that responses are honest and accurate, most surveys build in some means of validating responses. For example, responses on the amounts of shadow income earned can be compared with the total spent by purchasers of shadow work. Alternatively, interviewers can be asked to record their assessment of the respondent, as was the case in the Eurobarometer surveys (European Commission, 2007a, 2014).

Sample size
For qualitative studies, there have been studies reported on a single person (Woolfson, 2007). For extensive quantitative surveys, meanwhile, the sample size has ranged from 100 or so (Williams and Windebank, 2001) to nearly 27,000 interviews (European Commission, 2007a, 2014). The majority are in the range of about 400–1,000 interviews per country. Given the small proportion of participants engaging in shadow labour, this often leads to relatively small numbers of shadow workers being analysed.

Sampled populations
Most studies of the shadow economy have been conducted on populations in particular localities (for example, Fortin et al., 1996; Leonard, 1994; Pahl, 1984; Renooy, 1990; Warde, 1990; Williams, 2004a), socio-economic groups such as home-workers (for example, Phizacklea and Wolkowitz, 1995) or industrial sectors such as garment manufacturing (for example, Lin, 1995). Until recently, few nationally representative direct surveys had been conducted (an exception is Williams, 2006d) and even fewer cross-national comparative surveys (a notable exception is Pedersen, 2003). This has changed in recent years. In Europe, the 2007 and 2013 Eurobarometer surveys have conducted nationally representative samples (European Commission, 2007a, 2014), the International Labour Organization (ILO) has used common questionnaires in some 40 countries (ILO, 2013) and the World Bank Enterprise Surveys have conducted common harmonized questionnaires on the impact of shadow work on businesses in more than 130 countries (World Bank, 2014).

Sampling method
Various sampling methods have been used in studies of shadow labour. Here, we review a range of possible sampling methods.

Maximum variation sampling
One technique is to use maximum variation sampling, especially with small qualitative sample sizes. This seeks to continuously look for cases that display maximum diversity according to certain variables. For example, an affluent and deprived urban and rural locality may be chosen for study, as was the case in a UK localities study (Williams, 2004a). Within each locality, a spatially stratified sampling procedure was then used by estimating the number of households in the locality and then calling at every nth household. Although not a representative national sample, this provides data on the spatial variations in the extent and nature of work in the shadow economy. Similar sampling strategies could be applied starting with other variables such as age, gender, sector or occupation.

Random probability sampling

Random sampling is usually used in social surveys where the absolute measurement of prevalence is a core objective. The value of random sampling is, however, contingent on the ability to achieve high response rates to minimize the risk of non-response bias, and to achieve this within a given budget and timetable. Where this is not possible, quota sampling provides a practical alternative. In home interviewing, using a probability sampling approach would yield the highest response rates of all the available methods. It enables advance notification of respondents about the survey, although it is arguable that prior notification of the subject matter might deter the target population from taking part in the survey rather than encourage them to do so. However, the costs associated with adopting a bespoke probability sample approach are prohibitive. An alternative is an omnibus survey approach using probability sampling.

Quota sampling

There are two main drawbacks of quota samples relative to random samples. The first is that the quoted margins of error for quota samples rest on more assumptions than those required for random samples. Principally, the assumption is made that the sample variance for a quota sample is roughly equal to a random sample of the same scale. This seems to be borne out empirically and Bethlehem (2009) provides some statistical support for this assumption as part of his coverage of random samples with low response rates. Second, the risk of systematic bias in quota samples is usually ignored, even though this risk is greater than with random samples with high response rates. However, because quota samples have a lower per interview cost than random samples, a small degree of systematic bias can be absorbed without reducing the value of a quota sample to the point where it is no better than a smaller random probability sample. It should be noted that these drawbacks mainly pertain to cross-sectional estimates. So long as real life change is properly reflected in both random and quota samples, estimates of change should be equally accurate for both methods.

Despite the drawbacks of quota samples relative to random samples, a number of features of the shadow economy mean that a quota sampling method should be considered. First, while robust measurement of participation in the shadow labour force is usually a critical objective, perfect measurement is not expected. It is accepted that activity will in all likelihood be under-measured and this source of error will dwarf any non-response bias (as measurement error usually does when the topic is a sensitive one). A proportion of those active in the shadow labour force will be unwilling to admit to this activity, while other activity may be under-reported because participants do not think of or recall it in the context of the questioning. The degree of under-reporting can be mitigated through good questionnaire design, but it cannot be eliminated altogether. In this respect, it can be argued that the advantages of probability over quota sampling are less convincing than in studies where participation is more straightforward to measure.

Second, direct surveys of shadow labour are often particularly concerned with understanding the attitudes and motivations of people active in the shadow economy, and how these vary between different segments. While sizing of the individual segments is important, understanding how the segments differ in their attitudes and motivations is arguably more important. The key to this is to maximize the sample size. The cost per completed interview of a quota sample design is much lower than for a probability sample design, so this is a substantial advantage.

Random location sampling
A well-established hybrid of the random/quota sampling method is random location sampling. This eliminates the more unsatisfactory features of quota sampling without incurring the cost and other penalties involved in conducting surveys according to strict probability methods. The principal characteristic of the method that distinguishes it from other quota sample methods is that interviewers are given very little choice in the selection of participants. Random location uses a two-stage sampling method. The first stage replicates probability sampling approaches, whereby a stratified random sample of areas (primary sampling units) is drawn. The second stage deviates from probability sampling, insofar as the interviewer is free to call on any address within the primary sampling unit to achieve a set number of interviews. The underlying premise of random location sampling is that the quota controls and rules that govern when, where and with whom interviewers carry out their work replace the measures employed in probability sample surveys to maximize response rates. For this reason, interviewers working on random location surveys do not record the outcome of the contacts they make at each address in their assignment and, as is conventional in quota-based survey designs, response rates are not measured.

Sample composition is controlled via setting quotas defined by, for example, gender, age and working status, which are designed to combat the natural variation in response propensity (both contact and cooperation) among the local population. Combined with the area stratification, this method produces robust representative samples.

COMPARING DIRECT SURVEY METHODS: A CASE STUDY OF THE NETHERLANDS

In 1982, the Netherlands Central Bureau of Statistics started large-scale survey research on the supply of shadow labour. Given that it was unknown what type of survey would yield the best results (by which is meant the highest level of self-reporting by participants of their participation), eight survey variants were tested. They differed in the medium of communication between the researcher and respondent (face-to-face, mail and telephone) and in interview design (direct approach, gradual approach and 'free-form' conversation). Several criteria were used to assess the survey variants on their suitability for obtaining statistical information on the extent and nature of the shadow labour force. The finding was that in terms of pre-venting non-response and item non-response, face-to-face methods yielded the best results. In preventing incorrect responses, a gradual introduction to the more sensitive questions was better (Kazemier and van Eck, 1992). This section reports a more recent follow-up comparative evaluation of the effectiveness of different survey methods (Kazemier, 2014).

In 2006, and to enable the character of shadow work to be more fully understood, Statistics Netherlands decided to do research into what type of direct survey method should be used to provide such information. Similar to the research conducted by Statistics Netherlands during the 1980s, the decision was taken to investigate respondents both as suppliers and purchasers of shadow work. The research started in 2006 with an experiment to evaluate whether a mixed-mode survey would yield satisfac-tory results. In a mixed-mode survey, respondents are approached in a way that best suits the interviewee (internet, telephone, mail or face-to-face). In the tested mixed-mode survey, a random sample of people over 16 years old were sent a letter in which they were invited to complete an internet survey. Participants who did not have access to the internet and those not wanting to complete the survey online could ask for a questionnaire on paper. Non-respondents were phoned and asked to complete the online or paper questionnaire. They could also opt to be interviewed by phone. For a control, traditional random face-to-face survey research was also conducted. The numbers of responses and respondents who reported participation in shadow labour are presented in Table 3.1. This reveals that many opted to use the online survey with the majority of those not doing so selecting a telephone survey rather than a paper questionnaire. The finding, however, was that the face-to-face interviews not only yielded a higher response rate but also a higher participation rate in shadow labour than the mixed mode approach using the internet, paper and telephone interviews.

Table 3.1   Response and incidence by survey mode 2006

Mode	Number	Response rate	Respondents who admitted shadow economic activity, % (standard error)
Face-to-face	1,133	61%	9.1 (0.9)
Mixed mode	980	51%	5.7 (0.7)
– Internet	550		7.1 (1.1)
– Paper	127		3.1 (1.6)
– Telephone	303		4.3 (1.2)

Source: abridged version of Kazemier (2014, Table 1)

The finding, moreover, is that there is a statistically significant difference between the different modes. The participation rate in shadow labour identified in the face-to-face survey was significantly higher than in the mixed mode survey: $\chi 2 = 6.85$ ($\chi 20.95$ per cent; df $=1 = 3.84$). Without the written or telephone variant in the mixed-mode, the differences are not significant at a 95 per cent confidence level, but they are at a 90 per cent confidence level.

Despite these findings regarding the higher response rate and also higher incidence of shadow work being identified in face-to-face interviews, Statistics Netherlands continued to experiment with trying to develop online survey methods in the period 2007 to 2010, not least because it was seen as a cheaper option. Indeed, there is now a considerable literature on online surveys (Bethlehem, 2009; Couper, 2001, 2008; Dillman et al., 2009; Roberts, 2007; Sue and Ritter, 2007). One of the issues to be carefully considered is representativeness. Not everyone has access to the internet, and not everyone who has access is proficient in the use of the internet. This is especially the case for older people. Table 3.2 displays that there is a clear relationship between the age of the participants and response rates in the online survey of shadow work conducted in 2006. Moreover, no respondents over the age of 55 admitted to working in the shadow economy. To further cut research costs therefore, it was decided to focus future research on people aged 16–65, despite evidence in other surveys that people aged over 65 years commonly engage in shadow labour (European Commission, 2007a). Similarly, there is also a relationship between internet access and the level of education and income. In 2006, 76 per cent of all people with only primary education had access to the internet, compared to 88 per cent of all people with secondary education and 95 per cent of higher educated people. Moreover, the higher the income, the higher the internet access: ranging from 76 per cent for the poorest 20 per cent to 93 per cent for the richest 20 per cent. Moreover, not everyone who has internet access can make adequate use of it.

Table 3.2   Response, incidence and internet access by age, internet survey 2006

Age	Access to the internet	% of population	% of responses	Participation rate in shadow labour, % (st.error)
16–25 years	95	16	19	19.3 (3.8)
26–35 years	90	18	22	5.9 (2.2)
36–45 years	92	21	19	1.9 (1.4)
46–55 years	90	19	21	7.6 (2.4)
56–65 years	73	16	14	0.0
66–75 years	50	10	5	0.0
		100	100	7.1 (1.1)

Source: abridged version of Kazemier (2014, Table 2)

By repeated weighting (Houbiers et al., 2003; Knottnerus and van Duin, 2006; Gouweneel and Knottnerus, 2008), the outcomes of the surveys were at least partly corrected for selectivity. Variables used to calculate the weights were gender by age, ethnic origin by generation, level of education, socio-economic category, household type and monthly income. The average weight is 1.00; 90 per cent of the weights are between 0.35 (5 per cent quantile) and 1.95 (95 per cent quantile). Another disadvantage of online surveys is that one can never be certain that the questionnaire is completed by the participant. This is also a problem with paper surveys sent by post. It is not known to what extent this affects the outcomes.

The internet, therefore, is not the best mode for surveys on shadow work. Assuming that the best surveys are those with the highest number of respondents admitting to working in the shadow economy, face-to-face surveys are preferable. Indeed, the 2006 face-to-face surveys, as Table 3.1 reveals, reported a significantly higher participation rate in shadow labour than the 2006 internet surveys. To what extent this difference is because shadow workers refused to cooperate (non-response) or because they did not admit these activities in the survey remains unknown. If non-response is due to a refusal to cooperate, however, the response rate should be lower than with other survey research. This was not the case. The non-response rates of the online surveys on shadow work are in the range of the non-response rates of other online surveys conducted by Statistics Netherlands, albeit at the lower end. A comparison with response rates of other surveys, however, can be misleading. A few percentage points less response because shadow workers refused cooperation may not lead to suspect differences in the response rates, while it does lead to a significantly lower incidence in the response. Attempts to increase the response rate by improving the questionnaire were unsuccessful.

The total amount earned by shadow workers is also significantly underestimated in the online surveys. According to the 2006 face-to-face survey and the 2006/7 online surveys, the total amount paid for shadow activities is 3–10 times higher than the amount received for shadow work. Given that they should match, one can only conclude that the online surveys in this experiment did not provide reliable estimates of participation rates in the shadow economy nor the size (in monetary terms) of the shadow economy. Nevertheless, for some activities they seem reliable. The estimates of the amounts paid by households for cleaning and home maintenance, however, seem remarkably reliable. The results arrived at by face-to-face surveys and by online surveys are almost the same and matched by the results of research conducted by others. The main reason for this is that paying off-the-books is not against the law, and there is no obligation or incentive to report the payments to the tax authorities or social security authorities. Therefore, there is little reason to hide the payments from the survey. This is also a way forward. Asking questions about the demand for shadow labour may be more successful than asking about the supply.

CONCLUSIONS

As it has been recognized that it is not the size of the shadow economy, but rather the nature of shadow work and the characteristics and motives of the shadow labour force that need to be known if it is going to be tackled, there has been some shift away from indirect measurement methods to direct survey methods. This chapter has reviewed the various direct survey methods that can be used to conduct research on the shadow economy along with the issues that need to be addressed when designing a direct survey of the shadow labour force. This has revealed that decisions are required on, first, the unit of analysis to be examined; second, the data collection methodology used; third, a multifarious variety of questionnaire design issues; fourth, the sample size; fifth, the sampled populations; and sixth and finally, the sampling method used.

To reveal the results of using different types of survey method, we have then reported evidence from the Netherlands on the different results produced when using different mediums of communication between the researcher and respondent (face-to-face, mail and telephone). This has displayed that the face-to-face interviews not only yielded a higher response rate but also a higher incidence of shadow work being conducted than the mixed mode approach using the internet, paper and telephone interviews.

What type of conclusions, therefore, can we draw, or what have we learnt, during nearly four decades of shadow economy research? Here, we would like to make four summary points. First, there is no ideal or dominant method to estimate the size and development of the shadow economy and shadow labour force. All methods have serious methodological problems and weaknesses. Second, if possible, researchers should use several methods to come somewhat closer to the 'true' value of the size and development of the shadow economy. Third, much more research is needed both with respect to the estimation methodology as well as the production of primary survey data for different countries and periods, and fourth and finally, the focus should be now on micro-shadow economy research, and to undertake experiments, in order to reach two goals: a better micro-foundation, and a better knowledge of the nature of their work in the shadow economy, who engages, what their motivations are and what they earn.

Nevertheless, there remain some questions that remain open. First, a common and internationally accepted definition of the shadow economy is still missing. Such a definition or convention is perhaps needed in order to make comparisons between the shadow economies of different countries more reliable. Second, the link between theory and empirical estimation of the shadow economy is still unsatisfactory; in the best case theory provides us with derived signs of the causal factors, but which are the 'core' causal factors is still open and also in which 'core' indicators shadow economy activities are reflected. And third and finally, a satisfactory validation of the empirical results should be developed so that it is easier to judge the empirical results with respect to their plausibility. With these caveats in mind, attention now turns in Parts II and III of the book to reporting the results of some indirect and direct measurement methods regarding the cross-national variations in the shadow economy and shadow labour force.

PART II

The shadow economy in global perspective

4. The shadow economy in developing and transition economies[1]

For the casual observer, what appears to be instantly apparent is that the shadow economy is not evenly distributed across the globe. For example, it is obvious to anybody from a developed nation visiting some developing or transition economies that the shadow economy appears to be more prevalent than in their home nation. It is the case, however, that developing and transition economies do not all have shadow economies of the same magnitude. There are significant variations in the size of the shadow economy not only across different global regions but also across different developing countries within each region.

The aim of this chapter is to begin to chart these variations in the magnitude of the shadow economy across the developing and transition economies. To do this, we here employ the most commonly used of all indirect measurement methods, namely the MIMIC method. Having outlined in some detail in Chapter 2 how this method derives its estimates, this chapter reports the findings in relation to developing and transition economies. First, therefore, this chapter charts the variations in the size of the shadow economy across global regions so as to show the broad variations across the world in the prevalence of the shadow economy. Having identified these global regional variations, the second section of this chapter then turns its attention to outlining the variations in the size of the shadow economy between countries. The outcome of this chapter will be to provide a graphic portrait of the varying size of the shadow economy across the developing world and the transition economies.

VARIATIONS IN THE SIZE OF THE SHADOW ECONOMY ACROSS GLOBAL REGIONS

This section reports the results of using the MIMIC method to evaluate the size of the shadow economy across 162 countries over the period from 1999 until 2007. In this section, the intention is to aggregate these results so as to analyse the variations in the size of the shadow economy by global region. To do this, we here take the eight global regions distinguished by the

Table 4.1   Average informality (unweighted) by World Bank's regions

Acronym	Region	mean	median	min	max	sd
EAP	East Asia and Pacific	32.3	32.4	12.7	50.6	13.3
ECA	Europe and Central Asia	38.9	39.0	18.1	65.8	10.9
LAC	Latin America and the Caribbean	41.1	38.8	19.3	66.1	12.3
MENA	Middle East and North Africa	28.0	32.5	18.3	37.2	7.8
OECD	High-income OECD	17.1	15.8	8.5	28.0	6.1
OHIE	Other high-income	23.0	25.0	12.4	33.4	7.0
SAS	South Asia	33.2	35.3	22.2	43.9	7.0
SSA	Sub-Saharan Africa	40.2	40.6	18.4	61.8	8.3
World		33.0	33.5	8.5	66.1	12.8

Source: Schneider et al. (2010)

World Bank, namely East Asia and Pacific, Europe and Central Asia, Latin America and the Caribbean, Middle East and North Africa, High-Income OECD, Other High-Income, South Asia, and Sub-Saharan Africa. First, we present the unweighted size of the shadow economy in each of these global regions (simply taking the mean magnitude of the shadow economy of the countries in each global region) and, second, we present the weighted size of the shadow economy in each global region (by taking into account the varying population size in the countries in each global region).

Table 4.1 presents the results of the unweighted size of the shadow economy for each of these global regions. As can be seen, the unweighted mean size of the shadow economy across the world during the period 1999–2007 was 33 per cent of GDP. That is to say, one-third of economic activity in the global economy took place in the shadow economy. This is an important finding. It suggests that unless the shadow economy is taken into account, then economic studies will be missing one-third of all economic activity across the world. If there are significant variations in the share of the economic activity that is in the shadow economy across global regions and also across countries, moreover, this will lead to significant distortions in the resultant depiction of the distribution of economic activity across the globe.

Indeed, this table reveals that there are significant variations in the size of the shadow economy across different global regions. Its share of total economic activity is largest in the Latin America and Caribbean region where the equivalent of 41.1 per cent of GDP is in the shadow economy, followed by 40.2 per cent of GDP in sub-Saharan Africa, 38.9 per cent in Europe and Central Asia, 33.2 per cent in South Asia, 32.3 per cent in East Asia and the Pacific, 28 per cent in the Middle East and North Africa,

Table 4.2   Average informality (weighted) by total GDP in 2005

Acronym	Region	Mean	median	min	max	sd
EAP	East Asia and Pacific	17.5	12.7	12.7	50.6	10.6
ECA	Europe and Central Asia	36.4	32.6	18.1	65.8	8.4
LAC	Latin America and the Caribbean	34.7	33.8	19.3	66.1	7.9
MENA	Middle East and North Africa	27.3	32.5	18.3	37.2	7.7
OECD	High-income OECD	13.4	11.0	8.5	28.0	5.7
OHIE	Other high-income	20.8	19.4	12.4	33.4	4.9
SAS	South Asia	25.1	22.2	22.2	43.9	5.9
SSA	Sub-Saharan Africa	37.6	33.2	18.4	61.8	11.7
World		17.1	13.2	8.5	66.1	9.9

Source: Schneider et al. (2010)

23 per cent in other high-income countries and 17.1 per cent in high-income OECD nations.

There are also significant cross-national variations within each global region. In Latin America and the Caribbean, for example, the size of the shadow economy ranges from 66.1 per cent to 19.3 per cent, with a standard deviation of 12.3 per cent. Similar patterns are identified in each and every global region. Indeed, although the unweighted mean size of the shadow economy across the globe is 33 per cent, the size of the shadow economy varies from 66.1 per cent to 8.5 per cent across countries and the standard deviation is 12.8 per cent. These figures for each global region, however, are unweighted for population size.

When we examine the weighted size of the shadow economy in each global region by taking into account the varying population size in the countries in each global region, a different picture emerges. As Table 4.2 displays, the weighted mean size of the shadow economy across the world during the period 1999–2007, taking into account the population size of each country, was 17.1 per cent of GDP. That is to say, just under one-sixth of economic activity in the global economy was in the shadow economy. Weighting the values therefore, makes a considerable difference. Although the weighted average is smaller than the unweighted one, displaying that countries that are smaller in terms of population size have larger shadow economies nevertheless again reveals the importance of taking the shadow economy into account when examining economies. Unless the shadow economy is included in economic studies, just over one-sixth of all economic activity across the world will be omitted from analyses. This in turn will lead to a distorted portrayal of the unevenness of global economic activity. Given that the shadow economy is generally

larger in countries where official GDP is lower, wider economic disparities will be portrayed than is actually the case when the shadow economy
is included. In other words, there appears to be some convergence in economic disparities measured by official GDP, once the shadow economy
is included in calculations.

Table 4.2 also reveals the variations in the weighted size of the shadow
economy in different global regions. When the weighted rather than
unweighted mean is examined for each global region the ordering changes.
Its share of total economic activity is largest is sub-Saharan Africa where
the shadow economy constitutes the equivalent of 37.6 per cent of GDP
followed by 36.4 per cent in Europe and Central Asia, 34.7 per cent in Latin
America and the Caribbean, 27.3 per cent in the Middle East and North
Africa, 25.1 per cent in South Asia, 20.8 per cent in other high-income
countries, 17.5 per cent in East Asia and the Pacific, and 13.4 per cent
in high-income OECD nations. Indeed, although a weighted mean of
17.1 per cent of GDP is in the shadow economy globally, the standard
deviation is 9.9 per cent. This displays the highly uneven distribution of
the shadow economy globally across countries. Again moreover, there
are large variations within each global region with the standard deviation
ranging from 10.6 per cent in East Asia and the Pacific to 4.9 per cent
across other high-income countries.

Moving beyond the World Bank classification of global regions, we can
also compare how the size of the shadow economy varies between developed countries, developing countries and transition economies. Figure 4.1
aggregates the data according to these three global regions so as to examine
the varying size of the shadow economy across these three country
groupings. This presents data on the weighted averages for the 25 OECD
countries, 116 developing countries and 25 transition economies examined
using the MIMIC measurement methodology. Starting with the overall
findings for all 162 countries on how the size of the shadow economy has
changed over time, the important finding is that across the world there
has been a decrease in the size of the shadow economy between 1999
and 2007. In 1999, the weighted mean size of the shadow economy was
17.9 per cent of GDP, but this then decreased to 17.2 per cent in 2003 and
to 16.1 per cent in 2007. This is a decrease of nearly two percentage points
over just an eight-year period. On a global scale, therefore, the shadow
economy appears to be decreasing in size relative to the formal economy
according to this MIMIC method over this time period. Indeed, if this
rate of decline were to continue over the next three decades, the shadow
economy would have reduced to some 9 per cent of global GDP. This, of
course, is a linear extrapolation and over-simplistic. The important point
is that over this eight-year period at least, there has been a decline in the

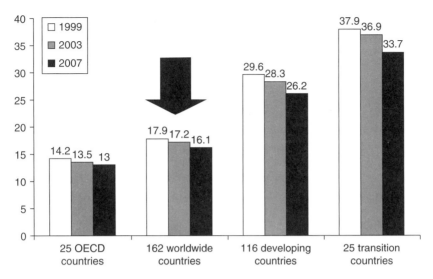

*Figure 4.1   Size and development of the shadow economy of various
country groups (weighted averages; as percentage of official
total GDP of the respective country group)*

size of the shadow economy on a global level according to the calculations of the MIMIC method.

There are, however, significant differences in the size of the shadow economy across OECD countries, developing countries and transition economies. In 2007, the weighted mean size of the shadow economy was 13 per cent in the 25 OECD nations, 26.2 per cent in the 116 developing countries and 33.7 per cent in the transition economies. This clearly displays, therefore, that transition economies have far larger shadow economies than developing countries. Across all three of these broad groupings of economies, however, there has been a decrease in the size of the shadow economy between 1999 and 2007. In the 25 OECD nations, the size of the shadow economy decreased from 14.1 per cent of GDP in 1999 to 13 per cent of GDP in 2007 (that is, a 7.8 per cent decrease in size), while in the 116 developing countries, the shadow economy decreased in size from 29.6 per cent to 26.2 per cent (that is, an 11.5 per cent decrease in size) and in the 25 transition economies the shadow economy decreased from 37.9 per cent to 33.7 per cent of GDP (that is, a decrease of 11.1 per cent). The result is that across these three broad groupings, the shadow economy has declined the slowest in the OECD nations where it was smallest to start with. In the developing and transition economies where the shadow economy was larger to begin with, the decrease in its size has been faster.

Although very tentative, the intimation therefore is that there is a partial convergence of these three broad regional groupings over this time period in terms of the size of their shadow economies.

CROSS-NATIONAL VARIATIONS IN THE SIZE OF THE SHADOW ECONOMY

In order to portray the cross-national variations in the size of the shadow economy, Figure 4.2 provides a graphic portrait of the varying size of the shadow economies across the world. This reveals the significant cross-national variations across the world in the size of the shadow economy. To begin to unravel these cross-national variations in this section, we here take each of the three broad regional groupings in turn, namely the OECD nations, developing countries and transition economies.

OECD Nations

These OECD nations will be dealt with in more depth in the next chapter. Here, it is only necessary to note the overarching trends in Table 4.3, which reveals the size of the shadow economy in this group of countries and the changes over time. This displays that the unweighted average was 17.7 per cent in 1999 and dropped to 16.6 per cent in 2007. This trend for a fall in the size of the shadow economy however, was not the case across all OECD nations. Some countries, such as Portugal, had ups and downs over this period rather than a continuous fall in the size of its shadow economy, while in others (for example, Australia) there was a steady decrease over this period. The countries with the smallest shadow economies are Switzerland, the United States, Luxembourg and Austria with an average over this period of 8.5 per cent, 8.6 per cent, 9.7 per cent and 9.8 per cent of GDP respectively. The largest shadow economies in OECD nations during this period were in Mexico, Greece and Italy where the shadow economy averaged 30.0 per cent, 27.5 per cent and 27.0 per cent of GDP respectively. Within this group of countries, therefore, there is considerable heterogeneity not only in the cross-national variations in the size of the shadow economy but also in terms of the trends over time.

Developing Countries

The size of the shadow economy in developing countries is on the whole larger than in OECD nations. Nevertheless, there are major variations in

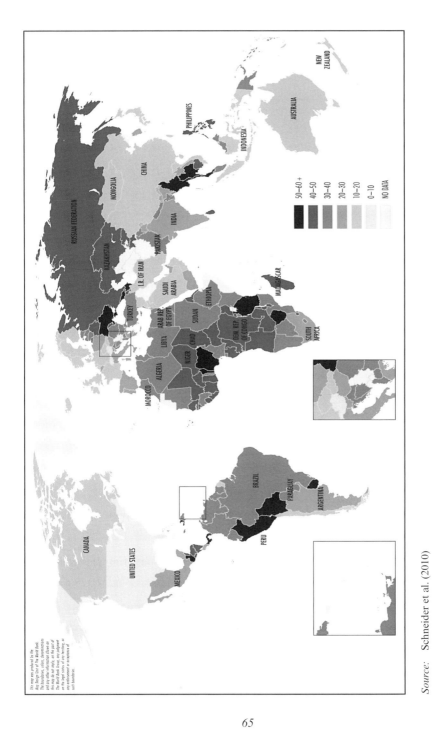

This map was produced by the Map Design Unit of The World Bank. The boundaries, colors, denominations and any other information shown on this map do not imply, on the part of The World Bank Group, any judgment on the legal status of any territory, or any endorsement or acceptance of such boundaries.

50–60 +
40–50
30–40
20–30
10–20
0–10
NO DATA

Source: Schneider et al. (2010)

Figure 4.2   Average size of the shadow economy of 162 countries over 1999–2007

Table 4.3   Size of the shadow economy in 25 OECD nations, 1999–2007

Country	Years									Country average
	1999	2000	2001	2002	2003	2004	2005	2006	2007	
Mexico	30.8	30.1	30.3	30.4	30.5	30.1	29.9	29.2	28.8	30.0
Greece	28.5	28.7	28.2	28.0	27.4	27.1	26.9	26.4	26.5	27.5
Italy	27.8	27.1	26.7	26.8	27.0	27.0	27.1	26.9	26.8	27.0
Korea, Rep.	28.3	27.5	27.3	26.9	26.8	26.5	26.3	25.9	25.6	26.8
Portugal	23.0	22.7	22.6	22.7	23.0	23.1	23.3	23.2	23.0	23.0
Spain	23.0	22.7	22.4	22.4	22.4	22.5	22.4	22.4	22.2	22.5
Belgium	22.7	22.2	22.1	22.0	22.0	21.8	21.8	21.4	21.3	21.9
Sweden	19.6	19.2	19.1	19.0	18.7	18.5	18.6	18.2	17.9	18.8
Norway	19.2	19.1	19.0	19.0	19.0	18.5	18.5	18.2	18.0	18.7
Finland	18.4	18.1	17.9	17.8	17.7	17.6	17.4	17.1	17.0	17.7
Denmark	18.4	18.0	18.0	18.0	18.0	17.8	17.6	17.0	16.9	17.7
Germany	16.4	16.0	15.9	16.1	16.3	16.1	16.0	15.6	15.3	16.0
Ireland	16.1	15.9	15.9	15.9	16.0	15.8	15.6	15.5	15.4	15.8
Canada	16.3	16.0	15.9	15.8	15.7	15.6	15.5	15.3	15.3	15.7
Iceland	16.0	15.9	15.8	16.0	15.9	15.5	15.1	15.0	15.0	15.6
France	15.7	15.2	15.0	15.1	15.0	14.9	14.8	14.8	14.7	15.0
Australia	14.4	14.3	14.3	14.1	13.9	13.7	13.7	13.7	13.5	14.0
Netherlands	13.3	13.1	13.1	13.2	13.3	13.2	13.2	13.2	13.0	13.2
United Kingdom	12.8	12.7	12.6	12.6	12.5	12.4	12.4	12.3	12.2	12.5
New Zealand	13.0	12.8	12.6	12.4	12.2	12.0	12.1	12.1	12.0	12.4
Japan	11.4	11.2	11.2	11.3	11.2	10.9	10.7	10.4	10.3	11.0
Austria	10.0	9.8	9.7	9.8	9.8	9.8	9.8	9.6	9.5	9.8
Luxembourg	10.0	9.8	9.8	9.8	9.8	9.8	9.7	9.6	9.4	9.7
United States	8.8	8.7	8.8	8.8	8.7	8.6	8.5	8.4	8.4	8.6
Switzerland	8.8	8.6	8.6	8.6	8.8	8.6	8.5	8.3	8.1	8.5
Average	17.7	17.4	17.3	17.3	17.3	17.1	17.0	16.8	16.6	–

Source: Own calculations

the magnitude of the shadow economy across these developing nations, or which might better be referred to as the 'majority' world (see Table 4.4). At the upper end of the developing countries, the average size of the shadow economy between 1999 and 2007 was 66.1 per cent in Bolivia, 63.5 per cent in Panama, 61.8 per cent in Zimbabwe, 58 per cent in Peru and 56.4 per cent in Haiti and Tanzania. Indeed, in 11 of these 116 developing countries (9.5 per cent of them), the shadow economy constituted more than half of all economic activity in the country. At the other end of the spectrum, however, the shadow economy constituted less than one-fifth of all economic activity in 16 of these 116 developing countries (13.7 per cent of them). Among the countries with the smallest shadow economies in the developing world between 1999 and 2007 is Macao at

Table 4.4   Size of the shadow economy in developing countries, 1999–2007

Country	Years									Country average
	1999	2000	2001	2002	2003	2004	2005	2006	2007	
Bolivia	67.0	67.1	67.6	67.7	67.7	66.9	64.3	62.8	63.5	66.1
Panama	64.8	64.1	64.7	65.1	64.4	63.5	61.7	60.0	–	63.5
Zimbabwe	59.6	59.4	61.5	62.8	63.7	62.3	62.0	62.3	62.7	61.8
Peru	60.1	59.9	60.2	59.1	58.6	57.9	57.2	55.7	53.7	58.0
Haiti	54.8	55.4	56.1	56.5	56.4	57.4	57.1	57.0	57.1	56.4
Tanzania	58.6	58.3	57.7	56.9	56.6	56.0	55.4	54.7	53.7	56.4
Nigeria	58.0	57.9	57.8	57.6	56.3	55.1	53.8	53.0	–	56.2
Uruguay	50.5	51.1	51.7	54.0	53.6	51.1	49.2	48.5	46.1	50.6
Thailand	53.4	52.6	52.4	51.5	50.2	49.6	49.0	48.5	48.2	50.6
Guatemala	51.6	51.5	51.6	51.2	50.7	50.5	50.2	49.0	47.9	50.5
Myanmar	51.6	52.6	51.5	50.7	49.0	49.1	47.8	–	–	50.3
Benin	51.2	50.2	49.8	49.6	49.3	49.5	49.8	49.6	49.1	49.8
Cambodia	50.4	50.1	49.6	50.0	49.2	48.8	47.8	46.8	46.0	48.7
Honduras	50.3	49.6	49.7	49.6	48.9	48.3	47.3	46.1	45.1	48.3
Gabon	46.2	48.0	47.4	47.6	47.5	48.0	47.7	48.0	47.3	47.5
Congo, Dem. Rep.	47.2	48.0	48.2	48.1	47.1	46.9	46.8	46.8	46.7	47.3
Zambia	49.3	48.9	48.3	48.1	47.5	46.8	46.3	45.0	43.9	47.1
Angola	48.8	48.8	48.4	47.4	47.3	47.1	45.0	44.0	42.1	46.5
Congo, Rep.	49.5	48.2	47.2	46.8	46.8	46.2	44.7	43.3	44.6	46.4
Sierra Leone	48.6	48.6	47.6	45.4	44.8	44.4	44.3	43.6	42.9	45.6
Côte d'Ivoire	41.4	43.2	44.3	45.5	46.0	46.1	46.3	46.8	47.0	45.2
El Salvador	46.5	46.3	46.2	45.6	45.2	44.9	44.5	43.8	43.0	45.1
Central African Republic	42.8	42.6	43.1	44.0	46.9	47.3	46.9	45.9	45.1	45.0
Nicaragua	45.7	45.2	45.3	45.5	45.0	44.2	43.8	43.5	43.1	44.6
Gambia, The	46.1	45.1	44.7	47.1	45.4	43.8	43.6	42.4	40.9	44.3
Liberia	44.2	43.2	43.2	43.1	45.0	45.4	44.9	44.5	44.2	44.2
Sri Lanka	45.2	44.6	44.6	44.1	43.8	43.9	43.4	42.9	42.2	43.9
Senegal	45.0	45.1	44.5	45.1	44.4	43.2	42.3	42.4	41.7	43.7
Chad	45.8	46.2	45.5	45.1	44.2	41.5	41.1	41.7	42.2	43.7
Belize	45.2	43.8	43.3	43.4	42.3	42.0	42.1	41.7	42.0	42.9
Uganda	43.5	43.1	42.9	42.9	42.5	42.4	42.2	41.0	40.3	42.3
Malawi	39.9	40.3	42.5	44.4	43.4	42.5	42.6	41.3	39.4	41.8
Philippines	43.8	43.3	43.0	42.5	42.0	41.6	40.1	39.5	38.3	41.6
Guinea-Bissau	40.4	39.6	39.6	40.7	41.5	41.9	41.7	41.5	41.6	40.9
Madagascar	40.1	39.6	38.7	44.8	43.4	41.6	40.8	39.8	38.5	40.8
Mali	42.5	42.3	40.8	40.2	39.9	40.6	40.1	39.9	39.9	40.7
Ghana	42.0	41.9	41.8	41.6	41.3	40.9	39.5	38.6	38.3	40.7
Swaziland	43.5	41.4	41.3	40.9	40.2	40.1	39.3	38.9	–	40.7
Burkina Faso	41.3	41.4	41.3	41.4	40.3	40.1	39.7	39.7	39.6	40.5
Niger	41.7	41.9	40.9	40.3	39.7	40.7	39.7	38.6	–	40.4
Rwanda	40.5	40.3	40.6	39.9	40.7	40.2	39.3	39.1	–	40.1
Eritrea	38.1	40.3	39.4	39.4	40.3	40.6	40.5	41.2	41.4	40.1
Mozambique	41.1	40.3	40.4	39.8	39.8	39.7	38.9	38.6	–	39.8
Burundi	39.1	39.5	39.6	39.4	39.6	39.6	39.7	39.6	39.6	39.5
Brazil	40.8	39.8	39.9	39.9	39.6	38.6	38.4	37.8	36.6	39.0

Table 4.4   (continued)

Country	1999	2000	2001	2002	2003	2004	2005	2006	2007	Country average
Guinea	39.7	39.6	39.3	38.7	38.8	38.5	38.4	38.9	39.2	39.0
Paraguay	38.0	39.8	39.7	40.1	39.1	38.3	38.2	37.4	–	38.8
Comoros	39.3	39.6	39.0	37.7	37.6	39.0	38.0	38.4	39.4	38.7
Ethiopia	40.6	40.3	39.5	39.6	40.1	38.6	37.7	36.3	35.1	38.6
Suriname	39.7	39.8	39.3	38.9	38.1	36.9	36.5	35.9	35.1	37.8
Colombia	39.4	39.1	38.9	38.9	37.9	37.1	36.1	35.1	33.5	37.3
Tunisia	38.7	38.4	37.8	37.8	37.4	36.9	36.7	35.9	35.4	37.2
Nepal	37.2	36.8	36.7	37.1	36.9	36.8	36.7	36.3	36.0	36.7
Papua New Guinea	35.5	36.1	36.8	37.1	37.1	37.0	37.2	37.1	36.5	36.7
Pakistan	37.0	36.8	37.0	36.8	36.2	35.3	34.9	33.8	33.6	35.7
Cape Verde	36.5	36.1	35.9	35.9	35.7	35.8	35.4	34.1	33.4	35.4
Bangladesh	36.0	35.6	35.5	35.7	35.6	35.5	35.1	34.5	34.1	35.3
Mauritania	35.5	36.1	36.0	35.8	35.8	35.1	34.4	31.7		35.1
Togo	34.4	35.1	35.4	34.5	34.9	35.0	35.0	34.6	–	34.9
Morocco	36.5	36.4	35.7	35.5	35.0	34.2	34.9	33.1	33.1	34.9
Egypt, Arab Rep.	35.5	35.1	35.2	35.7	35.4	35.0	34.8	34.1	33.1	34.9
Jamaica	36.4	36.4	36.2	36.2	34.4	33.9	34.0	32.9	32.5	34.8
Sudan	34.1	–	–	–	–	–	–	–	–	34.1
Venezuela, RB	33.8	33.6	33.5	35.5	36.9	34.9	33.5	32.0	30.9	33.8
Guyana	33.4	33.6	33.3	33.7	33.9	33.4	34.3	33.8	34.0	33.7
Libya	34.7	35.1	34.5	33.8	34.9	33.9	33.1	32.0	30.9	33.7
Solomon Islands	31.7	33.4	34.5	34.8	34.7	33.8	33.4	33.2	32.7	33.6
Trinidad and Tobago	34.7	34.4	34.3	34.4	33.4	33.1	32.9	31.9	31.5	33.4
Kenya	33.7	34.3	34.0	34.8	34.6	33.7	32.7	31.1	29.5	33.2
Lebanon	34.1	34.1	33.7	33.5	33.2	32.4	32.4	32.8	32.0	33.1
Botswana	33.9	33.4	33.2	33.3	33.0	32.8	32.7	32.3	31.9	32.9
Algeria	34.2	34.1	33.8	33.3	32.5	31.7	31.1	31.0	31.2	32.5
Fiji	32.9	33.6	33.3	32.6	32.5	31.9	31.4	31.0	32.6	32.4
Ecuador	34.2	34.4	33.7	33.3	32.8	31.6	30.8	30.4	30.4	32.4
Cameroon	33.3	32.8	32.4	32.1	31.7	31.6	31.6	31.4	31.4	32.0
Dominican Republic	32.4	32.1	32.4	32.1	32.1	32.4	31.7	31.0	30.5	31.9
Equatorial Guinea	32.7	32.8	32.0	31.5	31.2	30.8	30.5	30.6	30.1	31.4
Brunei Darussalam	31.3	31.1	31.0	30.2	29.9	31.2	31.8	30.8	31.2	30.9
Malaysia	32.2	31.1	31.6	31.5	31.2	30.7	30.4	30.0	29.6	30.9
Lesotho	31.7	31.3	31.1	31.0	30.7	30.1	30.2	29.3	28.8	30.5
Namibia	31.4	31.4	31.2	31.3	30.7	29.7	29.6	28.8	28.5	30.3
Lao PDR	30.9	30.6	30.2	30.0	29.8	29.4	28.9	28.4	28.0	29.6
Maldives	30.3	30.3	30.0	29.4	29.2	28.9	29.6	29.3	28.6	29.5
Bhutan	29.6	29.4	29.2	29.1	28.7	28.7	28.3	28.2	27.7	28.8
Cyprus	29.2	28.7	28.2	27.8	28.2	28.1	27.7	27.3	26.5	28.0
South Africa	28.4	28.4	28.4	28.0	27.8	27.1	26.5	26.0	25.2	27.3
Malta	27.4	27.1	27.3	27.3	27.5	27.6	27.3	27.0	26.5	27.2
Yemen, Rep.	27.7	27.4	27.3	27.2	27.0	27.0	26.6	26.8	26.8	27.1
Bahamas	26.3	26.2	26.4	26.5	27.0	27.4	26.7	26.2	26.2	26.5
United Arab Emirates	26.3	26.4	27.0	27.4	26.3	25.4	24.8	23.5	–	25.9

Table 4.4   (continued)

Country	Years									Country average
	1999	2000	2001	2002	2003	2004	2005	2006	2007	
Costa Rica	26.1	26.2	26.4	26.4	26.1	25.9	25.6	25.0	24.0	25.7
Argentina	25.2	25.4	26.1	27.6	26.4	25.5	24.7	23.8	23.0	25.3
Taiwan	25.7	25.4	25.7	25.4	25.2	24.7	24.5	24.2	23.9	25.0
Mauritius	23.3	23.1	22.9	23.0	22.7	22.4	22.4	22.2	21.9	22.7
India	23.2	23.1	22.8	22.6	22.3	22.0	21.7	21.2	20.7	22.2
Israel	22.7	21.9	22.3	22.7	22.7	22.1	21.8	21.2	20.7	22.0
Kuwait	20.1	20.1	20.2	20.3	19.3	18.8	18.1	17.9	–	19.4
Chile	19.9	19.8	19.6	19.6	19.4	19.1	18.9	18.7	18.5	19.3
Syrian Arab Republic	19.3	19.3	19.2	19.1	19.3	19.1	19.0	18.7	18.5	19.1
Indonesia	19.7	19.4	19.4	19.3	19.1	18.8	18.6	18.3	17.9	18.9
Jordan	19.4	19.4	19.2	18.9	18.7	18.3	18.0	17.5	17.2	18.5
Oman	19.1	18.9	18.5	18.5	18.4	18.3	18.0	17.6	–	18.4
Iran, Islamic Rep.	19.1	18.9	19.0	18.7	18.2	17.9	18.1	17.7	17.3	18.3
Saudi Arabia	18.7	18.4	18.7	19.2	18.3	17.7	17.4	17.4	16.8	18.1
Bahrain	18.6	18.4	18.2	18.0	17.8	17.4	17.1	–	–	17.9
Mongolia	18.4	18.4	18.3	18.0	17.7	17.4	17.1	16.7	16.4	17.6
Hong Kong, China	17.0	16.6	16.6	16.6	16.4	15.9	15.5	15.0	14.7	16.0
Vietnam	15.8	15.6	15.5	15.3	15.2	15.1	14.7	14.6	14.4	15.1
Qatar	–	19.0	19.3	19.0	19.6	17.4	18.4	–	–	14.1
Singapore	13.3	13.1	13.3	13.3	13.1	12.8	12.7	12.4	12.2	12.9
China	13.2	13.1	13.0	12.9	12.8	12.6	12.5	12.2	11.9	12.7
Macao, China	13.3	13.1	13.0	12.9	12.5	12.1	11.9	11.7	11.1	12.4
Time Average	37.0	36.7	36.8	36.8	36.5	36.1	35.5	35.1		

Source: Own calculations

12.4 per cent, China at 12.7 per cent, Singapore at 12.9 per cent, Qatar at 14.1 per cent and Vietnam at 15.1 per cent.

Across developing countries as a whole, there has been a decrease in the size of the shadow economy over the 1999–2007 time period. Nevertheless, there are variations. The majority of developing countries witnessed a decline in the size of their shadow economies. However, some countries over this period witnessed a growth, such as Zimbabwe and the Solomon Islands, with others witnessing ups and downs.

Transition Economies

The size of the shadow economy in transition economies is larger than in developing countries. Nevertheless, there are major variations in the magnitude of the shadow economy across these transition economies, or what might better be referred to as post-Soviet economies (see Table 4.5). At the

Table 4.5   Size of the shadow economy in transition economies, 1999–2007

Country	Year									Country average
	1999	2000	2001	2002	2003	2004	2005	2006	2007	
Georgia	68.3	67.3	67.2	67.2	65.9	65.5	65.1	63.6	62.1	65.8
Azerbaijan	61.0	60.6	60.3	60.0	59.1	58.6	56.7	54.0	52.0	58.0
Ukraine	52.7	52.2	51.4	50.8	49.7	48.8	47.8	47.3	46.8	49.7
Belarus	48.3	48.1	47.9	47.6	47.0	46.1	45.2	44.2	43.3	46.4
Moldova	45.6	45.1	44.1	44.5	44.6	44.0	43.4	44.3	–	44.5
Armenia	46.6	46.3	45.4	44.5	43.9	43.6	42.7	42.1	41.1	44.0
Russian Federation	47.0	46.1	45.3	44.5	43.6	43.0	42.4	41.7	40.6	43.8
Tajikistan	43.5	43.2	42.9	42.7	42.1	41.7	41.5	41.2	41.0	42.2
Kazakhstan	43.8	43.2	42.5	42.0	41.1	40.6	39.8	38.9	38.4	41.1
Kyrgyz Republic	41.4	41.2	40.8	41.4	40.5	39.8	40.1	39.8	38.8	40.4
Macedonia	39.0	38.2	39.1	38.9	38.4	37.4	36.9	36.0	34.9	37.6
Bulgaria	37.3	36.9	36.6	36.1	35.6	34.9	34.1	33.5	32.7	35.3
Albania	35.7	35.3	34.9	34.7	34.4	33.9	33.7	33.3	32.9	34.3
Bosnia & Herzegovina	34.3	34.1	34.0	33.9	33.5	33.6	33.2	32.9	32.8	33.6
Romania	34.3	34.4	33.7	33.5	32.8	32.0	31.7	30.7	30.2	32.6
Croatia	33.8	33.4	33.2	32.6	32.1	31.7	31.3	30.8	30.4	32.1
Lithuania	33.8	33.7	33.3	32.8	32.0	31.7	31.0	30.4	29.7	32.0
Turkey	32.7	32.1	32.8	32.4	31.8	31.0	30.0	29.5	29.1	31.3
Estonia	–	32.7	32.4	32.0	31.4	31.1	30.5	29.8	29.5	31.2
Latvia	30.8	30.5	30.1	29.8	29.4	29.0	28.4	27.7	27.2	29.2
Poland	27.7	27.6	27.7	27.7	27.5	27.3	26.9	26.4	26.0	27.2
Slovenia	27.3	27.1	26.7	26.6	26.4	26.2	25.8	25.3	24.7	26.2
Hungary	25.4	25.1	24.8	24.5	24.4	24.1	24.0	23.7	23.7	24.4
Czech Republic	19.3	19.1	18.9	18.8	18.7	18.4	17.8	17.3	17.0	18.4
Slovak Republic	18.9	18.9	18.8	18.6	18.3	18.1	17.6	17.2	16.8	18.1
Time Average	36.9	36.3	36.1	35.8	35.3	34.8	34.3	33.7	32.6	

Source: Own calculations

upper end of these transition economies, the average size of the shadow economy between 1999 and 2007 was 65.8 per cent in Georgia, 58 per cent in Azerbaijan, 49.7 per cent in Ukraine, 46.4 per cent in Belarus and 44.5 per cent in Moldova. Indeed, in 11 of these 25 transition economies (40 per cent of them), the shadow economy constituted more than 40 per cent of all economic activity in the country. At the other end of the spectrum, however, the shadow economy constituted less than 30 per cent of official GDP in six of these 25 transition countries (24 per cent of them). Among the countries with the smallest shadow economies in these transition countries between 1999 and 2007 are the Slovak Republic at 18.1 per cent, the Czech Republic at 18.4 per cent, Hungary at 24.4 per cent and Slovenia at 26.2 per cent.

Across transition economies as a whole, there is a decrease in the size of the shadow economy over this period of time. Nevertheless, there are again variations. Although most of the transition economies witnessed a steady decline in the size of the shadow economy over this time period, others such as the Kyrgyz Republic witnessed ups and downs. None, however, witnessed a growth of the shadow economy over this period of time.

CONCLUSIONS

This chapter has reported the results of applying the MIMIC method to estimate the size of the shadow economy across 116 developing countries and 25 transition economies, and compared these findings with OECD nations. This MIMIC approach is the most commonly used of all indirect measurement methods to estimate the magnitude of the shadow economy. The overarching finding is that the unweighted mean size of the shadow economy across the world during the period 1999–2007 was 33 per cent of GDP. That is to say, one-third of economic activity in the global economy took place in the shadow economy. However, when we examine the weighted mean size of the shadow economy across the world during the period 1999–2007, taking into account the population size of each country, the finding is that it was 17.1 per cent of GDP. This therefore reveals that unless the shadow economy is taken into account in economic studies, just under one-sixth of all economic activity across the world will be omitted from analyses.

There are nevertheless significant variations in its size across the world. When the weighted mean is examined, the finding is that the global region with the largest shadow economy is sub-Saharan Africa where the equivalent of 37.6 per cent of GDP is in the shadow economy, followed by 36.4 per cent in Europe and Central Asia, 34.7 per cent in Latin America and the Caribbean, 27.3 per cent in the Middle East and North Africa, 25.1 per cent in South Asia, 20.8 per cent in other high-income countries, 17.5 per cent in East Asia and the Pacific, and 13.4 per cent in high-income OECD nations. Indeed, although the weighted mean is 17.1 per cent of GDP globally, the standard deviation is 9.9 per cent, displaying the highly uneven distribution of the shadow economy globally across countries.

Comparing OECD (developed) nations, developing countries and transition economies, the finding is that in 2007, the weighted mean size of the shadow economy was 13 per cent in OECD nations, 26.2 per cent in developing countries and 33.7 per cent in transition economies. Transition economies, therefore, have larger shadow economies than developing countries. However, across all three of these broad groupings of economies, there has been a decrease in the size of the shadow economy between 1999 and 2007. In the OECD nations, the size of the shadow economy decreased from 14.1 per cent of GDP in 1999 to 13 per cent of GDP in 2007 (that is, a 7.8 per cent decrease in size), while in developing countries, the shadow economy decreased in size from 29.6 per cent to 26.2 per cent (that is, an 11.5 per cent decrease in size) and in the transition economies the shadow economy decreased from 37.9 per cent to 33.7 per cent of GDP (that is, a decrease of 11.1 per cent).

The result is that the shadow economy declined the slowest in the OECD nations where it was smallest to start with and quickest in the developing and transition economies where the shadow economy was larger. The very tentative intimation is therefore that there is a partial convergence of these three broad regional groupings over this time period in terms of the size of their shadow economies. Nevertheless, and as shown, marked variations exists across countries within each of these global regions not only in size of the shadow economy but also whether it is growing or declining, with some nations witnessing growing, others static and yet others declining shadow economies. Having provided this graphic portrait of how the size of the shadow economy varies across the developing world and the transition economies using the MIMIC method, attention turns in the next chapter to a more detailed analysis of the variations across the OECD nations as well as the determinants of the shadow economy.

NOTE

1.   The data and figures in this chapter are taken from Schneider et al. (2010).

5. The shadow economy in developed countries

In this chapter, we turn our attention to the size of the shadow economy in developed countries as well as what determines the magnitude of the shadow economy in such economies. To do this, we here report the results of the MIMIC method on not only the variations in the magnitude of the shadow economy across the developed world but also the major driving forces underpinning its existence. In doing so, our intention is to provide an estimate of the magnitude of the shadow economy in developed nations and an analysis of the extent to which particular determinants contribute to the size and development of the shadow economy and how that relative impact varies across countries. For example, is it the case that the tax burden is relatively more important than tax morale? And does welfare spending influence the size of the shadow economy? Identifying such determinants is crucial if action is to be taken to tackle the shadow economy. Unless the driving forces underpinning the shadow economy are understood, governments will not comprehend where they can intervene in order to reduce its size and neither will there be understanding of the way in which these interventions vary across different countries.

In the first section, therefore, we introduce the MIMIC results on the relative size of the shadow economy across OECD countries. Having provided this broad overview of the cross-national variations in the size of the shadow economy, the second section then turns to analysing the determinants of the shadow economy by presenting a MIMIC model estimation of the causal variables influencing its size. To do this, the model's specifications regarding the driving forces of the shadow economy along with hypotheses regarding its determinants are introduced, including an evaluation of the relative importance of these driving forces across the OECD countries, displaying how the determinants vary both across countries and also how their relative importance changes over time within each of these countries. To show this in more detail, the third section then takes case studies of the determinants of the shadow economy and how these are changing over time in Germany, Austria, France, Italy and Spain. The final section then draws some conclusions regarding the cross-national variations in the size of the shadow economy across developed countries and how the weight attached to the determinants of the shadow economy varies across different countries.

VARIATIONS IN THE SIZE OF THE SHADOW ECONOMY IN OECD COUNTRIES

In order to calculate the size and development of the shadow economies of OECD countries, one has to overcome the disadvantage of the MIMIC approach, which is that only the relative sizes of the shadow economy are obtained. As such, another approach has to be used to calculate the absolute figures. For the calculation of the absolute sizes of the shadow economies from these MIMIC estimations, the already available estimates are used from the currency demand approach for Austria, Germany, Italy and the United States, derived from Dell'Anno and Schneider (2003), Bajada and Schneider (2009) and Schneider and Enste (2000a, 2000b, 2002). As these values of the size of the shadow economy (in percentage of GDP) are available for various years for the above mentioned countries, these can then be used in a benchmark procedure to transform the index of the shadow economy from the MIMIC estimations into cardinal values (this procedure is described in detail in Dell'Anno and Schneider, 2003, 2009).

Table 5.1 reports the results of using this method to calculate the size of the shadow economy for OECD countries over the period 1999–2010. Starting with the overall findings, this reveals that in 2010, the average magnitude of the shadow economy across these OECD countries was 20.3 per cent of GDP. As such, and comparing these results with the findings for developing and transition countries in Chapter 4, what becomes quickly apparent is that the magnitude of the shadow economy in developed countries is smaller than in developing countries and transition economies. It also reveals that across the developed world as a whole, there was a steady general reduction in the size of the shadow economy over time until 2009, when it begins to increase again, which is due to the world financial and economic crisis. For example, in Canada the shadow economy was 14.9 per cent of official GDP in the year 2008 and had increased to 15.5 per cent in 2009. In Norway, the shadow economy was 17.7 per cent of official GDP in 2008 and increased to 18.6 per cent in 2009.

Turning to the cross-national variations in the size of the shadow economy across the developed world, Table 5.1 reveals significant differences. At one end are countries such as Bulgaria, Romania and Turkey, whose shadow economies are the equivalent of 34.6 per cent, 32.2 per cent

Table 5.1 Size and development of the shadow economy (in % of GDP)[1] in OECD countries

Country	1999	2000	2001	2002	2003	2004	2005	2006	2007	2008	2009	2010	Average
Australia	14.4	14.3	14.3	14.1	13.9	13.7	13.7	13.7	13.7	13.2	13.5	13.4	13.8
Austria	10.0	9.8	9.7	9.8	9.8	9.8	9.8	9.6	9.7	9.5	9.7	10.6	9.8
Belgium	22.7	22.2	22.1	22.0	22.0	21.8	21.8	21.4	20.8	20.3	20.5	20.7	21.5
Bulgaria	37.3	36.9	36.6	36.1	35.6	34.9	34.1	33.5	33.0	33.7	32.1	31.9	34.6
Canada	16.3	16	15.9	15.8	15.7	15.6	15.5	15.3	15.2	14.9	15.5	15.4	15.6
Chile	19.9	19.8	19.6	19.6	19.4	19.1	18.9	18.7	18.4	19.1	20.5	19.8	19.4
Cyprus	29.2	28.7	28.2	27.8	28.2	28.1	27.7	27.3	27.3	27.7	26.9	25.4	27.7
Czech Rep.	19.3	19.1	18.9	18.8	18.7	18.4	17.8	17.3	16.3	15.2	15.7	15.5	17.6
Denmark	18.4	18.0	18.0	18.0	18.0	17.8	17.6	17.0	16.5	15.3	16.2	16.2	17.3
Estonia	–	25.6	25.3	24.9	24.3	24.0	23.4	22.7	22.5	20.8	24.3	22.5	21.7
Finland	18.4	18.1	17.9	17.8	17.7	17.6	17.4	17.1	16.6	16.4	16.7	16.8	17.4
France	15.7	15.2	15.0	15.1	15.0	14.9	14.8	14.8	14.5	14.0	14.5	14.6	14.8
Germany	16.4	16.0	15.9	16.1	16.3	16.1	16.0	15.6	15.3	14.8	14.6	15.1	15.7
Greece	28.5	28.7	28.2	28.0	27.4	27.1	26.9	26.4	26.5	26.0	25.3	25.1	27.0
Hungary	25.4	25.1	24.8	24.5	24.4	24.1	24.0	23.7	23.7	23.1	23.1	23.1	24.1
Iceland	16.0	15.9	15.8	16.0	15.9	15.5	15.1	15.0	14.4	13.8	14.7	14.4	15.2
Ireland	16.1	15.9	15.9	15.9	16.0	15.8	15.6	15.5	15.9	15.9	17.5	16.5	16.1
Italy	27.8	27.1	26.7	26.8	27.0	27.0	27.1	26.9	26.8	26.7	26.5	26.7	26.9
Japan[2]	11.4	11.2	11.2	11.3	11.2	10.9	10.7	10.4	10.3	11.0	11.0	11.0	11.0
Korea, Rep.	28.3	27.5	27.3	26.9	26.8	26.5	26.3	25.9	25.8	25.6	24.5	24.7	26.3
Latvia	23.9	23.6	23.2	22.9	22.5	22.1	21.5	20.8	20.8	22.6	20.0	21.5	22.1
Lithuania	27.2	27.1	26.7	26.2	25.4	25.1	24.4	23.8	24.3	26.0	23.6	25.4	25.4
Luxembourg	10.0	9.8	9.8	9.8	9.8	9.8	9.7	9.6	9.3	9.1	9.3	9.6	9.6
Malta	27.4	27.1	27.3	27.3	27.5	27.6	27.3	27.0	26.8	27.0	26.7	28.1	27.3
Mexico[2]	30.8	30.1	30.3	30.4	30.5	30.1	29.9	29.2	28.8	30.0	30.0	30.0	30.0

Table 5.1 (continued)

Country	1999	2000	2001	2002	2003	2004	2005	2006	2007	2008	2009	2010	Average
Netherlands	13.3	13.1	13.1	13.2	13.3	13.2	13.2	13.2	13.1	12.7	12.9	13.6	13.2
New Zealand	13.0	12.8	12.6	12.4	12.2	12.0	12.1	12.1	12.0	11.8	12.0	12.0	12.2
Norway	19.2	19.1	19.0	19.0	19.0	18.5	18.5	18.2	18.1	17.7	18.6	18.2	18.6
Poland	27.7	27.6	27.7	27.7	27.5	27.3	26.9	26.4	25.4	24.7	24.6	23.8	26.4
Portugal	23.0	22.7	22.6	22.7	23.0	23.1	23.3	23.2	22.5	21.9	22.0	22.2	22.7
Romania	34.3	34.4	33.7	33.5	32.8	32.0	31.7	30.7	30.8	31.5	30.0	30.9	32.2
Slovak Rep.	18.9	18.9	18.8	18.6	18.3	18.1	17.6	17.2	16.6	16.0	15.8	15.8	17.5
Slovenia	27.3	27.1	26.7	26.6	26.4	26.2	25.8	25.3	25.3	24.6	23.5	23.7	25.7
Spain	23.0	22.7	22.4	22.4	22.4	22.5	22.4	22.4	22.3	22.9	24.5	23.5	22.8
Sweden	19.6	19.2	19.1	19.0	18.7	18.5	18.6	18.2	18.0	17.7	17.9	18.1	18.6
Switzerland	8.8	8.6	8.6	8.6	8.8	8.6	8.5	8.3	8.0	7.2	7.8	8.0	8.3
Turkey	32.7	32.1	32.8	32.4	31.8	31.0	30.0	29.5	28.0	28.6	29.4	29.0	30.6
United Kingdom	12.8	12.7	12.6	12.6	12.5	12.4	12.4	12.3	12.4	12.1	12.9	12.0	12.5
United States	8.8	8.7	8.8	8.8	8.7	8.6	8.5	8.4	8.6	8.6	9.3	9.1	8.7
Average	20.3	20.7	20.6	20.5	20.4	20.1	19.9	19.6	19.3	19.2	18.3	18.3	20.3

Notes:
1 Estimates before 2007 are taken from Buehn and Schneider (2012b).
2 Data for 2009 and 2010 are not available for all causes, hence 2009 and 2010 estimates are a linear interpolation of the 2008 estimate and the country average.

Source: Own calculations

and 30.6 per cent of GDP respectively. At the other end are countries such as Luxembourg, Switzerland and the United States whose shadow economies are the equivalent of 9.6 per cent, 8.3 per cent and 8.7 per cent of official GDP respectively. It is also important to analyse the changes over time in the size of the shadow economy across countries. In general, all countries have witnessed a decline in the size of their shadow economies from 1999 until 2009, when the world economic and financial crisis began, after which all countries witnessed a rise in the size of their shadow economies.

DETERMINANTS OF THE SHADOW ECONOMY IN DEVELOPED COUNTRIES

Having provided estimates of the size of the shadow economy, attention now turns to outlining the determinants of the shadow economy and then showing how the MIMIC method can be used to estimate the relative importance of each of these determinants both within each country and across countries. To do this, it is first necessary to outline the various determinants of the shadow economy used by the MIMIC method. Here, therefore, we present a MIMIC model estimation of the causal variables influencing the indicator variables of the shadow economies in OECD countries.

Based on a review of the theoretical literature (Buehn and Schneider, 2012a, 2012b; Tafenau et al., 2010; Schneider, 2005, 2009, 2011), seven hypotheses are here proposed that are to be tested in the MIMIC approach. These seven hypotheses are:

1. An increase in direct and indirect taxation increases the shadow economy.
2. An increase in social security contributions increases the shadow economy.
3. The more the country is regulated, the greater the incentives are to work in the shadow economy.
4. The lower the quality of state institutions, the higher the incentives to work in the shadow economy.
5. The lower the tax morale, the higher the incentives to work in the shadow economy.
6. The higher the unemployment, the more people engage in shadow economy activities.
7. The lower the GDP per capita in a country, the higher is the incentive to work in the shadow economy.

To evaluate these hypotheses, Table 5.2 outlines the indicators used to measure each variable along with the expected signs. For example, the effect of a larger shadow economy on official GDP figures can be expected to be negative, all other things being equal. The larger the shadow economy, the lower the government's tax revenues and thus the ability to provide public goods and services, i.e., public demand, that significantly contributes to official GDP. In addition, the more individuals participate in shadow economic activities, the less they work officially. Hence, the expected correlation between the shadow economy and official labour market indicators can also be expected to be negative, all other things being equal. Using currency in circulation as an indicator of shadow economic activities seems most reasonable, as cash is mostly used as means of payment in the shadow economy. The expected correlation is positive.

Table 5.3 presents the econometric results using the MIMIC approach (latent estimation approach) for a range of OECD countries using nine data points for the years 1990/1, 1994/5, 1997/8, 1999/2000, 2001/2, 2002/3, 2003/4, 2004/5 and 2006/7. Besides the usual causal variables such as direct and indirect taxation, social security contributions and state regulation, we have added two further causal factors (i.e., tax morale and the quality of state institutions). In addition to the employment rate, the annual growth rate of GDP and the change of currency per capita, we use the average working time (per week) as an additional indicator variable. Using this latter indicator variable, the problem might arise that this variable is influenced by state regulation, so that it is not exogenous; hence the usual narrative is that estimation may be biased. This problem, nevertheless, applies for almost all causal variables.

The estimated coefficients of all eight causal variables are statistically significant and have the theoretically expected signs. The tax and social security burden variables are quantitatively the most important ones, followed by the tax morale variable, which has the single biggest influence. Furthermore, the independent variable that measures the quality of state institutions is statistically significant and quite important to determine the shadow economy. The development of the official economy measured by both the levels of unemployment and GDP per capita has a quantitatively important influence on the shadow economy. Turning to the indicator variables, all have a statistically significant influence and the estimated coefficients have the theoretically expected signs. The quantitatively most important independent variables are the employment rate and the change of currency per capita (which is heavily influenced by banking innovations or payment, meaning that this variable is pretty unstable with respect to the length of the estimation). In sum, these econometric results demonstrate that in these developed OECD countries, the level of social security

Table 5.2   Indicators used to measure determinants of the shadow economy and expected signs

Causal variable	Description and source	Expected sign
Business freedom	Business freedom index measuring the time and efforts of business activity ranging; 0 = least business freedom, and 100 = maximum business freedom; Heritage Foundation	−
Corruption	Corruption index (score between 0 and 100 with higher values indicating more corruption); Heritage Foundation	+
Education	Secondary school enrolment rate (% gross); World Development Indicators (WDI)	−
GDP growth	GDP per capita growth, annual (%); WDI	+/−
Indirect taxes	Taxes on goods and services (% of total tax revenue); WDI	+
Payroll taxes	Taxes on income, profits and capital gains (% of total tax revenue); WDI	+
Personal income tax	Personal income tax (PIT) to GDP, government finance statistics; International Monetary Fund	+
Rule of Law	Rule of Law index summarizing the quality of contract enforcement, the police and the courts, as well as the likelihood of crime and violence, −2.5 = no compliance, and 2.5 = total compliance; World Bank Governance Indicators	−
Self-employment	Total self-employed workers (proportion of total employment); WDI	+
Tax morale	To assess the level of tax morale we use the following question: *'Please tell me for each of the following statements whether you think it can always be justified, never be justified, or something in between: . . . Cheating on tax if you have the chance.'* The question leads to a ten-scale index of tax morale with the two extreme points 'never justified' (1) and 'always justified' (10). Using the proportion of respondents who answered the question with a value of 6 or higher, higher values of our tax morale variable indicate a lower level of tax morale; European and World Value Surveys	−
Unemployment	Unemployment rate (% of total labour force); WDI	+
Currency in circulation	Monetary aggregates M0 over M1; International Monetary Fund, International Financial Statistics	+
GDP pc	GDP per capita, PPP (constant 2005 international $); WDI	−
Labour force participation	Labour force participation rate (% of total population); WDI	−

Table 5.3   *MIMIC estimation of the shadow economy of highly developed OECD countries, 1990/1, 1994/5, 1997/8, 1999/2000, 2001/2, 2002/3, 2003/4, 2004/5 and 2006/7*

Causal variables	Estimated coefficients
Share of direct taxation (in % of GDP)	$\lambda 1 = 0.392$** (3.34)
Share of indirect taxation (in % of GDP)	$\lambda 2 = 0.184$(*) (1.74)
Share of social security contribution (in % of GDP)	$\lambda 3 = 0.523$** (3.90)
Burden of state regulation (index of labor market regulation, Heritage Foundation, score 1 least regular, score 5 most regular)	$\lambda 4 = 0.226$(*) (2.03)
Quality of state institutions (rule of law, World Bank, score -3 worst and $+3$ best case)	$\lambda 5 = -0.314$* (-2.70)
Tax morale (WVS and EVS, Index, Scale tax cheating always justified $=1$, never justified $=10$)	$\lambda 6 = -0.593$** (-3.76)
Unemployment rate (%)	$\lambda 7 = 0.316$** (2.40)
GDP per capita (in US-$)	$\lambda 8 = -0.106$** (-3.04)

Indicator variables	Estimated coefficients
Employment rate (in % of population 18–64)	$\lambda 9 = -0.613$** (-2.52)
Average working time (per week)	$\lambda 10 = -1.00$ (Residuum)
Annual growth rate of GDP (adjusted for the mean of OECD countries)	$\lambda 11 = -0.281$** (-3.16)
Change of local currency per capita	$\lambda 12 = 0.320$** (3.80)
Test-statistics	$RMSE^1 = 0.0016$* (p-value $= 0.912$) $Chi\text{-}square^2 = 26.43$ (p-value $= 0.916$) $TMCV^3 = 0.051$ $AGFI^4 = 0.772$ $N = 189$ $D.F.^5 = 71$

Table 5.3 (continued)

Notes:

t-statistics are in parentheses. *; **; *** indicate significance at the 90%, 95% or 99% confidence levels.

1 Steiger's root mean square error of approximation (RMSEA) for test of close fit; RMSEA < 0.05; the RMSEA-value varies between 0.0 and 1.0.

2 If the structural equation model is asymptotically correct, then the matrix S (sample covariance matrix) will be equal to Σ (θ) (model implied covariance matrix). This test has a statistical validity with a large sample (N $\geq$ 100) and multinomial distributions; both are given for all three equations using a test of multinomial distributions.

3 Test of Multivariate Normality for Continuous Variables (TMNCV); p-values of skewness and kurtosis.

4 Test of Adjusted Goodness of Fit Index (AGFI), varying between 0 and 1; 1 = perfect fit.

5 The degrees of freedom are determined by 0.5 (p + q) (p + q + 1) − t; with p = number of indicators; q = number of causes; t = the number for free parameters.

contributions and the share of direct taxation have the biggest influence, followed by tax morale and the quality of state institutions (Feld and Schneider, 2010; Schneider et al., 2010). These findings will be returned to in Part III of this book on how the shadow economy can be tackled. Until now, as will be argued, policy approaches for tackling the shadow economy have put little emphasis on macro-level measures that deal with issues such as tax morale and the quality of state institutions. Before addressing this, however, it is necessary to examine their importance as determinants of the shadow economy both within and across countries.

Table 5.4 shows five different MIMIC model specifications to firstly demonstrate the robustness of our results. The second reason is that some of the causal variables cannot be included in the empirical models at the same time as they are highly correlated with each other. Turning firstly to the direct and indirect tax burden, we find that both causal variables are highly statistically significant and have the expected positive sign in all equations. This is not the case for the payroll taxes. However, the 'soft' factor of tax morale is highly statistically significant and has the predicted negative sign in all equations, i.e., a lower level of tax morale is correlated with larger shadow economies. Looking at the more economic causal variables, namely unemployment, business freedom and self-employment, we also find that all three causal variables have a highly statistically significant influence and carrying the expected signs. This holds also for GDP growth, which has a positive and again highly statistically significant influence. The 'rule of law' is only statistically significant in specification 1 and 2, while the alternative measure of institutions, i.e., the variable corruption, is not statistically significant at all. The causal variable education is also

Table 5.4   MIMIC model estimations (standardized coefficients)

Specification	1	2	3	4	5
Causes:					
Personal income tax	0.27***	0.33***	0.37***	0.40***	0.39***
	(3.27)	(3.99)	(4.30)	(4.80)	(4.74)
Payroll taxes	−0.08	−0.11			
	(0.98)	(1.35)			
Indirect taxes	0.24***	0.22***	0.31***	0.21***	0.24***
	(2.75)	(2.66)	(3.85)	(2.67)	(2.97)
Tax morale	−0.31***	−0.22***	−0.26***	−0.22***	−0.21***
	(3.29)	(2.40)	(2.84)	(2.51)	(2.38)
Unemployment	0.63***	0.65***	0.63***	0.55***	0.53***
	(5.92)	(6.30)	(5.96)	(5.56)	(5.47)
Business freedom	−0.29***	−0.26***	−0.29***	−0.35***	−0.35***
	(3.35)	(3.11)	(3.36)	(4.06)	(4.20)
Self-employment	0.29***	0.30***	0.34***	0.33***	0.27***
	(2.68)	(2.88)	(3.17)	(3.18)	(2.57)
Rule of law	−0.14*	−0.14*	−0.10	−0.08	
	(1.81)	(1.83)	(1.31)	(1.03)	
GDP growth		0.30***	0.31***	0.27***	0.29***
		(3.62)	(3.70)	(3.35)	(3.52)
Education				−0.31***	−0.26***
				(3.51)	(2.83)
Corruption					0.14
					(1.56)
Indicators:					
GDP pc	−0.52	−0.52	−0.48	−0.51	−0.50
Currency in circulation	0.09	0.07	0.10*	0.10*	0.08
	(1.39)	(1.07)	(1.75)	(1.69)	(1.26)
Labour force	−0.56***	−0.55***	−0.52***	−0.50***	−0.51***
participation	(6.42)	(6.58)	(6.36)	(6.48)	(6.46)
Observations	151	151	151	151	151
Degrees freedom	44	54	42	52	52
Chi-square	88.88	89.68	24.10	32.51	34.57
RMSEA	0.08	0.06	0.00	0.00	0.00

Note: The sample includes OECD countries and the estimation period is 1998 to 2010. Absolute z-statistics are reported in parentheses. *, **, *** indicate significance at the 10%, 5% and 1% level, respectively.

highly statistically significant and has the expected sign indicating that the more or better quality of education people receive on average, the less they operate in the shadow economy, all other things being equal. Concerning the indicators, the labour force participation indicator is highly statistically significant and has the predicted negative influence, while the measure of currency in circulation is only statistically significant in specification 3 and 4. In general the estimation results are quite satisfactory, especially as most causal variables have the predicted sign and are highly statistically significant.

The standardized coefficients presented allow us to directly compare the relative influence of different causal variables. Table 5.4 shows that the coefficient of the unemployment rate has the biggest influence on the shadow economy with a standardized coefficient between 0.53 and 0.65; followed by personal income tax with a standardized coefficient between 0.27 and 0.40; followed by business freedom with a standardized coefficient between 0.26 and 0.35. GDP growth and education display very similar standardized coefficients with value of 0.27 and 0.31 and between 0.26 and 0.31, respectively. Concerning the tax burden measures, personal income and direct taxes have standardized coefficients between 0.27 and 0.40 and the tax morale variable between 0.21 and 0.31. The dominating influence of the unemployment rate is not perhaps unexpected, as being unemployed quite often means a severe income loss; hence unemployed people try to compensate this income or utility loss by expanding their activities in the shadow economy, if social contributions are insufficient to enable them to maintain their living standards.

To reveal how the determinants of the shadow economy are not uniform across all developed countries, attention now turns to the determinants for OECD countries between 1998/9 and 2010. These developed countries are Australia, Austria, Belgium, Bulgaria, Canada, Chile, Cyprus, Czech Republic, Denmark, Estonia, Finland, France, Germany, Greece, Hungary, Iceland, Ireland, Italy, Japan, Korea, Latvia, Lithuania, Luxembourg, Malta, Mexico, Netherlands, New Zealand, Norway, Poland, Portugal, Romania, Slovak Republic, Slovenia, Spain, Sweden, Switzerland, Turkey, United Kingdom and the United States.

Table 5.5 presents the average relative influence (in percentage terms) of the causal variables on the size and development of the shadow economies for all OECD countries between 1999 and 2010. This reveals that tax morale, unemployment and self-employment are the most influential determinants of the shadow economy for the majority of countries. Looking at the average values for all developed OECD nations, we observe that unemployment and self-employment have the highest influence (14.6 per cent) across countries. This is followed by tax morale with an average relative

Table 5.5   *Average relative impact (in %) of the causal variables on the*
              shadow economy of OECD countries over 1999 to 2010

Country	Average size of the shadow economy	Personal income tax	Indirect taxes	Tax morale	Unemployment	Self-employment	GDP growth	Business freedom
Australia	13.8	12.4	13.4	14.1	18.1	15.8	13.2	13.0
Austria	9.8	12.4	14.6	14.1	11.8	16.8	15.9	14.4
Belgium	21.5	12.9	12.8	14.4	16.2	16.0	14.2	13.3
Bulgaria	34.6	14.9	13.5	14.8	14.8	14.2	13.7	14.2
Canada	15.6	12.7	14.9	14.9	18.4	11.7	13.8	13.6
Chile	19.4	16.1	14.1	14.1	14.2	12.9	14.4	14.3
Cyprus	27.2	13.8	14.5	14.5	14.3	14.5	13.8	14.6
Czech Rep.	17.6	15.1	16.0	14.0	11.5	13.1	14.3	15.9
Denmark	17.3	10.8	13.1	14.7	18.2	15.6	14.4	13.2
Estonia	21.7	16.4	14.4	14.5	12.4	13.1	14.0	15.2
Finland	17.4	15.4	13.0	14.8	12.9	16.9	13.7	13.3
France	14.8	9.1	14.4	14.8	15.1	17.3	15.1	14.3
Germany	15.7	16.6	13.2	15.0	13.0	12.8	15.2	14.2
Greece	27.0	10.3	16.2	14.5	10.4	18.7	14.3	15.5
Hungary	24.1	14.0	14.1	15.0	15.0	14.2	13.5	14.2
Iceland	15.2	12.4	14.3	14.7	15.1	14.4	14.8	14.3
Italy	26.9	13.0	13.9	14.0	14.5	14.0	16.6	13.9
Korea	26.3	13.3	14.4	14.9	13.3	14.6	15.3	14.2
Latvia	22.2	14.6	14.3	13.9	15.1	14.6	13.3	14.2
Lithuania	25.4	13.1	14.5	14.1	15.1	14.5	14.2	14.5
Luxembourg	9.6	14.7	14.3	14.2	13.0	14.9	14.5	14.3
Malta	27.3	14.3	14.3	15.1	14.3	14.3	13.4	14.3
Mexico	30.0	14.3	13.7	14.5	14.4	14.2	14.9	13.9
Netherlands	13.2	14.6	13.6	14.0	16.1	13.7	14.2	13.8
New Zealand	12.2	14.6	14.2	14.2	15.2	14.3	13.2	14.2
Norway	18.6	14.1	13.8	14.2	14.1	14.5	15.4	13.9
Poland	26.4	14.1	14.4	14.4	14.2	14.5	14.1	14.4
Portugal	22.7	12.5	14.1	14.9	14.2	14.4	15.9	14.1
Romania	32.2	15.5	14.2	13.9	14.2	14.1	14.0	14.2
Slovak Rep.	17.5	15.0	14.7	14.7	14.4	14.4	12.0	14.8
Slovenia	25.2	14.4	14.3	14.4	14.8	14.4	13.2	14.4
Spain	22.8	11.2	13.6	14.6	17.5	16.4	13.8	12.9
Sweden	18.6	14.9	14.3	14.6	13.3	14.2	14.2	14.5
Switzerland	8.3	13.8	13.0	15.7	13.4	14.4	14.8	14.8
Turkey	30.6	13.9	14.1	14.5	13.7	14.5	15.1	14.3
United Kingdom	12.5	13.6	14.0	14.3	18.1	12.4	13.7	14.0
United States	8.7	13.9	14.1	13.7	14.9	14.4	15.0	14.1
Average	20.3	13.8	14.1	14.5	14.6	14.6	14.3	14.2

impact of 14.5 per cent, then by GDP growth (14.3 per cent), business freedom (14.2 per cent), indirect taxes (14.1 per cent) and finally the personal income tax with an average relative impact of 13.8 per cent. However, as can be seen, the relative weighting attached to each of these determinants varies markedly across countries. In Australia, for example, unemployment is a far more important determinant of the shadow economy than in developed countries in general and the level of personal income tax a less important determinant, suggesting that relative to other developed world governments, Australia should place more emphasis on resolving the level of unemployment than reducing personal income tax rates if it wishes to reduce the size of its shadow economy.

Turning attention to an analysis of individual determinants in Table 5.5, meanwhile, it can again be seen that there are large variations in the relative impact of particular variables on the shadow economy across countries. Take, for example, the personal income tax level. This shows a large variance with respect to its relative impact on the shadow economy, having a very large relative impact in Germany (16.6 per cent) and Estonia (16.4 per cent), while its impact in France (9.1 per cent) and Greece (10.2 per cent) is smallest. This intimates that relative to other developed world governments, governments in Germany and Estonia should put more emphasis on personal income tax levels than France and Greece if they wish to reduce the size of their shadow economies. The relative impact of indirect taxes on the size of the shadow economy, meanwhile, is largest in Greece (16.1 per cent), followed by the Czech Republic (16.0 per cent); the relative impact of indirect taxes is smallest in Belgium (12.8 per cent) and Switzerland (13.0 per cent). The tax morale variable has the highest relative impact on the shadow economy in Switzerland with an average value of 15.7 per cent between 1999 and 2010, and the lowest in the United States (13.7 per cent). The unemployment variable has the largest impact in Canada (18.4 per cent) followed by Denmark (18.2 per cent). The relative impact of the unemployment rate is smallest in Greece (10.4 per cent), the Czech Republic (11.5 per cent) and Austria (11.8 per cent). Self-employment is on average most important in Greece (18.7 per cent), France (17.3 per cent), Finland (16.9 per cent), Austria (16.8 per cent) and Spain (16.4 per cent).

Overall therefore, and as one would expect, Table 5.5 demonstrates that the OECD countries are very different regarding the relative influence of the causal variables on the size and development of their shadow economies. Given this, attention now turns towards examining in more detail the shadow economy in specific developed world countries, the determinants of their shadow economies and how the relative impact of these determinants is changing over time.

DETERMINANTS OF THE SHADOW ECONOMY: COUNTRY CASE STUDIES

Determinants of the Shadow Economy in Germany

Table 5.6 presents the determinants of the shadow economy in Germany along with how the relative weighting attached to these determinants have changed over the period from 1998 to 2010. This reveals that the predominant causal variables of the shadow economy in Germany are personal income taxes and GDP growth with average relative impacts of 16.6 per cent and 15.2 per cent respectively, followed by the level of tax morale (15.0 per cent). This table also displays the shifts over this time period in the relative influence of these causal variables. While the influence of the indirect tax burden had markedly decreased from 16.3 per cent in 1998 to 11.0 per cent in 2010, the impact of the causal variable of unemployment shows the opposite movement, increasing significantly from 11.4 per cent in 1998 to 16.1 per cent in 2010. We also observe a strong increase in the relative impact of the causal variable of tax morale. The relative weighting was 12.4 per cent in 1998 but had increased to 16.6 per cent in 2010, suggesting that there is an ever-growing need for Germany to focus more attention on reducing the acceptability of participating in the shadow economy among the German population. This, of course, requires very different policy measures

Table 5.6   The relative impact of the causal variables on the shadow economy of Germany over 1998 to 2010

Year	Personal Income Tax (PIT)	Indirect taxes	Tax morale	Unemployment	Self-employment	GDP growth	Business freedom
1998	15.6	16.3	12.4	11.4	13.4	13.4	17.5
1999	15.3	15.0	12.8	14.2	14.0	13.8	15.1
2000	14.8	14.8	13.1	16.3	13.7	12.4	14.9
2001	13.7	13.9	13.5	16.0	13.3	14.7	14.9
2002	16.1	13.2	13.7	13.2	13.1	15.9	14.7
2003	17.6	13.1	14.3	11.2	12.7	16.2	15.0
2004	20.1	13.6	15.4	8.3	11.7	15.2	15.7
2005	20.4	13.5	16.3	5.7	11.7	16.2	16.2
2006	19.6	14.4	17.6	9.0	12.7	13.6	13.1
2007	17.3	12.0	17.2	14.6	12.6	13.8	12.5
2008	14.8	11.4	16.8	17.6	12.6	15.0	11.7
2009	14.7	9.9	15.9	16.0	12.1	20.4	11.0
2010	15.6	11.0	16.6	16.1	12.5	16.5	11.7
Average	16.6	13.2	15.0	13.0	12.8	15.2	14.2

to those conventionally pursued when seeking to tackle the shadow economy, as will be discussed in Part III of this book. The causal variable of self-employment, meanwhile, displays no clear trend. The average relative contribution to estimates of the German shadow economy is 12.8 per cent. Business freedom, on the other hand, shows a decreasing trend from 17.5 per cent in 1998 to 11.7 per cent in 2010, suggesting that the regulatory burden is now less of an influence than in the past.

Determinants of the Shadow Economy in Austria

Turning to Austria, Table 5.7 presents the relative impact of the causal variables on the size of the shadow economy. This clearly reveals that the predominant determinant is self-employment contributing most (i.e., 16.8 per cent) to the Austrian shadow economy. The second most influential causal variable is GDP growth with an average relative impact of 15.9 per cent, followed by indirect taxes, which has an average relative impact of 14.6 per cent, and the business freedom variable, measuring the impact of regulations on the ability and flexibility to run a business, which contributes 14.4 per cent. Meanwhile, the unemployment rate explains on average just 11.8 per cent of the shadow economy's variation and personal income taxes just 12.4 per cent.

Examining the evolution of the relative importance of the causal variables during the observation period, we observe a decreasing relative impact

Table 5.7   *The relative impact of the causal variables on the shadow economy of Austria over 1998 to 2010*

Year	Personal income tax (PIT)	Indirect taxes	Tax morale	Unemployment	Self-employment	GDP growth	Business freedom
1998	11.7	14.1	16.1	12.4	16.0	13.5	16.2
1999	10.9	13.0	15.4	16.0	15.6	13.4	15.6
2000	12.0	13.0	14.6	17.2	15.6	12.6	15.2
2001	9.6	14.1	13.9	16.1	15.5	15.9	14.9
2002	11.2	12.1	14.5	13.9	16.4	15.9	16.0
2003	11.3	11.3	14.3	11.6	18.0	17.2	16.3
2004	12.9	12.7	14.8	6.8	19.1	16.4	17.3
2005	14.8	14.2	14.4	4.1	18.4	16.7	17.5
2006	14.9	16.8	14.2	8.8	18.2	15.4	11.7
2007	14.5	17.4	13.7	11.7	16.2	14.7	11.9
2008	11.7	17.3	12.1	15.8	16.2	15.5	11.2
2009	12.9	16.3	12.1	7.2	16.9	22.3	12.2
2010	13.0	17.0	12.6	11.6	16.5	17.6	11.8
Average	12.4	14.6	14.1	11.8	16.8	15.9	14.4

of business freedom from 16.2 per cent in 1998 to 11.8 per cent in 2010, of tax morale from 16.1 per cent (1998) to 12.6 per cent (2010) and unemployment from 12.4 per cent to 11.6 per cent. Meanwhile, other causal variables have increased in importance, namely GDP growth from 13.5 per cent in 1998 to 17.6 per cent in 2010, indirect taxes from 14.1 per cent in 1998 to 17.0 per cent in 2010, and personal income taxes from 11.7 per cent to 13.0 per cent. Again, this suggests that policy approaches towards the shadow economy cannot be static in a country given its changing determinants and vice versa, that introducing different policies results in shifts in the major determinants of the shadow economy. This necessitates a continual need to revisit the predominant determinants of the shadow economy so as to tailor policy towards them. In Austria by 2010, this necessitated that the government pay greater attention to direct and indirect taxes as these were growing in importance as major causal variables.

Determinants of the Shadow Economy in France

In France, Table 5.8 reveals a rather different weighting of the various causal variables and also changes over time in the relative weighting attached to these causal variables. Starting with the relative importance of the causal variables, the finding is that self-employment accounts for 17.3 per cent and the causal variables of GDP growth and unemployment are equally important. Their relative contribution to the shadow

Table 5.8   The relative impact of the causal variables on the shadow economy of France over 1998 to 2010

Year	Personal income tax (PIT)	Indirect taxes	Tax morale	Unemployment	Self-employment	GDP growth	Business freedom
1998	11.8	13.3	15.7	7.2	20.2	15.7	16.0
1999	10.9	14.0	15.5	7.6	20.6	15.6	15.9
2000	8.9	14.0	13.7	13.1	18.4	13.1	18.8
2001	8.2	14.3	12.7	16.9	16.9	14.3	16.6
2002	8.8	12.4	13.2	16.5	17.0	15.6	16.5
2003	8.8	11.7	13.8	17.0	16.2	15.7	16.6
2004	9.3	12.8	14.8	15.3	17.1	13.6	17.0
2005	7.8	14.6	14.7	16.0	16.5	14.1	16.3
2006	8.7	15.9	16.1	16.9	17.1	13.9	11.3
2007	8.9	16.1	15.8	18.6	16.6	13.2	10.9
2008	8.0	16.5	15.2	19.1	15.9	15.4	9.9
2009	8.8	15.7	15.6	14.3	15.8	19.5	10.3
2010	8.6	16.1	15.5	17.3	16.1	16.1	10.3
Average	9.1	14.4	14.8	15.1	17.3	15.1	14.3

economy is on average 15.1 per cent. Examining the shifts over time in the determinants of the shadow economy, the finding is that the relative influence of indirect taxation has increased from 13.3 per cent in 1998 to 16.1 per cent in 2010. The impact of the unemployment rate, moreover, had markedly increased from 7.2 per cent in 1998 to 17.3 per cent in 2010. Meanwhile, the influence of tax morale had remained stable between 1998 and 2010, while self-employment had become less important; its impact had decreased from 20.2 per cent in 1998 to 16.1 per cent in 2010. The relative influence of the personal income tax was 11.8 per cent in 1998 and had decreased to 8.6 per cent in 2010. The same holds for the business freedom index, which contributed 16.0 per cent in 1998 and 10.3 per cent in 2010. Again, therefore, there has been a shift over time in what the French government should focus upon if it wishes to tackle the shadow economy. As can be seen, the weighting accorded to for example unemployment has significantly increased, suggesting the need for greater attention to be paid to labour market interventions that reduce the unemployment rate, especially among vulnerable populations who may otherwise enter the shadow economy in order to gain a means of livelihood.

Determinants of the Shadow Economy in Italy

Turning to Southern Europe and the case of Italy, the simulation results concerning the relative impact of the causal variables on the Italian shadow economy are shown in Table 5.9. This demonstrates that the causal variable of GDP growth has the highest influence, which was 15.3 per cent in 1998 and had increased even further to 19.6 per cent in 2010. The second most important variable is unemployment with a relative impact of 12.9 per cent in 1998, which had increased to 14.8 per cent in 2010. The average relative impact of indirect taxes is 13.9 per cent, the causal variable of personal income tax contributed 13.8 per cent to the shadow economy estimate in 1998 and 12.2 per cent in 2010. The relative impacts of the variables tax morale and business freedom show a similar pattern. Both had decreased slightly between 1998 and 2010. The decrease in the tax morale variable was 1.1 per cent from 14.5 per cent in 1998 to 13.4 per cent in 2010, and that of the business freedom index 1.6 per cent from 14.7 per cent in 1998 to 13.1 per cent in 2010. Again, therefore, the macro-level determinants requiring attention differ to other nations and also change over time, suggesting that what is important at one period in time is less important at another point in time.

Table 5.9   The relative impact of the causal variables on the shadow economy of Italy over 1998 to 2010

Year	Personal income tax (PIT)	Indirect taxes	Tax morale	Unemployment	Self-employment	GDP growth	Business freedom
1998	13.8	14.3	14.5	12.9	14.5	15.3	14.7
1999	13.5	14.3	14.6	13.2	14.6	15.2	14.7
2000	14.2	14.8	15.0	14.2	15.0	11.8	15.1
2001	13.5	14.3	14.5	14.4	14.4	14.4	14.5
2002	13.2	13.9	14.0	14.2	14.0	16.6	14.1
2003	13.0	13.7	13.8	14.1	13.8	17.8	13.8
2004	13.2	13.9	14.0	14.9	13.9	16.0	14.1
2005	13.0	13.7	13.9	14.9	13.9	16.7	13.9
2006	13.2	14.0	14.2	15.8	14.3	14.6	13.9
2007	12.9	13.9	14.0	16.0	14.1	15.5	13.7
2008	12.2	13.5	13.4	15.0	13.6	19.2	13.2
2009	11.6	12.9	12.8	13.6	13.0	23.7	12.5
2010	12.2	13.4	13.4	14.8	13.5	19.6	13.1
Average	13.0	13.9	14.0	14.5	14.0	16.6	13.9

Determinants of the Shadow Economy in Spain

Finally, Table 5.10 presents the relative impact of the causal variables on the Spanish shadow economy between 1998 and 2010. In Spain, we find perhaps more fluctuation over time in the predominant causal variables, perhaps a reflection of the significant changes that have taken place in this country over this period of time. The predominant overall causal variable is unemployment. Over this time period, its average contribution to the development of the Spanish shadow economy is 17.5 per cent, having increased from 11.8 per cent in 1998 to 17.0 per cent in 2010 but rising to 22 per cent in 2006 and 2007. The second most important determinant is self-employment with an average relative impact of 16.4 per cent. Relative to the variable of unemployment, its contribution to determining the shadow economy has been more stable between 1998 and 2010. The indirect tax burden contributed 13.6 per cent to the shadow economy and its impact had increased between 1998 and 2010 from 11.8 per cent to 16.4 per cent. The average impact of the two causal variables GDP growth and tax morale is similarly important for the size and development of the shadow economy. GDP growth contributed 13.8 per cent on average and the mean relative impact of tax morale was 14.6 per cent. Finally, the business freedom index had lost importance between 1998 and 2010: its relative impact had decreased from 17.3 per cent in 1998 to 9.5 per cent in 2010,

Table 5.10   The relative impact of the causal variables on the shadow economy of Spain over 1998 to 2010

Year	Personal income tax (PIT)	Indirect taxes	Tax morale	Unemployment	Self-employment	GDP growth	Business freedom
1998	12.6	11.8	17.7	11.8	16.3	12.5	17.3
1999	12.4	10.4	17.7	15.1	16.3	11.7	16.4
2000	12.5	10.0	16.8	16.8	16.6	11.3	15.9
2001	11.5	10.0	15.5	19.8	15.7	12.7	14.9
2002	10.9	13.5	14.5	17.9	15.6	13.5	14.2
2003	11.2	13.5	14.1	17.9	16.0	13.3	14.2
2004	11.4	13.7	13.8	18.1	15.9	13.0	14.1
2005	10.9	13.5	13.4	20.0	15.7	12.5	14.0
2006	10.9	14.7	13.9	22.0	16.9	12.8	8.9
2007	9.8	15.6	13.4	22.0	16.8	13.2	9.2
2008	10.2	16.4	13.0	18.4	16.8	16.0	9.2
2009	11.0	17.4	13.1	10.7	17.3	20.6	10.0
2010	10.3	16.4	13.2	17.0	17.0	16.6	9.5
Average	11.2	13.6	14.6	17.5	16.4	13.8	12.9

as other variables became more important determinants of the shadow economy.

CONCLUSIONS

This chapter has documented using the MIMIC method the cross-national variations in the magnitude of the shadow economy across developed OECD nations and investigated the causal determinants of the shadow economy and how the relative weighting attached to these causal determinants changes both across countries and over time. The finding is that although the shadow economy is overall smaller in the developed world than in the developing world, there are nevertheless marked variations. In countries such as Bulgaria, Romania and Turkey the shadow economy is the equivalent of 34.6 per cent, 32.2 per cent and 30.6 per cent of GDP respectively, while countries in which the shadow economy is smallest are Luxembourg, Switzerland and the United States, whose shadow economies are the equivalent of 9.6 per cent, 8.3 per cent and 8.7 per cent of official GDP respectively.

To explain the shadow economy, the average relative influence (in percentage terms) of various causal variables has then been investigated for all OECD countries between 1999 and 2010. This has revealed that tax morale, unemployment and self-employment are the most influential determinants of the shadow economy. Examining the average values for all developed OECD nations, we observe that unemployment and self-employment have the highest influence (14.6 per cent) across countries. This is followed by tax morale with an average relative impact of 14.5 per cent, then GDP growth (14.3 per cent), business freedom (14.2 per cent), indirect taxes (14.1 per cent) and finally the personal income tax with an average relative impact of 13.8 per cent.

However, the relative importance of these causal variables changes both across countries and over time within countries. In Australia, for example, unemployment is a far more important determinant of the shadow economy than in developed countries in general and the level of personal income tax a less important determinant, suggesting that relative to other developed world governments, Australia should place more emphasis on resolving the level of unemployment than reducing personal income tax rates if it wishes to reduce the size of its shadow economy. Indeed, this chapter has provided a detailed review of both the relative importance of these causal variables in France, Germany, Austria, Spain and Italy, as well as how the importance of each of these causal variables has changed over time in each of these countries. The result is that it has been clearly revealed that it is not possible to adopt a universally similar approach to tackling the shadow economy across all countries and neither is the approach that needs to be adopted static over time. The emphasis given to tackling particular macro-level determinants needs to vary across countries. Moreover, as the relative weighting attached to different causal variables shifts over time, there is a need for the focus of the policy approach adopted by individual national governments to also change to reflect these shifts.

Despite these differences, this chapter has revealed that besides the indirect tax and personal income tax burden, which the government can directly influence by policy actions, self-employment and unemployment are two very important driving forces of the shadow economy. Unemployment may be controllable by the government through economic policy in a traditional Keynesian sense; alternatively, the government can try to improve the country's competitiveness to increase foreign demand. The impact of self-employment on the shadow economy is less or only partly controllable by the government and may be ambiguous from a welfare perspective. A government can deregulate the economy or incentivize 'entrepreneurship', which would make self-employment easier, potentially reducing unemployment and positively contributing to efforts in controlling the size of the shadow economy. Such actions, however, need to be accompanied with a strengthening of institutions and tax morale to reduce the probability that the self-employed shift unreasonable proportions of their economic activities into the shadow economy, which, if it happened, would make government policies incentivizing self-employment less effective. What is important overall, however, and is seldom voiced, is that tackling the shadow economy requires macro-level determinants of the shadow economy to be addressed. It cannot be tackled simply by increasing the probability of detection and increasing the level of penalties, which deals only with the effects rather than causes of the problem. This issue will be returned to in Part III of this book.

PART III

The shadow labour force in global perspective

6. The shadow labour force in developing and transition economies[1]

Part II revealed the cross-national variations and determinants of the size of the shadow economy using the MIMIC indirect measurement method. Here, in Part III, we seek to uncover the cross-national variations in participation in the shadow labour force using data collected from direct surveys and to explore the determinants of these cross-national variations. In this chapter, the aim is to evaluate the variations in the size and character of the shadow labour force across developing and transition economies along with the country-level determinants that shape the magnitude and nature of employment in the shadow labour force. To do this, we here report International Labour Organization (ILO) estimates of the level and nature of what it terms 'employment in the informal economy' across 36 developing and transition economies for which the ILO has collected data. The outcome will be to reveal not only significant cross-national variations in the extent and nature of participation in the shadow labour force across developing and transition economies but also that there are significant correlations between cross-national variations in the extent and nature of participation in the shadow labour force and cross-national variations in GNP per capita, corruption, poverty, taxation and social contribution levels.

From the middle of the twentieth century until the 1970s, the dominant view was that the existence of employment in the shadow economy was largely a developing country phenomenon and represented a pre-modern mode of production that was steadily disappearing with the advent of modernization and economic development (Geertz, 1963; Gilbert, 1998; Lewis, 1959). This depiction arguably persists in contemporary discourse. For example, based on the assumption that the shadow labour force is merely some remnant of a past production system that is disappearing and therefore unimportant, the dominant classificatory schemas of economies continue today to differentiate countries only by the nature of their formal economic production systems, such as by their levels of gross domestic product (GDP) or gross national income (GNI) per capita (World Bank, 2013), whether they are control, market or mixed economies (Arnold, 1996; Rohlf, 1998), or liberal or coordinated varieties of capitalism (Hall and Soskice, 2001). This, of course, would be highly appropriate if the majority of employment globally was indeed in the formal economy. Since the turn of the new millennium, however, there has been growing recognition that in many developing and transition economies, a sizeable proportion of the non-agricultural labour force have their main employment in the shadow economy (Dibben and Williams, 2012; Jütting and Laiglesia, 2009; ILO, 2012, 2013; Williams and Lansky, 2013). The result has been the emergence of fresh ways of classifying and differentiating economies that foreground work in the shadow economy (Williams, 2014c, 2014d, 2014e, 2015a, 2015b, 2015c).

First, therefore, a simple heuristic typology is outlined that classifies economies according to the level and nature of participation in the shadow labour force and, second, a review is undertaken of the competing explanations for the cross-national variations in the prevalence and character of the shadow labour force. Third, the ILO dataset of country surveys that contains data on the level and nature of employment in the shadow economy in 36 developing and transition countries is introduced, followed in the fourth section by the descriptive findings on the cross-national variations in the level and nature of the shadow labour force. The fifth section then evaluates the competing explanations for these cross-national variations before the sixth and final section summarizes the findings.

At the outset, however, the way in which the shadow labour force is here defined needs to be briefly addressed. In developing and transition economies, what we term the shadow labour force in this book is usually termed 'employment in the informal economy'. To define this, the widely accepted enterprise-based definition of the informal sector is combined with the jobs-based definition of informal employment developed by the 15th and 17th International Conference of Labour Statisticians (ICLS) respectively (Hussmanns, 2005; ILO, 2011, 2012). As Table 6.1 graphically displays, taking the enterprise as the unit of analysis results in the shadow labour force being viewed as comprised of both formal and shadow jobs in shadow enterprises (A+B), while taking jobs as the unit of analysis results in shadow employment including shadow jobs in both shadow and formal enterprises (A+C). 'Employment in the informal economy' (A+B+C)

Table 6.1   The anatomy of the labour force

Economic units	Informal jobs	Formal jobs
Informal economic units	A	B
Formal economic units	C	D

Source: ILO (2012)

thus covers all persons who in their main job are employed either in the shadow sector (A + B) or in shadow jobs (A + C), counting only once those persons who are classified in both categories.

As Chapter 1 discussed in some detail, the shadow sector (A + B) is composed of all those employed in shadow enterprises which the 15th ICLS in 1993 defined as private unincorporated enterprises that are unregistered or small in terms of the number of employed persons (Hussmanns, 2005; ILO, 2011, 2012). Given that this does not include those in shadow jobs in formal enterprises, the 17th ICLS in 2003 adopted a jobs-based definition that views shadow employment (A + C) as jobs that lack basic social or legal protections or employment benefits and that may be found in the formal sector, shadow sector or households (ILO, 2011). With these definitions in hand, attention can turn towards how economies can be classified according to the level and nature of employment in the shadow economy.

CLASSIFYING ECONOMIES BY THE EXTENT AND NATURE OF THE SHADOW LABOUR FORCE

Until now, to repeat, the employment relations systems of countries have been differentiated by analysing the character of their formal economies, such as whether they are control, market or mixed economies (Arnold, 1996; Rohlf, 1998) or liberal or coordinated varieties of capitalism (Hall and Soskice, 2001). This way of classifying employment relations systems, however, ignores that most employment globally is not in the formal economy. Some 60 per cent of the global workforce have their main employment in the shadow labour force (Jütting and Laiglesia, 2009), with many countries especially in the majority (third) world having more people employed in the shadow labour force than the formal sector (Dibben and Williams, 2012; ILO, 2013; Williams and Youssef, 2014). Based on this, recent years have witnessed the advocacy of new classificatory schemas of employment relations systems that recognize the prominence of the shadow labour force (Williams, 2014c, 2014d, 2014e, 2015a, 2015b 2015,c; Williams and Shahid, 2015; Williams and Youssef, 2014).

Any classification of economies that compares the variable size and heterogeneous character of the shadow labour force across the globe needs, first, to convey the proportion of jobs that are in the shadow labour market and, second, how the nature of the shadow labour force varies across economies. Figure 6.1 provides a simple way of classifying the proportion of non-agricultural jobs that are in the shadow labour market in any economy. All economies can be positioned at some point along this continuum.

When interpreting the different positions countries occupy on this

*Figure 6.1   Typology of economies: by level of employment in the shadow
economy as % of all non-agricultural employment*

continuum, caution is required. Sometimes a temporal sequencing has
been overlaid onto this continuum by assuming that there is a natural
and inevitable temporal trajectory towards the left of the continuum
(that is, ever-greater levels of formalization) and therefore a 'development
queue' has been portrayed with the more formal economies of the West
to the left of the spectrum and the less formalized economies of the third
(majority) world located at the right (Massey, 2005). Nevertheless, the
position any economy inhabits on this spectrum does not necessarily represent the stage they are at in their trajectory towards formalization, but
rather difference, and as such, a natural and inevitable temporal trajectory in a particular direction should not be assumed. Indeed, the lesson
learned from the past few decades is that different economies are moving
in different directions along this spectrum (Schneider, 2013; Williams,
2007a).

To capture the character of the shadow labour force and how this
varies across developing and transition economies, meanwhile, any
typology needs to outline the different forms of employment in the
shadow labour market in a country. Various alternative options are available to do so. One option is to examine the share of total employment
in the shadow economy that is carried out on a waged, own-account or
household basis (see Williams and Lansky, 2013). Here, however, and
using Table 6.1 above, a distinction is drawn between shadow employment in shadow enterprises (A), shadow jobs in formal enterprises (B)
and formal jobs in shadow enterprises (C). How the character of the
shadow labour force varies cross-nationally can be then classified
according to the 'intensity' of employment in the shadow economy,
namely the share of the shadow labour force that is in shadow employment in shadow enterprises (A). This is here considered a measure of a
more intense form of employment in the shadow economy since both
the job and the enterprise are in the shadow economy, which is not the
case with shadow jobs in formal enterprises (B) and formal employment
in shadow enterprises (C). Once economies are classified according to
the scale and intensity of employment in the shadow economy, then
these variations need to be explained.

CROSS-NATIONAL VARIATIONS IN THE SHADOW LABOUR FORCE: COMPETING EXPLANATIONS

Until now, there have been three competing explanations for the cross-national variations in the scale of employment in the shadow economy. These view higher levels of employment in the shadow economy to be a result of either economic underdevelopment (modernization explanation), high taxes, public sector corruption and state interference in the free market (neo-liberal explanation) or inadequate state intervention to protect workers from poverty (political economy perspective). Each is here considered in turn.

Modernization Perspective

In the modernization perspective, which dominated for most of the twentieth century, employment in the shadow economy was widely portrayed as a remnant from a pre-modern mode of production and fading as the modern formal economy took hold (Geertz, 1963; Gilbert, 1998; Lewis, 1959; Packard, 2007). As Bromley (2007, p. xv) asserts, from this perspective, employment in the shadow economy is viewed as 'unimportant and destined to disappear'. Such work is therefore a manifestation of underdevelopment that will disappear with economic advancement and modernization. Cross-national variations in the extent and nature of the shadow labour force, in consequence, signal the position of a country on a one-dimensional linear trajectory towards formalization. Classifying countries using indicators such as GNP per capita thus enable the relative level of economic advancement and modernization to be measured and for countries to be placed according to their place in the development queue with nations at the fore being 'advanced', 'modern' and 'progressive' and nations at the back of the queue with low levels of formalization being deemed 'backward', 'traditional' and 'underdeveloped' (Geertz, 1963; Gilbert, 1998; Lewis, 1959; Packard, 2007). To explore the validity of this explanation for the cross-national variations in the extent and nature of the shadow labour force, therefore, the following hypothesis can be tested:

Modernization hypothesis (H1): the shadow labour force will be more prevalent in less developed economies.

In recent decades, however, there has been recognition that employment in the shadow economy is widespread and persistent (Buehn and Schneider, 2012b; Feld and Schneider, 2010; ILO, 2011, 2012, 2013; Rani et al., 2013;

Rodgers and Williams, 2009; Schneider, 2011). This has led to the emergence of alternative explanations. Each is here reviewed in turn (for a fuller discussion, see Williams and Lansky, 2013).

Neo-liberal Perspective

Bhattacharya (2014) classifies neo-liberal discourse as composed of seven core components: it attacks labour 'rigidities' rather than focusing on labour's hard-won rights; treats low-cost labour as a comparative advantage; views labour rights as obstacles and luxuries; advocates the doctrine and practice of flexibility in advanced countries; adopts the paradigm of informality; calls to formalize informal workers as a way of disguising the ever-greater informality of formal workers; and celebrates enterprise culture and informal entrepreneurialism.

From this neo-liberal perspective, the persistence and extensiveness of employment in the shadow economy is thus deemed to be a manifestation of a populist reaction to high taxes, a corrupt state system and too much interference in the free market. Participation in shadow employment is thus viewed as a rational economic decision. People and businesses are viewed as voluntarily exiting the formal economy so as to avoid the costs, time and effort associated with formal employment (for example, Becker, 2004; De Soto, 1989, 2001; London and Hart, 2004; Nwabuzor, 2005; Sauvy, 1984; Williams and Gurtoo, 2012). As Nwabuzor (2005, p. 126) asserts: 'Informality is a response to burdensome controls, and an attempt to circumvent them.' Or as Becker (2004, p. 10) puts it, 'informal work arrangements are a rational response by micro-entrepreneurs to over-regulation by government bureaucracies'. For such neo-liberal commentators, therefore, shadow employment is a rational economic strategy resulting from high taxes and state-imposed institutional constraints (De Soto, 1989, 2001; Perry and Maloney, 2007). The ongoing prevalence and even growth of shadow employment is consequently viewed as resulting from high taxes, public sector corruption, over-regulation and state interference in the free market and the remedy is to pursue tax reductions, reduce corruption, deregulation and minimal state intervention. To explore the validity of this neo-liberal explanation, the following hypothesis can be tested:

Neo-liberal hypothesis (H2): the shadow labour force will be more prevalent in less developed countries with higher tax rates, greater public sector corruption and higher levels of state interference in the free market.

Political Economy Perspective

From a political economy perspective, however, this persistence and expansion of jobs in the shadow economy is regarded as a direct by-product of the advent of a deregulated open world economy (Bhattacharya, 2014; Castells and Portes, 1989; Gallin, 2001; Harriss-White, 2014; Hudson, 2005; Portes, 1994; Sassen, 1996; Slavnic, 2010; Taiwo, 2013). The increasing functional integration of a single global economic system is resulting in subcontracting and outsourcing becoming a primary way of integrating employment in the shadow economy into contemporary capitalism, causing a further downward pressure on wages and the erosion of incomes, social services and benefits, and the growth of yet more jobs in the shadow economy. As Fernandez-Kelly (2006, p. 18) states, 'the informal economy is far from a vestige of earlier stages in economic development. Instead, informality is part and parcel of the processes of modernization.' Indeed, for Davis (2006, p. 186), such 'primitive forms of exploitation . . . have been given new life by postmodern globalization'.

Viewed through this conceptual lens, employment in the shadow economy is a largely unregulated, low-paid and insecure kind of survival-driven employment undertaken under 'sweatshop-like' conditions by marginalized populations excluded from formal jobs and formal welfare support, who turn to such work as a last resort (Castells and Portes, 1989; Davis, 2006; Gallin, 2001; Hudson, 2005; ILO, 2002a; Sassen, 1996). Employment in the shadow economy from this perspective will therefore be higher in economies where there is inadequate state intervention to protect workers from poverty. To evaluate the validity of this political economy perspective, the following hypothesis can be tested:

Political economy hypothesis (H3): the shadow labour force will be more prevalent in those less developed and transition countries with lower levels of state intervention to protect workers from poverty.

Evaluations of the Competing Theories

Until now, most literature explaining cross-national variations in the prevalence of the shadow labour force has supported the tenets of just one of these perspectives. For example, Yamada (1996) argues that such employment is a matter of choice, as argued largely by neo-liberals. Over the past decade, however, more nuanced understandings have begun to emerge. These view each explanation as more relevant to some forms of shadow labour and some contexts than others, and believe that only by combining them can a finer-grained understanding be achieved. For example, although the existence of shadow labour is in all contexts due to a mix of exit and exclusion rationales, it has been argued that: the political economy explanation is more valid when explaining waged work in the shadow economy and the neo-liberal perspective when explaining self-employment in the shadow economy (Perry and Maloney, 2007; Williams, 2013a, 2013b); the political economy perspective is more relevant when explaining the shadow labour of relatively deprived populations and the neo-liberal perspective when explaining such labour in relatively affluent populations within countries (Evans et al., 2006; Gurtoo and Williams, 2009; Pfau-Effinger, 2009; Williams et al., 2012b, 2013a); that exit rationales are more common in developed economies and exclusion rationales in developing and transition economies (Oviedo et al., 2009); and that women are more likely to be driven by exclusion motives and men more commonly driven by voluntary exit motives as the neo-liberals assert (Franck, 2012; Grant, 2013; Williams, 2009a, 2011; Williams and Youssef, 2013).

Here, however, attention turns to evaluating their validity to explaining the cross-national variations in developing and transition economies. Is it as the 'modernization' perspective asserts that the shadow labour force is lower in wealthier developing economies than poorer developing economies? Is it as neo-liberals assert that the shadow labour force is more prevalent in countries with greater public sector corruption, higher taxes and more state interference in work and welfare? Or alternatively, is the shadow labour force more prevalent in countries where there is greater poverty and less protection of workers, forcing marginalized populations into such endeavour in the absence of alternatives?

METHODOLOGY: EXAMINING THE SHADOW LABOUR FORCE IN DEVELOPING AND TRANSITION ECONOMIES

To differentiate countries according to the level and intensity of participation in the shadow labour force and evaluate the contrasting explanations for the cross-national variations, the ILO surveys conducted in 47 developing countries are analysed here. In total, data is available for 36 of these 47 countries on both the level and intensity of employment in the shadow economy. So far as is known, this is the only cross-nationally comparable data currently available on participation in shadow labour in developing and transition countries that uses a common broad definition across all countries and a similar harmonized survey methodology to collect data using either an ILO Department of Statistics questionnaire sent to countries or information from national labour force or informal sector surveys (for further details, see ILO, 2012).

It is important to state that this survey examines only whether the main employment of a person is in the shadow labour force. Moreover, it excludes employment in agriculture, hunting, forestry and fishing. If this was to be included, as well as people who had second jobs in the shadow labour force, the prevalence of shadow employment would be higher. Whether this dataset provides an accurate description of participation in the shadow labour force is, of course, unknown because there is no benchmark available against which this can be evaluated. It is also often stated that direct surveys underestimate the scale of the shadow economy and shadow labour force relative to indirect measurement methods (Bardasi et al., 2010), particularly in relation to women's shadow work (Franck and Olsson, 2014; Langsten and Salen, 2008). If anything, therefore, participation in shadow employment might be higher than suggested by this survey. Moreover, people in different countries may well have differing tendencies to report or not report their shadow work due to variations in whether this is deemed acceptable in terms of national norms, values and codes of conduct. Although this cannot be ruled out, by adopting the same definition of shadow employment and the same survey method and interview schedule for collecting the data, this survey minimizes the effects of this possibility. As such, some caution is required with regard to this dataset. It is likely to provide a lower-bound estimate of the level of participation in the shadow labour force.

To select the indicators for evaluating the competing explanations, proxy indicators for the various tenets of each theorization are taken from the World Bank development indicators database for the year in which the survey was conducted in each country (World Bank, 2013). The only indicators taken from non-official sources are on perceptions of public sector corruption, which has been taken from Transparency International's corruption perceptions index for the relevant year in each country (Transparency International, 2013), the Human Development Index (HDI) and the Social Progress Index as a measure of 'development' (Social Progress Imperative, 2014; United Nations Development Programme, 2014).

To evaluate the modernization hypothesis (H1) that the shadow labour force will be more prevalent in less developed economies, the conventional indicator used in previous studies is GNP per capita (ILO, 2012; Yamada, 1996). Given that there is widespread criticism of this indicator as a proxy measure of the 'development' of an economy or the standard of living of its citizens (Kuznets, 1962), both this and additional measurements of the level of 'development' are used, namely:

- GNP per capita.
- Household final consumption expenditure per capita (that is, private consumption per capita) – this covers the market value of all goods and services, including durable products (for example, cars, washing machines and home computers), purchased by households (World Bank, 2013).
- Human Development Index (HDI) – this is a composite of life expectancy, education and income indices intended to shift the focus of development from national income accounting to people-centred policies (United Nations Development Programme, 2014).
- Social Progress Index (SPI) – this measures the extent to which countries provide for the social and environmental needs of their citizens; 52 indicators in the areas of basic human needs, foundations of wellbeing, and opportunity show the relative performance of nations (Social Progress Imperative, 2014).

To evaluate the neo-liberal hypothesis (H2) that participation in the shadow labour force will be higher in countries where there are high taxes, corruption and state interference in the free market, meanwhile, indicators previously used when evaluating the assumptions of neo-liberal thought are employed (Eurofound, 2013; European Commission, 2013; Williams, 2013a, 2013b, 2013c, 2013d), namely the World Bank (2013) country-level data on:

- Taxes on goods and services as a percentage of revenue, which includes general sales and turnover or value added taxes, selective excises on goods, selective taxes on services, taxes on the use of goods or property, taxes on extraction and production of minerals, and profits of fiscal monopolies.
- Taxes on revenue (excluding grants) as a percentage of GDP: revenue is cash receipts from taxes, social contributions and other revenues such as fines, fees, rent and income from property or sales. Grants are also considered as revenue but are excluded here.
- Tax revenue as a percentage of GDP: tax revenue refers to compulsory transfers to the central government for public purposes. Certain compulsory transfers such as fines, penalties and most social security contributions are excluded. Refunds and corrections of erroneously collected tax revenue are treated as negative revenue.

In addition, the public sector corruption tenet of the neo-liberal perspective is evaluated using:

- Transparency International's Corruption Perceptions Index (CPI) (Transparency International, 2013) – this is a composite index of perceptions of public sector corruption that draws on 14 expert opinion surveys and scores nations on a 0–10 scale, with zero indicating high levels and ten indicating low levels of perceived public sector corruption.
- The percentage of firms stating that they are expected to give gifts in meetings with tax officials.
- The percentage of firms giving informal payments to public officials.

To analyse both the neo-liberal hypothesis that state interference leads to greater levels of participation in the shadow labour force, and the political economy hypothesis that it is due to inadequate levels of state intervention, the indicators analysed are those previously used when evaluating these assumptions of neo-liberal and political economy thought (European Commission, 2013; Eurofound, 2013; Williams, 2013c, 2013d), namely:

- Social contributions as a percentage of revenue. Social contributions include social security contributions by employees, employers and self-employed individuals, and other contributions whose source cannot be determined. They also include actual or imputed contributions to social insurance schemes operated by governments.
- State revenue (excluding grants) as a percentage of GDP.
- Expense of government as a percentage of GDP, which is a measure of the size of government and therefore a loose proxy of the degree of intervention. The expense of government is the level of cash payments for the operating activities of the government in providing goods and services. It includes compensation of employees (such as wages and salaries), interest and subsidies, grants, social benefits and other expenses such as rent and dividends (World Bank, 2013).

Meanwhile, and to analyse the tenet of the political economy perspective that participation in the shadow labour force is correlated with the level of poverty, two indicators are analysed:

- The percentage of the population living below the national poverty line (ILO, 2012).
- The size of the poverty gap at $1.25 per day in personal purchasing power standards. The poverty gap is here taken as the mean shortfall from the poverty line (counting the non-poor as having

zero shortfall), expressed as a percentage of the poverty line. This measure reflects the depth of poverty as well as its incidence (World Bank, 2013).

To analyse the relationship between cross-national variations in the level and intensity of participation in the shadow labour force and these economic and social characteristics that each theorization views as determinants, and given the small sample size of 36 countries and lack of necessary controls to include in a multivariate regression analysis, it is only possible here to conduct bivariate regression analyses. To do this, Spearman's rank correlation coefficient (r_s) is used due to the non-parametric nature of the data. As will be revealed, despite the limitation of only using bivariate regression analysis, some meaningful findings are produced regarding the validity of the different perspectives.

Below, therefore, first the variable level and intensity of participation in the shadow labour force across the 36 countries will be reported and, second, a preliminary analysis of the wider economic and social conditions that each perspective deems to be associated with higher levels of participation so as to evaluate the competing perspectives.

CROSS-NATIONAL VARIATIONS IN THE SHADOW LABOUR FORCE

Table 6.2 reports the findings on the scale of employment in the shadow economy. This reveals that the simple unweighted average is that the majority (57.4 per cent) of the non-agricultural workforce in these 36 developing and transition economies have their main employment in the shadow economy. However, a weighted average figure is used here, which takes into account the variable workforce size in each country. Across all 36 countries, three out of every five (59.8 per cent) non-agricultural workers have their main employment in the shadow economy. The shadow labour force, therefore, is not some minor residue of little importance but a large realm employing the majority of the workforce in these developing and transition countries.

However, this overall weighted average figure masks some major variations across global regions. To analyse this, the 36 countries for which data are available are divided, using the World Bank (2013) classification into six regions (see Table 6.3). The finding is that the weighted proportion of the non-agricultural workforce whose main job is in the shadow labour market ranges from just under a quarter (24.8 per cent) of the working population in Europe and Central Asia, through to 75.6

Table 6.2   Employment in the shadow economy as percentage of non-agricultural employment (unweighted and weighted): by global region

Global region	Total employment in the informal economy as % of non-agricultural employment, unweighted	Total employment in the informal economy as % of non-agricultural employment, weighted	Number of countries
East Asia and Pacific	64.8	47.4	4
Europe and Central Asia	22.8	24.8	4
Latin America and Caribbean	58.2	51.1	16
Middle East and North Africa	59.0	58.5	1
South Asia	75.9	75.6	3
Sub-Saharan Africa	64.8	53.1	8
All global regions	57.4	59.8	36

Source: derived from ILO (2012)

per cent in South Asia. Consequently, the share of the working population whose main job is in the shadow economy is not evenly distributed globally.

As Table 6.3 reports, there are also marked cross-national variations in the proportion of the workforce whose main job is in the shadow economy, ranging from 84.7 per cent of the non-agricultural workforce in Mali to 6.5 per cent in Serbia. Indeed, in 24 (67 per cent) of the 36 nations, the majority of the non-agricultural workforce have their main job in the shadow labour market. There is, however, significant variation between countries. Using the classificatory schema in Figure 6.1, although no developing countries have all their workforce in either formal or shadow employment and none are 'nearly shadow' economies (with 90–99 per cent of the workforce in shadow jobs), 11 per cent are 'dominantly shadow' economies (with 80–89 per cent in shadow jobs), 25 per cent are 'largely shadow' economies (with 70–79 per cent in shadow jobs), 22 per cent are 'mostly shadow' economies (60–69 per cent in shadow jobs), 8 per cent are 'semi-shadow' economies (50–59 per cent in shadow jobs), 17 per cent are 'semi-formal' economies (40–49 per cent in shadow jobs), two are 'mostly formal' economies (30–39 per cent in shadow jobs), none are 'largely formal' economies (20–29 per cent in shadow jobs), 8 per cent are 'dominantly formal' economies (10–19 per cent in shadow jobs) and 3 per cent 'nearly formal' economies (1–9 per cent in shadow jobs). These developing and transition countries, in consequence, are heavily clustered in the middle of the continuum towards the shadow end of the continuum.

Table 6.3　　*Extent and nature of employment in the shadow economy, 36 developing and transition economies*

Country	Global region (World Bank classification)	Year of survey	Employment in shadow economy as % of non-agricultural employment (A+B+C)	% of all employment in shadow economy that is shadow employment in shadow enterprises	Type of economy
Mali	Sub-Saharan Africa	2004	84.7	85.2	Dominantly shadow
India	South Asia	2009/10	84.3	79.2	Dominantly shadow
Philippines	East Asia and Pacific	2008	84.0	69.8	Dominantly shadow
Pakistan	South Asia	2009/10	81.3	86.2	Dominantly shadow
Zambia	Sub-Saharan Africa	2008	76.3	75.8	Largely shadow
Bolivia	Latin America and Caribbean	2006	75.6	68.3	Largely shadow
Honduras	Latin America and Caribbean	2009	75.3	75.6	Largely shadow
Madagascar	Sub-Saharan Africa	2005	73.7	70.1	Largely shadow
Uganda	Sub-Saharan Africa	2010	73.5	75.8	Largely shadow
Indonesia	East Asia and Pacific	2009	72.4	83.1	Largely shadow
Lesotho	Sub-Saharan Africa	2008	70.7	18.8	Largely shadow
Paraguay	Latin America and Caribbean	2009	70.7	53.6	Largely shadow
Peru	Latin America and Caribbean	2009	70.7	68.2	Largely shadow
Nicaragua	Latin America and Caribbean	2009	69.4	73.1	Mostly shadow
Vietnam	East Asia and Pacific	2009	68.5	63.1	Mostly shadow
El Salvador	Latin America and Caribbean	2009	68.2	75.7	Mostly shadow
Tanzania	Sub-Saharan Africa	2005/6	66.7	68.5	Mostly shadow
Sri Lanka	South Asia	2009	62.1	81.1	Mostly shadow
Colombia	Latin America and Caribbean	2010	61.5	82.0	Mostly shadow
Ecuador	Latin America and Caribbean	2009	61.3	60.2	Mostly shadow
Liberia	Sub-Saharan Africa	2010	60.3	81.6	Mostly shadow

Table 6.3   (continued)

Country	Global region (World Bank classification)	Year of survey	Employment in shadow economy as % of non-agricultural employment (A+B+C)	% of all employment in shadow economy that is shadow employment in shadow enterprises	Type of economy
West Bank & Gaza	Middle East and North Africa	2010	59.0	36.9	Semi shadow
Mexico	Latin America and Caribbean	2009	54.3	61.7	Semi shadow
Argentina	Latin America and Caribbean	2009	50.0	63.6	Semi shadow
Dominican Rep	Latin America and Caribbean	2009	48.8	59.6	Semi-formal
Venezuela	Latin America and Caribbean	2009	48.2	74.1	Semi-formal
Costa Rica	Latin America and Caribbean	2009	48.2	67.6	Semi-formal
Panama	Latin America and Caribbean	2009	44.0	62.5	Semi-formal
Uruguay	Latin America and Caribbean	2009	43.7	68.6	Semi-formal
Brazil	Latin America and Caribbean	2009	42.3	57.2	Semi-formal
China	East Asia and Pacific	2010	34.4	58.4	Largely formal
South Africa	Sub-Saharan Africa	2010	32.7	54.4	Largely formal
Armenia	Europe and Central Asia	2009	19.8	51.5	Dominantly formal
Moldova Rep	Europe and Central Asia	2009	15.9	45.9	Dominantly formal
Macedonia	Europe and Central Asia	2010	12.8	57.8	Dominantly formal
Serbia	Europe and Central Asia	2010	6.5	46.2	Nearly formal

There is also a strong cross-national correlation between the scale of shadow employment (that is, the proportion of the non-agricultural workforce in employment in the shadow economy) and the intensity of employment in the shadow economy (that is, the share of all employment in the shadow economy that is shadow employment in shadow

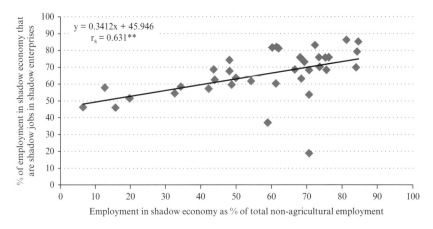

Figure 6.2   Extent and nature of employment in the shadow economy, 36 developing and transition economies

enterprises). To see this, columns 4 and 5 of Table 6.3 report the scale and intensity of employment in the shadow economy respectively. Examining the intensity of employment in the shadow economy, the finding is that across all 36 developing and transition countries, three-quarters (74 per cent) of all employment in the shadow economy is shadow employment in shadow enterprises. Again, however, marked cross-national variations exist, ranging from 86.2 per cent in Pakistan to 18.8 per cent in Lesotho. To analyse the correlation between the level and intensity of employment in the shadow economy, Figure 6.2 graphically displays the statistically significant association. The greater the level of employment in the shadow economy, the higher the intensity of shadow employment (that is, the more likely shadow jobs are to be located in shadow enterprises). Indeed, using Spearman's rank correlation coefficient (r_s) due to the non-parametric nature of the data, the finding is that this is statistically significant within a 99 per cent confidence interval ($r_s = -0.631**$).

Given these findings concerning the cross-national variations in the level and intensity of employment in the shadow economy, attention now turns towards critically evaluating the competing explanations for these variations.

ANALYSIS: EVALUATING COMPETING EXPLANATIONS FOR THE CROSS-NATIONAL VARIATIONS IN THE SHADOW LABOUR FORCE

To undertake a preliminary analysis of the validity of the three theoretical perspectives, the association between the cross-national variations in the degree and intensity of employment in the shadow economy and the cross-national variations in the various characteristics that each perspective deems important determinants are evaluated here.

Evaluating the Modernization Perspective

Beginning with the modernization explanation that the level of employment in the shadow economy is higher the less developed the economy is, the correlation between cross-national variations in participation in shadow employment and cross-national variations in GNP per capita is analysed across these 36 developing and transition economies. Using Spearman's rank correlation coefficient, the finding is that there is a strong statistically significant relationship within a 99 per cent confidence interval ($r_s = -0.520**$), as Figure 6.3 portrays. The direction of this relationship is that the level of participation in shadow employment is higher in developing and transition economies with lower levels of GNP per capita. There is also a statistically significant association within a 95 per cent confidence interval between the nature of shadow employment and GNP per capita ($r_s = -0.351*$). The intensity of shadow employment (that is, the share of the shadow labour force in shadow jobs in shadow enterprises) is greater in developing and transition economies with lower levels of GNP per capita.

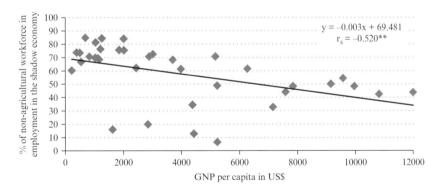

Figure 6.3   *Relationship between participation in shadow labour and GNP per capita*

However, and similar to previous studies reaching the same conclusion (ILO, 2012; Yamada, 1996), it is not possible to here establish the direction of the correlation in terms of any cause–effect relationship. This, in consequence, is a limitation of both this and previous studies.

In recent years, however, alternative indicators of the level of 'development' have emerged taking into account a wider range of variables other than simply economic productivity. Evaluating these measures of 'development' more widely defined, the finding is that there is a strong statistically significant correlation between cross-national variations in the level of shadow employment and cross-national variations in not only household consumption expenditure per capita ($r_s = -0.613**$) but also the Human Development Index ($r_s = -0.497**$) and Social Progress Index ($r_s = -0.509**$). Shadow employment therefore, across a range of indicators of 'development', is larger in less developed economies, thus confirming H1.

Evaluating the Neo-liberal Perspective

Examining the neo-liberal view that employment in the shadow economy is an outcome of higher tax rates, public sector corruption and interference by the state in the operation of the free market, the first step is to analyse the neo-liberal tenet that the scale of shadow employment is greater when public sector corruption is higher because this results in citizens exiting the formal economy so as to seek livelihoods beyond the corrupt public sector officials. The finding is that there is a strong statistically significant association between countries with higher perceived levels of public sector corruption and a greater prevalence of shadow employment ($r_s = -0.502**$). Although the association between public sector corruption and the intensity of shadow employment is not statistically significant ($r_s = -0.253$), the direction of the relationship is that countries with higher perceived levels of public sector corruption have a greater intensity of shadow employment (i.e., the share of the shadow labour force in shadow jobs in shadow enterprises).

Is it the case therefore, that the level of shadow employment is a product of 'exit' from the formal economy due to high taxes? Given that this is a core aspect of neo-liberal explanations, several measures of taxation are analysed here. Beginning with the relationship between the cross-national variations in the level of participation in shadow employment and the level of taxes on goods and services as a percentage of revenue, a statistically significant correlation is identified ($r_s = -0.430*$). However, its direction is the inverse of what neo-liberals suggest. The scale of shadow employment decreases as taxes on goods and services increase. Meanwhile, although the relationship between the intensity of shadow employment and the level of taxes on goods and services is not significant ($r_s = -0.216$), the direction is that the intensity of shadow employment again decreases as taxes on goods and services increase.

Given that these findings are contesting a core aspect of neo-liberal theory, two further measures of taxation are evaluated here. Analysing cross-national variations in the level of revenue (excluding grants) as a share of GDP and cross-national variations in employment in the shadow economy, a statistically significant association is identified with both the level of participation in shadow employment ($r_s = -0.510**$) and intensity of shadow employment ($r_s = -0.656**$). Again nevertheless, it is in the opposite direction to neo-liberal theory. This is also the case when the association between cross-national variations in the level of tax revenue as a proportion of GDP and cross-national variations in the level and intensity of shadow employment are analysed. Once more a strong statistically significant association is identified with both the level ($r_s = -0.451*$) and intensity ($r_s = -0.679**$) of shadow employment, but it is the inverse of what neo-liberal theory asserts. Across all three measures of tax rates, therefore, the level and intensity of shadow employment is lower in nations with higher tax rates. One reason that higher tax levels might be correlated with lower levels and intensities of shadow employment may be that taxes provide greater state revenue to enable social transfers so that citizens can receive some level of social protection, thus obviating their need to participate in the shadow labour force.

Political Economy Perspective

To evaluate the neo-liberal argument that state interference in the operation of the market leads to a greater level and intensity of shadow employment, as well as the contrary political economy stance that the magnitude and intensity of shadow employment reduces with greater state intervention, the relationship between cross-national variations in the level and intensity of shadow employment and the level of social contributions as a percentage of revenue can be analysed. A strong significant correlation is identified between the level of social contributions and both the level ($r_s = -0.609**$) as well as intensity ($r_s = -0.582*$) of shadow employment. Both the level and intensity of shadow employment reduces as social contributions rise as a share of revenue, intimating support for the political economy perspective. No support is thus found for the neo-liberal argument that state intervention leads to shadow employment. Instead, the political economy tenet is validated that shadow employment is correlated with too little state intervention in the form of social protection.

Similar findings are reached when other indicators of state intervention are explored, namely state revenue as a share of GDP as well as the expense of government as a share of GDP. There is a steep decline in the level of participation in the shadow labour force as both state revenue as a share of GDP increases ($r_s = -0.605**$) as well as the expense of government as a share of GDP ($r_s = -0.555**$). Bigger government results in a decrease, rather than increase, in the level of shadow employment. The neo-liberal assertion that state interference leads to higher levels of participation in shadow employment is therefore refuted and instead, the political economy view is supported that such employment is associated with too little state intervention in the form of social protection.

Finally, and turning to the political economy tenet that cross-national variations in the level and intensity of shadow employment are associated with the level of poverty, a statistically significant relationship is identified between cross-national variations in the proportion of the population living below the national poverty line and the level of participation in shadow employment ($r_s = -0.355*$) but not the intensity of shadow employment ($r_s = 0.194$). As Chen (2014, p. 404) puts it: 'In developing countries, most of the working poor are informally employed, and most informal workers are poor.' There is also a statistically significant relationship between cross-national variations in the size of the poverty gap, expressed as a percentage of the poverty line of \$1.25 per day in personal purchasing power standards, and cross-national variations in the level of participation in shadow employment ($r_s = 0.692**$). The greater the share of the population living below the national poverty line, the greater is the level and intensity of shadow employment, intimating that turning to the shadow labour market may well be a last resort for marginalized groups when no other means of livelihood or support are available, as asserted by the political economy explanation.

CONCLUSIONS

This chapter has provided an analytical framework for differentiating economies that places countries on continua in terms of the level and intensity of participation in the shadow labour force. Analysing the results of ILO surveys carried out in 36 countries, three in five (59.8 per cent) of the non-agricultural workforce have their main employment in the shadow economy and just under three-quarters (74 per cent) of these are in shadow employment in shadow enterprises. Nevertheless, there are cross-national variations. The proportion of the non-agricultural workforce with their main employment in the shadow economy ranges from 84.7 per cent in Mali to 6.5 per cent in Serbia. Similarly, the share of those employed in the shadow sector who engage in shadow employment in shadow enterprises ranges from 86.2 per cent in Pakistan to 18.8 per cent in Lesotho. Nevertheless, in two-thirds (67 per cent) of the 36 countries surveyed, more than half of the non-agricultural workforce have their main job in the shadow economy and in 32 (89 per cent) countries over half of this employment in the shadow sector is in the form of shadow employment in shadow enterprises.

Exploring the reasons for these cross-national variations in the level and intensity of shadow employment, three competing perspectives have been critically evaluated that argue that the degree and intensity of shadow employment is associated with economic underdevelopment (modernization perspective), higher taxes, corruption and state interference (neo-liberal perspective) and/or inadequate state intervention to protect workers from poverty (political economy perspective). Support has been found for the modernization and political economy perspectives that associate the shadow labour force with underdevelopment and inadequate state protection of workers from poverty respectively and the neo-liberal corruption thesis that the level of shadow employment is higher in countries where the perception of public sector corruption is greater. However, no support has been found for the neo-liberal theses that shadow employment is associated with higher taxes and more state interference. Instead, the finding is quite the opposite. Higher taxes and more state intervention reduce the level and intensity of shadow employment, presumably due to the ability of governments to have efficient enforcement systems, make social transfers and reduce the need of the population to resort to employment in the shadow economy to survive.

This now requires further evaluation in relation to a wider range of developing and transition economies as well as using time-series data for individual countries and, if possible, multivariate regression analysis on a larger sample size to determine how important each characteristic is to the final outcome while controlling for other characteristics. The major barrier to doing this nevertheless, is the lack of availability of cross-national comparative data on employment in the shadow economy to conduct such analyses. These findings, moreover, have important policy implications. For the moment, these are left aside. They will be returned to in Part III of this book. Instead, attention now turns towards evaluating the level and nature of participation in shadow employment in developed nations.

NOTE

1. This is a derived version of Williams, C.C. (2015), 'Explaining cross-national variations in the scale of informal employment: an exploratory analysis of 41 less developed economies', *International Journal of Manpower*, **36** (2) 118–35.

7. The shadow labour force in developed countries[1]

The aim of this chapter is to evaluate the cross-national variations in the size and character of the shadow labour force, but this time in relation to developed countries. To do this, the same analytical framework examining the degree of informalization will be used to reveal the varying extent of the shadow labour force. To examine the nature of the shadow labour force, meanwhile, a slightly different approach is adopted in this chapter. In the developed world, there has been an emergent recognition that participation in the shadow labour force is not always necessity-driven and a result of the exclusion of workers from the formal economy (Gerxhani, 2004; Maloney, 2004; Perry and Maloney, 2007; Snyder, 2004; Williams, 2010a, 2010b). Here, therefore, we examine the nature of the shadow labour force by examining whether participants are driven by exclusion from the formal economy or by a voluntary decision to exit the formal economy. The data here used is the 2007 Eurobarometer survey of the then 27 member states of the European Union (EU-27). The outcome will be to reveal that although there is a lower prevalence of a shadow labour force in developed countries, not only are there cross-national variations in the level of employment in the shadow economy but also in the character of such employment. Indeed, this chapter will reveal that lower levels of employment in the shadow economy and voluntary engagement in the shadow labour force are significantly correlated with wealthier, less corrupt and more equal societies possessing higher levels of taxation, social protection and effective redistribution via social transfers.

To show this, the first section will briefly review the literature on the extent and nature of employment in the shadow economy in the developed world, along with the analytical frameworks used to examine the cross-national variations in its magnitude, on the one hand, and its character, on the other hand. The second section then applies this analytical framework to understanding the cross-national variations in the level and nature of shadow employment across the EU-27. The third section will then explain the cross-national variations in the level and nature of shadow employment in terms of the different regulatory environments across the EU-27. The final section concludes by summarizing the findings.

Before commencing, however, how employment in the shadow economy is defined in this chapter needs to be made explicit. An employment relationship is the central legal concept around which labour law and collective bargaining agreements have sought to recognize and protect the rights of workers. The conventional notion of the employment relationship, thought to be universal, is that 'between a person, called the employee (frequently referred to as "the worker") with another person, called the employer to whom she or he provides labour or services under certain conditions in return for remuneration' (ILO, 2002a). In this chapter, akin to other chapters in this book, an employment relationship in the shadow economy is defined as remunerated activity that is not declared to the state for tax, social security and labour law purposes as should be the case, but is legal in all other respects (European Commission, 1998, 2007b; OECD, 2012; Renooy et al., 2004; Pfau-Effinger, 2009; Sepulveda and Syrett, 2007; Williams, 2006a). Forms of employment involving other absences or insufficiencies, such as when illegal goods and services are provided or that the work is unpaid, are therefore not considered informal employment but instead part of 'criminal' or unpaid spheres respectively. Here, moreover, work is only deemed shadow employment if money is exchanged between the employer/purchaser and employee/supplier. In this chapter, moreover, two major forms of shadow employment are distinguished: wholly shadow employment where the worker is not formally employed by the employer and the remunerated activity is not declared to the state for tax, social security and labour law purposes, and 'envelope wages' where a formal employee receives from their formal employer not only a declared salary but also an additional undeclared ('envelope') wage (Karpuskiene, 2007; Neef, 2002; Sedlenieks, 2003; Williams, 2007b, 2009c; Woolfson, 2007; Žabko and Rajevska, 2007).

EMPLOYMENT RELATIONS SYSTEMS AND THE SHADOW LABOUR FORCE

Existing classificatory schemas of employment relations systems in the developed world again denote the variations across countries by examining the differential character of their formal economies, by whether they are control, market or mixed economies (Arnold, 1996; Rohlf, 1998) or liberal or coordinated varieties of capitalism (Hall and Soskice, 2001). Here, however, and akin to the last chapter, we differentiate employment relations systems by the level of employment in the shadow economy. To achieve this, and as Figure 7.1 displays, we position employment relations systems on a continuum from wholly formal to wholly shadow.

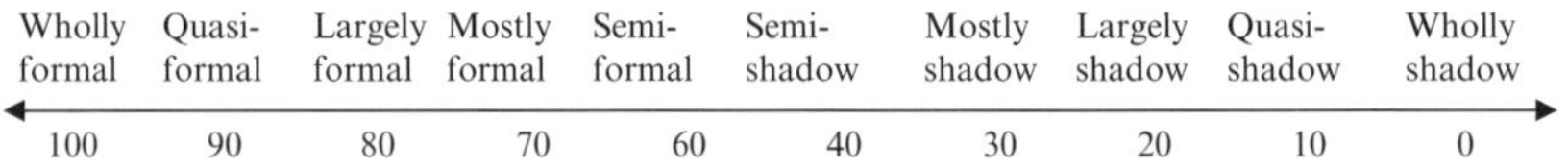

Wholly formal	Quasi-formal	Largely formal	Mostly formal	Semi-formal	Semi-shadow	Mostly shadow	Largely shadow	Quasi-shadow	Wholly shadow
100	90	80	70	60	40	30	20	10	0

*Figure 7.1   Classificatory schema of employment relations systems:
           percentage of employment in shadow economy*

For example, if less than 10 per cent of employment relations are in the shadow economy, then the system is categorized as 'quasi-formal', if less than 20 per cent then it is 'largely formal' and so forth. The outcome is that countries are positioned according to the level of employment relations in the shadow economy.

Second, and to evaluate the nature of employment relations in the shadow economy, whether shadow employment in a country results from the exclusion of participants from the formal economy or whether it results from a desire to voluntarily exit the formal economy is evaluated here. This is because in recent decades, two contrasting perspectives have dominated the literature, each adopting a different view of the nature of employment in the shadow economy and the reasons for its prevalence and growth. On the one hand, a political economy perspective has represented the nature of shadow employment as unregulated, low-paid and insecure work conducted under 'sweatshop-like' conditions by marginalized populations who undertake such work out of necessity due to their exclusion from the formal economy and no other options being open to them (Ahmad, 2008; Amin et al, 2002; Castells and Portes, 1989; Davis, 2006; Gallin, 2001; Hudson, 2005; Sassen, 1996). For these political economy commentators, employment in the shadow economy is explained to be a direct by-product of the new downsizing, subcontracting and outsourcing arrangements emerging under deregulated global capitalism that provide businesses with a shadow economy production channel to attain flexible production, profit and cost reduction (Amin et al, 2002; Castells and Portes, 1989; Davis, 2006; Gallin, 2001; Hudson, 2005; Sassen, 1996; Slavnic, 2010). The outcome, it is asserted, is the demise of the full-employment/comprehensive formal welfare state regime characteristic of the Fordist and socialist era (Amin et al., 2002; Fernandez-Kelly, 2006; Hudson, 2005) and its replacement by a new post-Fordist and post-socialist regime of deregulation, liberalization and privatization (Amin et al., 2002; Castells and Portes, 1989; Sassen, 1996). Participants in shadow employment, in short, are unwilling and unfortunate pawns within an exploitative global economy that has made work more precarious and poorly paid.

However, other commentators have argued that not all participants undertake shadow employment out of necessity due to their exclusion from the formal economy. Much shadow employment has been argued to be conducted more as a matter of choice rather than due to a lack of choice (Cross, 2000; Gerxhani, 2004; Maloney, 2004; Perry and Maloney, 2007; Snyder, 2004; Williams, 2010a). This has been recognized not only in a third (majority) world context (Cross, 2000; Cross and Morales, 2007; De Soto, 1989, 2001; Neuwirth, 2011) and in post-Soviet transition economies (Chavdarova, 2002; Round et al., 2008; Williams et al., 2013a) but also, importantly for this chapter, the Western world (Lazaridis and Koumandraki, 2003; OECD, 2012; Renooy et al., 2004; Small Business Council, 2004; Snyder, 2004; Venkatesh, 2006; Williams, 2006a).

This representation of participation in shadow employment as driven by a desire to exit the formal economy has found much support from neo-liberal commentators seeking to portray employment in the shadow economy as a populist reaction to high taxes, a corrupt state system and too much interference in the free market, resulting in workers making a rational economic decision to voluntarily exit the formal economy in order to avoid the costs, time and effort of formal registration (e.g., Becker, 2004; De Soto, 1989, 2001; London and Hart, 2004; Nwabuzor, 2005; Sauvy, 1984; Small Business Council, 2004). In contrast to the political economy explanation that views shadow employment to result from de-regulation and sees the remedy as greater regulation (Davis, 2006; Gallin, 2001; Slavnic, 2010), this neo-liberal explanation first views the growth of shadow employment to result from high taxes, corruption, over-regulation and state interference in the free market and the solution to be tax reductions, reducing corruption, deregulation and minimal state intervention and, second, portrays the nature of shadow employment to be an outcome of people deciding to voluntarily exit from the formal economy, rather than a product of involuntary exclusion. As Gerxhani (2004, p. 274) puts it, workers 'choose to participate in the informal economy because they find more autonomy, flexibility and freedom in this sector than in the formal one'.

Here, therefore, and to evaluate the nature of employment in the shadow economy, the degree to which shadow employment is a product of either exclusion from the formal economy or a desire to voluntarily exit the formal economy can be evaluated. As Figure 7.2 displays, this can be achieved by positioning the rationales underpinning participation in shadow employment on a spectrum from all shadow work being driven by exclusion rationales at one end of the continuum to all shadow work being driven by exit rationales at the other end. For example, if greater than 90 per cent of shadow employment is driven by exclusion rationales, the nature of shadow employment can be categorized as driven by 'on the whole exclusion' rationales, if greater than 80 per cent then it is driven by

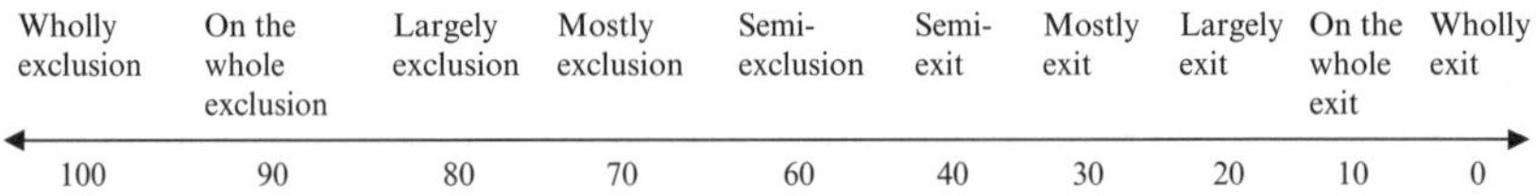

Wholly exclusion	On the whole exclusion	Largely exclusion	Mostly exclusion	Semi-exclusion	Semi-exit	Mostly exit	Largely exit	On the whole exit	Wholly exit
100	90	80	70	60	40	30	20	10	0

Figure 7.2   Classificatory schema of the nature of shadow employment: percentage driven by exclusion rationales

'largely exclusion' rationales and so forth. By classifying countries in this manner, a map of the nature of shadow employment across regions and countries can be then produced. More broadly, this also then enables an evaluation of the validity of the political economy and neo-liberal explanations for shadow employment in different contexts.

Having set out this analytical framework for differentiating employment relations systems by the extent and nature of employment in the shadow economy, attention now turns to applying it to understanding the cross-national variations across the Western world. To do this, the cross-national variations in the extent and nature of shadow employment across the EU-27 are compared.

EVALUATING EMPLOYMENT RELATIONS IN THE EUROPEAN UNION

Methodology

Most studies of the level and nature of employment in the shadow economy in the EU-27 have been small-scale surveys of particular nations, population groups and/or types of shadow work. Such studies have been conducted in Baltic nations (Meriküll and Staehr, 2010), Bulgaria (Centre for the Study of Democracy, 2008; Chavdarova, 2002; Loukanova and Bezlov, 2007), Estonia (Estonian Institute of Economic Research, 2012), Germany (Feld and Larsen, 2012), Lithuania (Karpuskiene, 2007; Krumplyte, 2010), Romania (Ghinararu, 2007; Kim, 2005; Stănculescu, 2002), Slovenia (Ignjatović, 2007), Sweden (Skatteverket, 2006, 2012) and the UK (Williams and Windebank, 2001). However, these studies cannot be used in aggregate to compare the differential level and nature of employment in the shadow economy across the EU-27 because of the varying definitions and measurement methods used.

Here, therefore, one of the few extensive cross-national surveys currently available on this subject is analysed, the *Special Eurobarometer No. 284: Undeclared Work in the European Union*, conducted as part of wave 67.3

of the 2007 Eurobarometer survey (European Commission, 2007a). As with Eurobarometer surveys in general, a multi-stage random (probability) sampling method is employed in each member state. A number of sampling points are drawn with probability proportional to population size (for total coverage of the country) and to population density according to the basic regions classified under the Eurostat nomenclature of territorial units for statistics (NUTS) 2 (or equivalent) and the distribution of the resident population in terms of metropolitan, urban and rural areas. In each of the selected sampling units, a starting address is then drawn at random. Further addresses (every nth address) are subsequently selected by standard 'random route' procedures from the initial address. In each household surveyed, meanwhile, the participant is drawn at random from adults aged 15 and over (following the 'closest birthday rule'). All interviews are conducted face-to-face in people's homes and in the appropriate national language. To collate the data collected, computer-assisted personal interviewing (CAPI) is used where available. A national weighting procedure is then employed for data analysis purposes, using marginal and intercellular weighting by comparing the sample with the universe description taken from Eurostat population data and national statistical offices. All results reported here are based on this weighting procedure, which ensures that the gender, age, region and size of locality of the sample were proportionate to the universe.

To evaluate the extent and nature of employment in the shadow economy, the face-to-face interview schedule adopted a gradual approach to the more sensitive research questions. First, participants were asked for their opinions and attitudes regarding shadow employment; and having established some rapport, the second section asked questions regarding their purchase of goods and services on an undeclared basis in the last 12 months. Third, participants in formal employment were asked about whether they received envelope wage payments, and whether they were happy with this arrangement or whether they would have preferred to have received their full gross salary on a declared basis. Fourth and finally, questions were asked about their participation in wholly shadow employment, including the nature of the work they conducted (e.g., the number of hours per week and weeks worked, wage rates) and for whom, as well as their reasons for participating in this form of work in terms of whether it was due to exit and/or exclusion rationales. The results are analysed below.

Results

To evaluate the variable extent to which employment is in the shadow economy across the EU-27, first, the 11,587 participants surveyed who were found to be in formal employment were asked whether they had received envelope wages from their formal employer in the last 12 months and, second, the number of the full sample of 26,659 participants surveyed who had undertaken wholly shadow employment in the last 12 months was investigated. Here, and to estimate participation in wholly shadow employment, one-off jobs conducted for kin, friends, neighbours and acquaintances for reasons related to redistributing money or help to somebody in need are excluded from the analysis since such 'paid favours' are more akin to unpaid community exchange than a formal employment relationship in terms of the social relations and motives involved. However, all other forms of wholly shadow employment are included from permanent full-time shadow jobs conducted either as an employee or on a self-employed basis, through to all part-time, temporary or short-term work regardless of its duration, just as is the case when analysing the findings regarding the level of participation in formal employment.

The headline finding is that 9.2 per cent of all reported employment in the EU-27 conducted during the 12 months prior to the survey was shadow employment in the sense that some or all of the remunerated activity was not declared to the state for tax, social security and labour law purposes when it should have been, but the activity is legal in all other respects (see Table 7.1). Applying the analytical framework presented in Figure 7.1, therefore, the EU-27 can be classified as a 'quasi-formal' employment relations system; this global region is almost but not quite a wholly formal employment relations system. It is important to be aware, however, that although the vast majority of jobs are formal, it is still the case that nearly one in ten jobs are in the shadow economy, which equates to some 20.6 million of the 224 million jobs in the EU-27.

However, the level of employment in the shadow economy varies across different countries. To see this, Table 7.1 groups member states into four EU regions: Western Europe (Belgium, Germany, France, Ireland, Luxembourg, Netherlands, Austria and the UK); East-Central Europe (Bulgaria, Czech Republic, Estonia, Latvia, Lithuania, Hungary, Poland, Romania, Slovenia and Slovakia); Southern Europe (Cyprus, Greece, Spain, Italy, Malta and Portugal) and the Nordic countries (Denmark, Finland and Sweden). This reveals that while Western Europe and the Nordic nations have 'quasi-formal' employment relations systems (i.e., 4.6 per cent and 8.4 per cent of employment respectively is in the shadow economy), Southern Europe has a 'largely formal' employment relations system (i.e., 10.3 per cent of employment is in the shadow economy) and East-Central Europe a 'mostly formal' employment relations system with 20.1 per cent of jobs being in the shadow economy. In consequence, there is a marked east-to-west and south-to-north divide in

Table 7.1   Extent and nature of shadow employment in EU-27

Country	Extent of shadow employment		Nature of shadow employment: % of shadow employment driven by:			
	% of jobs that are formal	Type of employment relations system	Exit	Exclusion	Both exit and exclusion	Type of shadow labour force
EU-27	90.8	Quasi-formal	*51*	*46*	*3*	Semi-driven by exit
Nordic nations	*91.6*	*Quasi-formal*	*77*	*21*	*2*	*Mostly driven by exit*
Finland	96.5	Quasi-formal	78	22	0	Mostly driven by exit
Sweden	92.1	Quasi-formal	67	33	0	Semi-driven by exit
Denmark	87.7	Largely formal	93	7	0	On the whole exit
Western Europe	*95.4*	*Quasi-formal*	*71*	*27*	*2*	*Mostly driven by exit*
Luxembourg	99.0	Wholly formal	–	–	–	–
UK	97.0	Quasi-formal	100	0	0	Wholly driven by exit
Germany	96.9	Quasi-formal	78	22	0	Mostly driven by exit
France	95.4	Quasi-formal	56	44	0	Semi-driven by exit
Ireland	93.3	Quasi-formal	67	33	0	Semi-driven by exit
Austria	91.4	Quasi-formal	65	35	0	Semi-driven by exit
Netherlands	90.3	Quasi-formal	89	8	3	Largely driven by exit
Belgium	88.6	Largely formal	73	23	4	Mostly driven by exit
East-Central Europe	*79.9*	*Mostly formal*	*39*	*56*	*5*	*Semi-driven by exclusion*
Czech Rep	93.0	Quasi-formal	58	38	4	Semi-driven by exit
Slovenia	91.8	Quasi-formal	75	25	0	Mostly driven by exit
Slovak rep	87.0	Largely formal	56	44	0	Semi-driven by exit
Estonia	82.8	Largely formal	67	33	0	Semi-driven by exit
Hungary	82.7	Largely formal	50	36	14	Semi-driven by exit
Lithuania	81.8	Largely formal	53	40	7	Semi-driven by exit
Poland	81.3	Largely formal	27	66	7	Semi-driven by exclusion
Bulgaria	76.2	Mostly formal	59	41	0	Semi-driven by exit
Latvia	70.4	Mostly formal	70	30	0	Mostly driven by exit
Romania	64.3	Semi-formal	23	74	3	Mostly driven by exclusion
Southern Europe	*89.7*	*Largely formal*	*40*	*56*	*4*	*Semi-driven by exclusion*
Malta	99.0	Wholly formal	–	–	–	–
Cyprus	94.1	Quasi-formal	50	50	0	Semi-driven by exit
Portugal	91.3	Quasi-formal	33	67	0	Semi-driven by exclusion
Spain	90.2	Quasi-formal	49	46	5	Semi-driven by exit
Greece	90.2	Quasi-formal	53	47	0	Semi-driven by exit
Italy	88.6	Largely formal	26	70	4	Mostly driven by exclusion

Source: 2007 Eurobarometer survey on undeclared work dataset

the EU-27. Employment relations on the eastern/southern side are more commonly in the shadow economy than on the western/Nordic side, although the east-to-west divide is more marked than the south-to-north divide.

There are also variations within each European region. For example, the 'mostly formal' employment relations system of East-Central Europe is composed of a range of country-level systems from the 'quasi-formal' employment relations systems of the Czech Republic and Slovenia (where 7 per cent and 8.2 per cent of employment is in the shadow economy respectively), through the 'largely formal' employment relations systems of the Slovak Republic, Estonia, Hungary, Lithuania and Poland, to the 'semi-formal' employment relations system of Romania where 35.7 per cent of all employment is in the shadow economy. Similarly, the 'quasi-formal' employment relations system of Western Europe ranges from near wholly formal systems such as Luxembourg through to the 'largely formal' employment relations system of Belgium where 11.4 per cent of employment is in the shadow economy. There are thus variations in employment relations systems not only between European regions but also within each European region.

To examine the *nature* of employment in the shadow economy in the EU-27 in relation to Figure 7.2, the proportion driven by exit and exclusion rationales in each country and European region can be analysed. On the one hand, those engaged in envelope wages were asked 'Were you happy with getting part of your salary without having it declared to the tax or social security authorities or would you have preferred to have your total gross salary declared?' Those happy with this envelope wage arrangement are deemed to engage in this form of shadow employment out of choice (i.e., for 'exit' rationales), while those who would prefer it to be declared are denoted as engaging in this endeavour due to their lack of choice (i.e., for exclusion rationales). On the other hand, to analyse whether wholly shadow employment was carried out for exit or exclusion rationales, the responses to three questions are analysed here:

- Did you do this activity because you could not find a regular job?
- Did you do this activity because the bureaucracy/red tape to carry out a regular job is too complicated?
- Did you do this activity because taxes and/or social security contributions are too high?

Those agreeing with the first statement but not the latter two are deemed to be driven into shadow employment out of necessity, while those agreeing with either or both of the two latter statements but not the first are engaged in shadow employment as a matter of choice. Those agreeing with the first statement and either or both of the latter two are doing so for both exit and exclusion rationales.

Analysing the responses of those participating in shadow employment (i.e., envelope wages and wholly undeclared employment), the finding is that 51 per cent is conducted for 'exit' rationales, 46 per cent for 'exclusion' rationales and 3 per cent for a combination of the two reasons across the EU-27. Applying this to Figure 7.2, the EU-27 as a whole is thus characterized by a shadow labour force 'semi-driven by exit' rationales. However, this is not universally the case. As Table 7.1 displays, East-Central Europe and Southern Europe are 'semi-driven by exclusion' rationales, but Western Europe and Nordic nations in stark contrast are 'mostly driven by exit' rationales. A clear east-to-west and north-to-south division thus exists with the Eastern and Southern side driven more by exclusion rationales and the western and northern sides more by exit rationales.

However, and akin to the level of employment in the shadow economy, it is again the case that within each European region, variations exist in the nature of the shadow labour force. For example, of the ten East-Central European member states, while six have a shadow labour force 'semi-driven by exit' rationales, the shadow labour force in Slovenia and Latvia are 'mostly driven by exit' rationales while the shadow labour force in Poland is 'semi-driven by exclusion' rationales and in Romania 'mostly driven by exclusion' rationales.

In sum, the EU-27 is a 'quasi-formal' employment relations system where the majority of shadow employment results from voluntary exit, rather than involuntary exclusion from, the formal economy. However, there are variations from west to east and north to south, with lower levels of employment in the shadow economy and voluntary participation in the shadow labour force in Western Europe and the Nordic nations but higher levels of employment in the shadow economy mostly driven by exclusion rationales in East-Central and Southern Europe.

EXPLAINING CROSS-NATIONAL VARIATIONS IN EMPLOYMENT RELATIONS SYSTEMS

How, therefore, might these variations in the character of employment relations systems in terms of the level and nature of employment in the shadow economy across the EU-27 be explained? Is it as the 'modernization' thesis asserts that 'developed' wealthier economies have lower levels of employment in the shadow economy than 'developing' or 'underdeveloped' economies? Is it as neo-liberals assert, that participation in the shadow labour force is a voluntary choice and direct result of high taxes, corruption and state interference in the free market and that the remedy is therefore to reduce taxes, corruption and state intervention in work and welfare? Or is it as political economists assert, that participation in the shadow labour force is out of necessity and a direct by-product of a deregulatory regime and inadequate levels of state intervention and that the solution is therefore to pursue greater intervention by raising taxes and funding higher levels of social protection and redistribution via social transfers?

To evaluate these competing explanations, an analysis of the relationship between the level and nature of employment in the shadow economy and different regulatory environments is provided here. Given the small sample size of 27 member states and the lack of the necessary controls to include in a multivariate regression analysis, it is only possible to conduct bivariate regression analysis of the relationship between the level and nature of employment in the shadow economy and different characteristics of the wider regulatory environment. Nevertheless, and as will be shown, meaningful findings are produced.

First, and to evaluate the modernization thesis assertion that 'developed' wealthier economies have lower levels of employment in the shadow economy and 'developing' or 'underdeveloped' economies higher levels, and that it is more out of choice in wealthier economies, GDP per capita across the EU-27 in 2007 is analysed here (European Commission, 2011, Table 7.3a). As Figures 7.3a and 7.3b reveal, and using Spearman's rank correlation coefficient due to the non-parametric nature of the data, there is a strong significant relationship between the level and nature of employment in the shadow economy and the levels of GDP per capita ($r_s = -0.633**$ and $r_s = 0.510*$ respectively). Member states with higher levels of GDP per

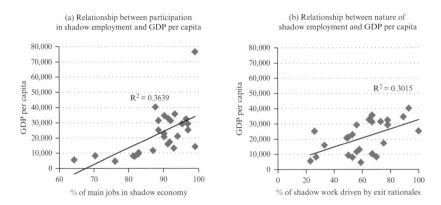

Figure 7.3   Evaluation of the modernization thesis

capita have more formalized employment relations systems where a greater proportion of shadow employment is conducted for exit rationales. This is similarly the case when purchasing power standards (PPS) are investigated (Eurostat, 2013a), which, unlike GDP per capita, takes into account the differences in the cost of living in different countries. Again, a strong correlation exists between the level and nature of employment in the shadow economy and the level of PPS ($r_s = -0.666^{**}$ and $r_s = -0.510^*$ respectively). Employment in the shadow economy, in sum, is lower in wealthier countries and more likely to be conducted for exit rationales.

Turning to the relationship between the employment in the shadow economy and the type of regulatory environment, one can commence by evaluating the neo-liberal tenet that employment in the shadow economy results from high taxation levels. To do this, firstly, implicit tax rates (ITR) on labour can be analysed, which is a summary measure of the average effective tax burden on the income of employed labour (Eurostat, 2010). This calculates the sum of all direct and indirect taxes and employees' and employers' social contributions levied on employed labour income, and then this is divided by the total compensation of employees. As Figures 7.4a and 7.4b display, no statistically significant correlation exists between the ITR on labour and either the level of employment in the shadow economy across the EU-27 ($r_s = 0.042$) or the nature of shadow employment ($r_s = 0.062$).

Given how this finding that there is no relationship between tax rates and the level of shadow employment contests a core assumption of the neo-liberal perspective, this relationship is here further analysed using another measure of tax rates, namely total tax revenue (excluding social contributions) as a percentage of GDP (Eurostat, 2007). Total tax revenue here includes all taxes on production and imports (e.g., taxes enterprises incur such as for professional licences, taxes on land and building and payroll taxes), all current taxes on income and wealth (including both direct and indirect taxes) and all capital taxes. As Figures 7.4c and 7.4d graphically display, a significant relationship does here exist between the total tax revenue and the level and nature of employment in the shadow economy ($r_s = -0.516^{**}$ and $r_s = 0.412^*$ respectively). However, and contrary to neo-liberal discourse, employment relations are more formal in member states where the total tax revenue as a proportion of GDP is higher. In support of the neo-liberal thesis, nevertheless, as total tax revenue as a proportion of GDP increases, a greater proportion of shadow employment is conducted for exit rationales, intimating that raising tax rates leads to a greater proportion of the shadow labour force doing so in order to voluntarily exit the formal economy. Higher tax rates, nevertheless, are not associated with higher levels of employment in the shadow economy across the EU-27.

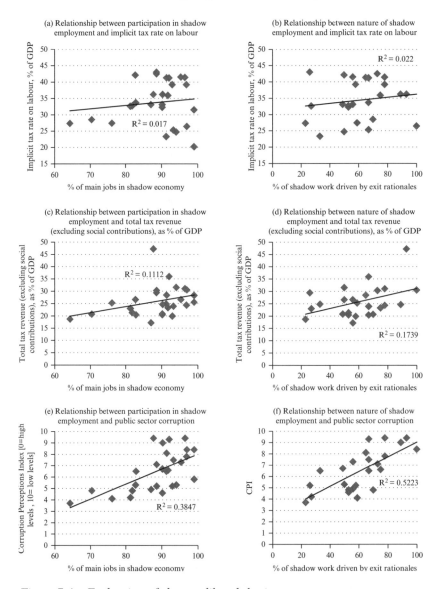

Figure 7.4   Evaluation of the neo-liberal thesis

Turning to the mostly neo-liberal thesis that public sector corruption leads to higher levels of employment in the shadow economy due to a greater desire to exit the formal economy, Transparency International's 2007 Corruption Perceptions Index (CPI) is used, which examines perceptions of public sector corruption, and is a composite index that draws on 14 expert opinion surveys (Transparency International, 2013). This index scores countries on a scale from zero to ten, with zero indicating high levels and ten indicating low levels of perceived public sector corruption. Figure 7.4e reveals a strong correlation between the level of public sector corruption and the level of employment in the shadow economy ($r_s = -0.635**$). The higher the perceived level of public sector corruption is, the greater the level of employment in the shadow economy is. This supports the mostly neo-liberal thesis that shadow employment is an exit strategy pursued by workers confronted by bribes and corruption when seeking to enter or remain in the formal economy. However, Figure 7.4f reveals a strong correlation between perceptions of corruption and the nature of shadow employment ($r_s = 0.614**$), displaying that exit rationales decrease in importance as corruption increases. This intimates that shadow employment is not a result of own-account workers voluntarily exiting the formal economy, as neo-liberals suggest, but more a tactic pursued by employers, which they then impose on their shadow employees.

Reviewing the neo-liberal perspective, therefore, no evidence has been found to support the assertion that shadow employment is correlated with higher tax levels, and although higher levels of shadow employment are correlated with greater levels of public sector corruption, it is not due to the voluntary exit of informal workers, as suggested by neo-liberals. Is it nevertheless the case that greater levels of state interference in the free market, as neo-liberals assert, result in higher levels of shadow employment? Or is it the case, as political economists assert, that the employment in the shadow economy is a direct by-product of a lack of state intervention?

To evaluate these competing views on the role of state intervention, Figures 7.5a and 7.5b analyse the relationship between the extent and nature of employment in the shadow economy and the levels of state social protection expenditure (excluding old age benefits) as a proportion of GDP (European Commission, 2011, Table 3). There is a strong statistically significant correlation: the greater the level of social protection expenditure, the lower the level of employment in the shadow economy ($r_s = -0.510**$) and the more likely it is to be conducted for exit rationales although this is not a significant relationship ($r_s = 0.368$). Therefore, support is found for the political economy rather than neo-liberal perspective. In regulatory environments in which there is greater social protection of citizens, employment in the shadow economy is lower.

Does it therefore follow that in populations where a greater proportion of the population is at risk of poverty, and unprotected by the state, that the level of shadow employment is higher? To analyse this, the percentage of the total population at risk of poverty is analysed, which is defined as

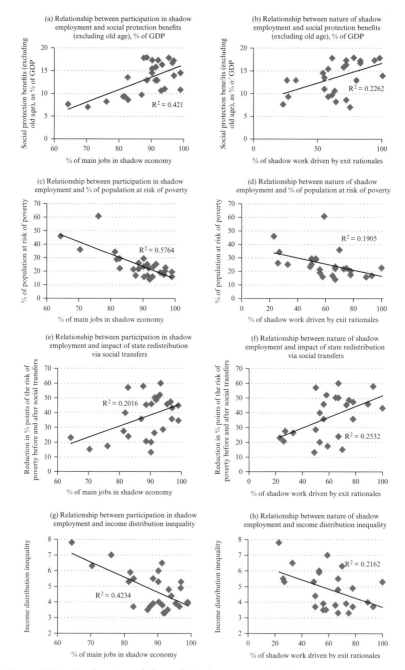

Figure 7.5   Evaluation of the political economy thesis

persons with an equivalized disposable income below the risk-of-poverty threshold, which is set at 60 per cent of the national median equivalized disposable income, after social transfers (Eurostat, 2013b). As Figures 7.5c and 7.5d display, there is a strong correlation between the proportion of the population at risk of poverty and the level ($r_s = 0.627**$) and nature ($r_s = 0.490*$) of employment in the shadow economy. The higher the proportion of the population at risk of poverty, the higher is the level of employment in the shadow economy and the more likely is shadow employment to be undertaken for exclusion rationales.

Moreover, the more states intervene to reduce the proportion of the population at risk of poverty using social transfers, the lower is employment in the shadow economy. To see this, the effectiveness of state redistribution via social transfers is analysed. Here, the poverty level is again defined as the share of the population with an income below 60 per cent of the national median income, and then the reduction in percentage points of poverty after social transfers is calculated to determine the effectiveness of state redistribution (European Commission, 2011, Table 3). As Figures 7.5e and 7.5f display, a strong statistically significant correlation exists; the more effective is state redistribution via social transfers in reducing poverty, the lower is the level of employment in the shadow economy ($r_s = -0.405**$) and the shadow employment is less likely to be conducted for exclusion rationales ($r_s = 0.452*$). This further supports the political economy perspective that greater state intervention in work and welfare regimes reduces employment in the shadow economy and shadow employment conducted for exclusion rationales.

So too is it the case that the level of societal equality and shadow employment are associated. Examining the inequalities in the distribution of income (Eurostat, 2013c), measured by evaluating the ratio of total income (by which is meant equivalized disposable income) received by the 20 per cent of the population with the highest income (top quintile) to that received by the 20 per cent of the population with the lowest income (lowest quintile), a strong correlation is found to exist between the inequalities in the distribution of income and the level of employment in the shadow economy ($r_s = 0.418*$). As Figures 7.5g and 7.5h display, the more equal the societies in terms of the distribution of income, the lower is the level of employment in the shadow economy and the less likely is the shadow employment to be conducted for exclusion rationales ($r_s = 0.419*$).

CONCLUSIONS

Examining employment relations systems in the EU-27 from the perspective of the level and nature of employment in the shadow economy, the 2007 Eurobarometer survey reveals that the majority (90.8 per cent) of employment in the EU-27 is formal employment, and the EU-27 is as a whole a 'quasi-formal' employment relations system where the majority of shadow employment results from a desire to voluntarily exit, rather than exclusion from, the formal economy. However, major variations exist across the EU-27 in both the extent and nature of employment in the shadow economy.

First, there are variations in the extent of employment in the shadow economy. Western Europe and the Nordic nations have 'quasi-formal' employment relations systems (4.6 per cent and 8.4 per cent of employment respectively is in the shadow economy), while Southern Europe has a 'largely formal' employment relations system (10.3 per cent of employment is in the shadow economy) and East-Central Europe has a 'mostly formal' employment relations system with 20.1 per cent of employment in the shadow economy. Consequently, there is a divide from east to west and south to north in the EU-27 with greater levels of employment in the shadow economy on the eastern/southern side than on the western/Nordic side, although the east-to-west divide is more marked than the south-to-north divide. Second, there are also differences in the nature of employment in the shadow economy. Although shadow employment in the EU-27 as a whole is largely driven by a desire to voluntarily exit, rather than exclusion from, the formal economy, a clear east-to-west and north-to-south divide exists. While East-Central Europe and Southern Europe are 'semi-driven' by exclusion rationales, Western Europe and Nordic nations are 'mostly driven' by exit rationales.

To tentatively explain these variations in employment relations systems, competing perspectives have been evaluated. These include the 'modernization' thesis, which asserts that as economies develop and become wealthier, there is a natural and inevitable shift towards formalization, and two theorizations that explain the level and nature of employment in the shadow economy in terms of the type of regulatory regime in a country. These are the neo-liberal perspective, which argues that employment in the shadow economy directly results from high taxes, corruption and state interference in the free market, and a political economy perspective, which explains shadow employment to result from a deregulatory regime and inadequate levels of state intervention to provide social protection for citizens. The finding, using bivariate regression analysis, is that these competing perspectives need to be combined. In short, wealthier more equal societies with less public sector corruption that pursue higher levels of taxation, social protection and more effective redistribution via social transfers, are significantly correlated with lower levels of employment in the shadow economy that are driven largely by exit rather than exclusion rationales. Indeed, this explains the higher levels of shadow employment and preponderance of exclusion rationales in East-Central and Southern European countries, which are generally less wealthy and less equal societies with higher rates of public sector corruption and lower levels of taxation, social protection and state redistribution via social transfers compared with West European and Nordic nations.

This finding regarding the relationship between employment in the shadow economy and different regulatory environments has clear policy implications. In stark contrast to previous literature on tackling employment in the shadow economy, which has focused upon whether deterrence measures need to be introduced or more enabling measures that smooth the transition to formality and provide incentives (OECD, 2012; Williams, 2004b, 2004c, 2006b, 2008a, 2008b), Parts II and III have revealed that the wider regulatory environment is important. It is to the issue of how to tackle the shadow economy and shadow labour force therefore, that attention now turns.

NOTE

1. This is a derived version of Williams, C.C. (2014), 'Explaining cross-national variations in the prevalence and character of undeclared employment in the European Union', *European Spatial Research and Policy*, **21** (2), 115–32.

PART IV

Tackling the shadow economy and shadow labour force

8.   Current policy approaches

Compared with the voluminous academic literature on measuring and explaining the shadow economy and shadow labour force, much less has been written on how to tackle this realm. Given that the major reason for measuring and explaining the shadow economy and shadow labour force is so that it can be tackled, this major gap in the literature needs to be filled. Part IV of this book seeks to do so. To achieve this, this chapter begins by providing an analytical framework for understanding the current policy approaches that are available and used across the world to tackle the shadow economy and shadow labour force.

To commence this analysis of the policy approaches, it is necessary to recognize that until very recently, governments have largely sought to tackle the shadow economy and shadow labour force by seeking to repress this sphere. Today, however, a growing number of governments are no longer seeking to eradicate the shadow economy and shadow labour force. Rather, there has been growing recognition across governments that they are seeking to move the shadow economy and shadow labour into the formal economy (Dekker et al., 2010; European Commission, 2007a; ILO, 2015; Small Business Council, 2004, Williams, 2006a; Williams and Nadin, 2012a, 2012b, 2013, 2014; Williams and Renooy, 2013). The rationale for this shift is several-fold.

For governments, the benefits of moving the shadow economy and labour into the formal economy are that it improves the level of public revenue, thus enabling governments to pursue higher expenditure on social integration and mobility projects (Williams and Windebank, 1998). It also enables the creation of more formal jobs and facilitates a joining-up of policy towards the shadow economy and labour with the policy approaches towards entrepreneurship and social inclusion (Dekker et al., 2010; European Commission, 2007a; Small Business Council, 2004). To explain, given that a large proportion of shadow work is own-account entrepreneurial endeavour and some two-thirds of businesses start up test-trading the viability of their venture in the shadow economy (Autio and Fu, 2015), seeking to eradicate the shadow economy resulted in one hand of government repressing precisely the entrepreneurship and enterprise culture than with the other hand it was seeking to foster. Similarly, given that much work in the shadow economy, especially in Western economies, is composed of paid favours between close social relations conducted for redistributive rationales and to help out others (Williams, 2004a), repressing the shadow economy also resulted in one hand of government eradicating precisely the active citizenship that its other hand sought to nurture. Seeking to harness endeavour in the shadow economy by facilitating its transfer into the formal economy, rather than seeking to eradicate it, these contradictions are overcome. There is a joining-up of government policy towards the shadow economy and policy towards entrepreneurship and active citizenship. It is not only beneficial to governments, however, to move the shadow economy and labour into the formal economy.

For formal businesses, it prevents unfair competition and enables the business community to pursue a 'high road' rather than 'low road' approach by shifting towards greater regulatory standards on working conditions such as health and safety and labour standards (Grabiner, 2000; Renooy et al., 2004; Williams and Windebank, 1998). For shadow workers meanwhile, the key benefits are that they can achieve the same levels of legal protection as formal workers (ILO, 2015; Morris and Polese, 2014). For customers, furthermore, the advantages of legitimizing the shadow economy and labour are that such customers benefit from legal recourse if a poor job is done, have access to insurance cover, enjoy guarantees with regard to the work conducted, and have more certainty that health and safety regulations are being followed (Williams and Martinez-Perez, 2014c). Across most governments, therefore, the aim now is less to stamp out the shadow economy and shadow labour and more to move the shadow economy and labour into the formal realm. How, therefore, can this be achieved?

To unpack the toolbox of policy approaches and measures available to governments and others seeking to move the shadow economy and shadow labour into the formal sector, the first section of this chapter will draw upon the contrasting approaches to eliciting behaviour change at the organizational level to learn lessons for those seeking to elicit behaviour change at the societal level in relation to tackling the shadow economy. This will reveal that those wishing to move the shadow economy and labour into the formal sector at the societal level have much to learn from human resource management and organizational behaviour, which have been promoting behaviour change at the organizational level for many decades, where there has been a shift from the use of a 'hard' compliance approach to a 'soft' commitment approach. In the second section, therefore, the scale of analysis is then shifted from the organizational to the societal level and a conceptual framework provided of the range of 'hard' compliance and 'soft' commitment tools available to governments for tackling the shadow economy and shadow labour. Using this analytical framework, the third section then reviews the available evidence on the policy approaches and measures currently used, albeit only across the 31 countries within the European Economic Area. This will reveal that unlike the shift towards a soft commitment approach at the organizational level, at the societal level when tackling the shadow economy and labour, the use of a hard compliance approach in general and a hard compliance approach that punishes non-compliant ('bad') behaviour in particular, remains the common approach and other interventions based on either using a hard compliance approach that rewards compliant ('good') behaviour or a soft commitment approach that fosters a culture of commitment remain widely underused and perceived as less effective. This will thus set the scene for the following chapter, which provides a comprehensive review and evaluation of a way forward for tackling the shadow economy and labour.

UNPACKING THE POLICY TOOLBOX: LESSONS FROM THE ORGANIZATIONAL LEVEL

When seeking to elicit behaviour change at the organizational level, the lesson learned from both the human resource management and organizational behaviour literature is that there has been a gradual shift of approach in organizations. In the human resource management literature, this is referred to as a shift from 'hard' to 'soft' human resource management or from 'direct' to 'indirect' controls, while in the organizational behaviour literature it is often referred to as a shift from 'bureaucratic' to 'post-bureaucratic' management (du Gay, 2000, 2005; Grey, 2005; Legge, 1995; Parker, 2002; Reed, 1992, 2005; Thompson, 1993; Thompson and Alvesson, 2005). Here, we briefly review this literature. The intention in doing so is to provide an analytical framework for understanding the full range of policy approaches available for those seeking to elicit behaviour change at the societal level.

To understand the 'hard' approach and its successor, the 'soft' approach, a useful starting point is the work of Weber who, in *Wirtschaft und Gesellschaft*, published after his death in 1921, presents an ideal-type model of bureaucracy. This ideal-type bureaucracy has the following characteristics: all operating rules and procedures are formally recorded; tasks are divided up and allocated to people with formally certified expertise to carry them out; activities are controlled and coordinated by officials organized in a hierarchy of authority; communications and commands pass up or down the hierarchy without missing out steps; posts are filled and promotions achieved by the best-qualified people; office-holder posts constitute their only employment; posts cannot become the property or private territory of the office-holder, the officer's authority derives from their appointed office and not from their person; and all decisions and judgements are made impersonally and neutrally, without emotion, personal preference or prejudice. In such an ideal-type bureaucracy in consequence, business is conducted 'without regard for person' (Weber, 1978, p. 226) and according to purely objective criteria. The usual narrative in the management studies literature is that this bureaucratic mode of organization reached its apogee in the post-1945 period (Bell, 1960; Kerr et al., 1973).

From the mid-twentieth century onwards, however, the assumptions of this bureaucratic model of organizational efficiency began to come under scrutiny. The origins of this critique were a series of studies undertaken during the 1920s and 1930s at the Hawthorne works of the Western Electric Company near Chicago in the United States (Mayo, 1933; Roethlisberger and Dickson, 1939), which spawned a human relations movement that drew attention to the social character of work and how interpersonal dynamics were important in the maintenance of motivation and productivity (Blau and Scott, 1963; Etzioni, 1961; Merton, 1949). Their argument was that if management met employees' social needs in the workplace by providing them with the satisfaction of working together, by making them feel important and needed in the organization and by displaying interest in their personal issues, industrial unrest and social breakdown could be avoided (see Grey, 2005). This discovery of the human factor produced a new focus upon the needs of workers (Alvesson and Willmott, 1996).

While the earlier era of scientific management had sought to capture the body, this human relations movement was thus seeking to capture the heart and was later extended to a 'soft' approach that sought to capture the soul of the worker (Ciulla, 2000) by encouraging them to become what Bunting (2004) somewhat negatively terms 'willing slaves' or what Zohar and Marshall (2001, 2005) more positively view as creating 'spiritual intelligence' or 'spiritual capital'. Rather than seek to control the behaviour of workers using a 'hard' compliance approach, what has been witnessed is the emergence of a 'soft' commitment approach that has sought to capture the hearts, minds and souls of workers with the intention of engendering self-regulation. Instead of applying external controls to enforce compliance, the intention has become to facilitate commitment so that self-regulation occurs.

Table 8.1 provides a summary of these contrasting 'hard' compliance and 'soft' commitment approaches to eliciting behaviour change in organizations. As it reveals, bureaucratic work organizations grounded in the 'hard' compliance approach focus upon engendering compliance

Table 8.1   Hard and soft HRM approaches in work organizations

Hard approach	Soft approach
Centralized structures	Decentralized structures
A tightly bureaucratic structure and culture	A loosely bureaucratic structure and culture
Highly prescribed procedures	Flexible procedures
Close supervision and monitoring of activities	Empowerment and discretion applied to activities
Tight rules	Loose rules
Low commitment culture	High commitment culture
Low trust culture	High trust culture
Adversarial culture	Culture of mutual interest

Source: derived from Watson (2003, Table 5.2)

using close supervision and monitoring of workers, tight rules, prescribed procedures and centralized structures, resulting in a low-commitment, low-trust and adversarial culture, but one where the power wielded by the organization ensures compliance. Post-bureaucratic organizations using a 'soft' approach meanwhile, focus more upon the creation of loose rules, flexible procedures and decentralized structures that elicit a high-commitment, high-trust culture of mutual interest. Commitment to the organization is elicited by ensuring that there is an alignment between the mission and vision of the organization and the norms, values and beliefs of the individual workers. When achieved, the result is that workers can be set free as willing slaves of the organization since they will engage in the self-regulation of their own behaviour and that of others, thus replacing the need for a 'hard' compliance approach except for the few who do not align their values with the mission and vision of the organization.

In this soft commitment approach, there is thus a shift from external to internal controls. The focus is more upon instilling values and peer reinforcement of appropriate behaviour rather than ensuring compliance with rule-following. No longer is compliance sought through the use of externally imposed bureaucratic control systems, which results in reactive rather than proactive behaviours. Instead, commitment is sought through internalizing values and views congruent with the interests of the organization in order to elicit self-regulation from both the individual and the team of people surrounding them (for example, Guest, 1987; Legge, 1989, 1995; Wilkinson and Willmott, 1994). How, therefore, might this shift in approach towards eliciting behaviour change be applied to understanding the range of policy approaches available for tackling the shadow economy and shadow labour at the societal level?

TACKLING THE SHADOW ECONOMY: HARD AND SOFT APPROACHES

Reviewing the literature on the different approaches towards tackling the shadow economy, two contrasting approaches are often discerned. These are variously labelled: an 'economic deterrence' approach versus a 'fiscal psychology' approach (Hasseldine and Li, 1999); a 'chauvinistic' versus 'softy' approach (Cullis and Lewis, 1997); a 'deterrence model' versus an 'accommodative model' (Murphy, 2005, 2008); 'regulatory formalism' versus 'responsive regulation' (Braithwaite, 2002); 'market-based' versus 'rights-based' (Vainio, 2012); 'deterrence' versus 'tax morale' (Ahmed and Braithwaite, 2005); 'command and control' versus 'responsive regulation' (Commonwealth Association of Tax Administrators, 2006); a 'sticks' versus 'carrots' approach (Small Business Council, 2004) or a 'deterrence' versus an 'enabling' approach (Williams, 2004b, 2004c, 2006a). Much of this literature is merely differentiating between a 'hard' compliance approach that seeks to elicit behaviour change by punishing non-compliant ('bad') behaviour and a 'soft' compliance approach that seeks to elicit behaviour change by rewarding compliant ('good') behaviour. However, there is more than a hint when reading the depictions of 'regulatory formalism' and 'responsive regulation' of Braithwaite (2002) and the 'command and control' versus 'responsive regulation' approaches of the Commonwealth Association of Tax Administrators (2006) that a similar transformation to the organizational-level shift from a hard to a soft approach is being sought when tackling the shadow economy and shadow labour at the societal level.

Table 8.2 provides a summary of how these hard compliance and soft commitment approaches can be and are applied to tackling the shadow economy and shadow labour. In the hard compliance approach, the emphasis is firmly on engendering compliance to the rules. To achieve this, people are viewed as rational economic actors and, as such, the hard compliance approach seeks to ensure that the benefits of working in the shadow economy are outweighed by the benefits of operating in the formal economy. This can be accomplished either by using deterrence measures that increase the costs of non-compliance ('sticks') and/or by making the conduct of work in the formal economy more beneficial and easier ('carrots'). In the soft commitment approach, meanwhile, there is a shift away from using 'sticks' and 'carrots'. Instead, the focus is upon

Table 8.2   Policy approaches for tackling the shadow economy and shadow labour

Approach	Tools	Policy measures
Hard approach: deterrents	Improved detection	Data matching and sharing Joined-up strategy Joint operations
	Increased penalties	Increased penalties
	Increase perception of risk	Advertise penalties Advertise effectiveness of detection procedures
Hard approach: 'bribes'	For employers	Simplification of compliance Direct and indirect tax incentives Support and advice
	For employees	Supply-side incentives (e.g., society-wide amnesties; voluntary disclosure; smoothing transition to formalization)
	For customers	Demand-side incentives (e.g., targeted direct and indirect taxes)
Soft approach: reduce asymmetry between state and citizens	Change citizens (informal institutions)	Tax education Normative appeals Awareness raising of benefits of declaring full salaries
	Change state (formal institutions)	Procedural and redistributive fairness and justice Wider economic and social developments

developing the psychological contract (or what might also be called the social contract) between the state and its citizens by nurturing a high-trust, high-commitment culture and therefore the self-regulation of citizens. Here, therefore, we review each approach in turn.

Hard Compliance Approach

To tackle the shadow economy and shadow labour, a first way of doing so is to use a hard compliance approach that treats people as rational economic actors and seeks to change the costs of operating in the shadow economy and benefits of operating formally. As the OECD (2008, p. 82) states: 'Combating informal employment requires a comprehensive approach to reduce the costs and increase the benefits to business and workers of operating formally.' To outline this hard compliance approach, therefore, the measures it uses to detect and punish non-compliant behaviour are reviewed, followed by its use of 'bribes' or incentives that reward compliant behaviour.

Hard approach: detecting and punishing non-compliance

The use of deterrents (that is, increasing the costs of non-compliant behaviour) to elicit behaviour change has its origins in the classic utilitarian theory of crime. Developed by Jeremy Bentham ([1788] 1983) and Cesare Beccaria ([1797] 1986), this argues that people are rational actors seeking to maximize their expected utility; they weigh up the opportunities and risks of an action and disobey the law if the expected penalty and probability of being caught are small relative to the benefits of disobeying the law. As Bentham ([1788] 1983, p. 399) put it, 'the profit of the crime is the force which urges a man to delinquency: the pain of the punishment is the force employed to restrain him from it. If the first of these forces be the greater, the crime will be committed; if the second, the crime will not be committed.'

In the study of criminal behaviour, this rational actor approach was popularized by Becker (1968) in the late 1960s who argued that governments must change the costs of non-compliance and benefits of compliance so that compliant behaviour becomes the rational choice for citizens. By increasing the risks of detection and level of sanctions for criminal behaviour, such activity would become irrational behaviour. Prior to this rational economic actor model, criminal behaviour had been widely viewed as resulting from mental illness and/or the social environment, with criminals depicted as victims of their circumstances. Becker's rational actor view of crime therefore represented a paradigm shift.

During the early 1970s, Becker's rational economic actor approach was seized upon by Allingham and Sandmo (1972) and applied to the issue of tax non-compliance. The non-compliant were depicted as rational economic actors who evade tax as long as the pay-off is greater than the expected cost of being caught and punished. For them, therefore, the goal was to change the cost/benefit ratio confronting those engaged or thinking about participating in tax non-compliance. This rational economic actor approach was subsequently widely adopted (for example, Bernasconi, 1998; Grabiner, 2000; Gramsick and Bursik, 1990; Hasseldine and Li, 1999; Job et al., 2007; Lewis, 1982; Milliron and Toy, 1988; Richardson and Sawyer, 2001; Sandford, 1999). Akin to the Beckerian approach to crime, emphasis was put on increasing the actual and perceived risks and costs associated with participation in non-compliant behaviour. This was to be achieved by, first, increasing the perceived or actual likelihood of detection and/or, second, increasing the penalties and sanctions for those caught.

This hard compliance approach based on detecting and punishing non-compliance thus uses 'sticks' to punish non-compliant ('bad') behaviour. As such, its approach runs counter to the dominant and accepted belief in many other spheres that punishing bad behaviour is ineffective compared with rewarding compliant ('good') behaviour. For example, few parents when seeking to change the behaviour of their children would today assert that smacking their children for doing something wrong is a better approach than rewarding their good behaviour. Yet when it comes to tackling the shadow economy, the same recognition does not appear to be apparent.

Examining the vast body of literature on the effectiveness of detecting and punishing tax non-compliance, however, it becomes quickly apparent that there is little conclusive evidence regarding its effectiveness. Some earlier literature seeking to support this rational actor approach argues that increasing the probability of audit and detection will reduce participation in the shadow economy, at least for some income groups (Alm et al., 1992, 1995; Beron et al., 1992; Dubin and Wilde, 1988; Dubin et al., 1987; Kinsey and Gramsick, 1993; Klepper and Nagin, 1989; Slemrod et al., 2001; Varma and Doob, 1998; Witte and Woodbury, 1985). Similarly, some earlier literature argues that increasing fines reduces participation in the shadow economy (Alm et al., 1995; De Juan et al., 1994; Elffers et al., 1987; Feld and Frey, 2002; Friedland, 1982; Friedland et al., 1978; Klepper and Nagin, 1989; Schwartz and Orleans, 1967; Spicer and Lunstedt, 1976; Varma and Doob, 1998; Webley and Halstead, 1986; Wenzel, 2004a, 2004b).

However, the vast majority of literature does not support this hard approach based on detecting and punishing non-compliance (see Williams, 2008a, 2008b). A substantial literature reveals that increasing penalties leads to a growth in the shadow economy and labour, has no effect or only has a short-term effect (Elffers et al., 1987; Feld and Frey, 2002; Friedland, 1982; Murphy, 2005; Spicer and Lunstedt, 1976; Varma and Doob, 1998; Webley and Halstead, 1986). A similarly large body of evidence reveals that increasing the probability of detection does not result in higher levels of compliance (for example, Dubin et al., 1987; Dubin and Wilde, 1988; Elffers et al., 1987; Shaw et al., 2008; Webley and Halstead, 1986). Instead, a substantial and growing literature reveals that it leads to increased non-compliance, not least due to a breakdown of trust between the state and its citizens (Ayres and Braithwaite, 1992; Blumenthal et al., 1998; Brehm and Brehm, 1981; Kagan and Scholz, 1984; Murphy and Harris, 2007; Tyler et al., 2007). Indeed, the perhaps most telling criticism of the rational actor model is the finding that many people are voluntarily compliant even when the level of penalties and risks of detection compared with the benefits of being compliant warrant them acting in a non-compliant manner (Baldry,

1986; Erard and Feinstein, 1994; Murphy, 2008). If compliance ensues even when the benefits of doing so are outweighed by the benefits of non-compliance, there must be other factors engendering this commitment to compliance beyond simply the risk of detection and level of punishment. The result has been that many have begun to question the value of using deterrents alone.

Hard approach: compliance through 'bribes'/incentives

One response to this concern about the effectiveness of increasing the costs and risks of non-compliance has been to put more emphasis on increasing the benefits of compliance (that is, the benefits of formalization). This desire to increase the benefits of compliance has been further reinforced by the recognition that the aim of governments is not simply to eradicate the shadow economy and shadow labour but rather to shift the shadow economy and shadow labour into the formal economy. The outcome has been a stream of literature that has sought to shift away from measures to detect and punish non-compliance and towards incentivizing formalization by making it easier and more beneficial to operate on a formal basis (Hite, 1989; Renooy et al., 2004; Small Business Council, 2004; Slemrod, 1992; Williams, 2006a).

Here, therefore, punishment for non-compliance is replaced with rewarding compliant behaviour, rather than taking it as given. Indeed, evidence that this is more effective is found in studies of many areas of human activity, ranging from engendering effective leadership in organizations (for example, Prewitt, 2003; Romero and Kleiner, 2000), through toilet training young children (Cicero and Pfadt, 2002), smoking cessation (Glautier, 2004) and the personal management of diabetes (for example, Parra-Medina et al., 2004) to the tackling of anti-social behaviour in schools (Beaman and Wheldall, 2000; Luiselli et al., 2002). In all these fields of human behaviour and many others, it is now rare to find an emphasis on punishing 'bad' behaviour, while rewarding 'good' behaviour is widely adopted.

In the realm of tackling the shadow economy, such a positive reinforcement approach based on the use of incentives (or what might better be seen as 'bribes') to elicit behaviour change can take at least three forms (see Table 8.2). First, it can be made easier and/or more beneficial for businesses to engage in compliant behaviour. Second, it can be made easier and/or more beneficial for individuals supplying shadow work to engage in compliant behaviour. Third and finally, it can be made easier and/or more beneficial for customers to use the formal rather than the shadow economy to source goods and services.

Indeed, recently a significant focus has been put on evaluating initiatives to simplify and reduce the costs of formalization. Examining a simplified 'single business permit' for small firms in Kenya, Devas and Kelly (2001) report that this encouraged formalization, as does Sander (2003) who finds that in a very similar pilot project in Entebbe, Uganda, where reforms reduced the costs of formalization, a 43 per cent increase in compliance resulted. Similarly, Garcia-Bolivar (2006) reports the results of reducing the costs of formalization in Bolivia, which resulted in a 20 per cent increase in the number of firm registrations, and he reports similar increases in Vietnam. Jaramillo (2009), reporting the results of a field experiment in Lima, Peru, finds that only one in four firms offered free business licences and support with the registration process were willing to formalize, which he attributes to the recurrent costs of being formal along with the low perceived benefits of formalization, limited growth ambitions, and low trust in government. De Mel et al. (2012) similarly finds that a financial offer equivalent to half to one month's median profits induced registration of about 20 per cent of firms, while a financial offer equivalent to two months' profits led to 50 per cent of firms registering. Greater attention, therefore, is being paid to identifying whether the perceived benefits of formalization are adequate and how this can be improved, rather than simply focusing upon increasing the risks and costs of non-compliance. Remaining prevalent in such an approach, however, is a rational economic actor view of people as weighing up the opportunities and risks of non-compliance against the benefits of compliance.

Soft Commitment Approach

The problem with using a hard compliance approach to elicit behaviour change is that individuals are not always rational economic actors with perfect information available to them. They are limited in their ability to compute the costs and benefits, often misperceive or do not perceive the true costs of their actions, have limited self-control and are influenced by their social context. Perhaps most importantly, they are motivated not just by self-interest and what is most profitable for them but also by additional motives including redistribution, fairness, reciprocity, social customs, norms and morality (Alm, 2011). They are not just rational economic actors. They are also social actors.

Based on this recognition, the soft commitment approach moves away from the use of 'sticks' and 'carrots' to change behaviour. Rather, the focus is upon improving the psychological (or social) contract between the state and its citizens through the development of a high-trust, high-commitment culture (Alm et al., 1995; Andreoni et al., 1998; Torgler, 2003; Weigel et al., 1987; Wenzel, 2002). The intention in doing so is to engender willing or voluntary commitment to legitimate behaviour, rather than force citizens to comply using threats, harassment and/or bribes. This approach that seeks to engender a psychological and social commitment to acting in a compliant manner has a long history. More than a century ago, Georg von Schanz (1890) stressed the relevance of a tax contract between the state and its citizens. Some 60 years later, the German 'Cologne school of tax psychology' conducted surveys and tried to measure tax morale among taxpayers (see Schmölders, 1951/2, 1960, 1962; Strümpel, 1969), viewing it as an important and integral attitude that was strongly related to tax non-compliance (see Schmölders, 1960). Although such research went into abeyance with the rise of the rational economic actor model, since the turn of the millennium, it has once again begun to resurface (see for example, Kirchler, 1997, 1998, 1999, 2007; Torgler, 2003, 2005a, 2005b, 2006a, 2006b, 2007, 2011).

Seen through the lens of institutional theory (North, 1990), the underlying premise of this soft commitment approach is that the shadow economy and shadow labour arises when there is an asymmetry between the laws, codes and regulations of formal institutions and the norms, beliefs and values of informal institutions. When these are wholly in symmetry, the shadow economy and shadow labour will not exist, except unintentionally, since all citizens will believe in acting in a legitimate manner. However, when the norms, values and beliefs differ from the laws and regulations, resulting in what formal institutions deem to be illegal activities being legitimate in terms of the norms, values and beliefs of the society or particular population groups, the shadow economy and shadow labour arises (Webb et al., 2009; Williams and Shahid, 2015). To tackle the shadow economy, therefore, there is a need to reduce this institutional asymmetry. Two ways of achieving this exist.

On the one hand, one can alter the norms, values and beliefs of the population (informal institutions) regarding the acceptability of the shadow economy and shadow labour so that these informal institutions align with the laws, regulations and codes of formal institutions. On the other hand, one can alter the formal institutions to align better with the norms, values and beliefs of the wider society. By doing so, formal and informal institutions can become more aligned, resulting in a reduction in the shadow economy and shadow labour due to greater self-regulation brought about by an intrinsic psychological and social commitment to the formal economy. Similar to the 'soft' human resource management approach at the level of the organization, this soft commitment approach thus seeks at the societal level the same goal of engendering a commitment to compliance or what Torgler (2003, p. 285) terms an 'intrinsic motivation to pay taxes'. Here, therefore, individuals and businesses are viewed not as rational economic actors but as social actors and their cooperation is sought rather than seek to coerce them to comply.

On the other hand, changes in formal institutions can be sought. These are of two types. First, changes can be sought in the processes of formal institutions in terms of tax fairness, procedural justice and redistributive justice. Fairness here refers to the extent to which people believe they are paying their fair share compared with others (Wenzel, 2004a). Redistributive justice refers to whether they receive the goods and services they believe that they deserve given the taxes that they pay (Richardson and Sawyer, 2001) and procedural justice to the degree to which they believe that the tax authority has treated then in a respectful, impartial and responsible manner (Braithwaite and Reinhart, 2000; Murphy, 2005).

Second, changes can be sought to the products of formal institutions, by which is meant wider economic and social developments in recognition that the shadow economy and shadow labour are in large part a by-product of broader economic and social conditions. Until now, and as Parts II and III of this book revealed, there have been three contrasting theoretical standpoints regarding what broader economic and social policies might encourage citizens to pursue legitimate behaviour and not to engage in work in the shadow economy. First, the 'modernization' thesis purports that the shadow economy decreases as economies modernize and develop and therefore that economic development and growth is required to reduce the shadow economy. Second, the 'neo-liberal' thesis argues that its prevalence is a direct result of high taxes, public sector corruption and state interference in the free market and therefore that tax reductions, resolving public sector corruption and reducing the regulatory burden are the ways forward. Third and finally, the 'political economy' thesis argues that its pervasiveness is the outcome of inadequate levels of state intervention in work and welfare that leaves workers unprotected and that the focus should be less upon formalizing work and more upon introducing social protection for workers, reducing inequality and pursuing labour market interventions to help vulnerable groups. For the moment, the policies required to bring about economic and social developments that reduce the shadow economy and shadow labour are left aside. The next chapter will return to this in more detail. Here, all that is necessary is to recognize that the soft commitment approach requires not only changes in informal institutions but also the processes of formal institutions and products in terms of wider economic and social developments.

CURRENT POLICY APPROACHES: A CASE STUDY OF EUROPEAN NATIONS

Which of these approaches is most commonly used by governments when tackling the shadow economy and shadow labour? Although much anecdotal evidence exists that most governments rely on the hard compliance approach in general, and the deterrence approach more particularly, very little research has been conducted on this issue. Few studies have sought to evaluate which policy approaches and measures are being adopted either in individual countries or cross-nationally. The exception is a study conducted in 2010 across European nations that sought to evaluate whether a range of hard compliance and soft commitment policy measures were being used to tackle the shadow economy and shadow labour (see Dekker et al., 2010; Williams and Nadin, 2012b; Williams et al., 2013b). Here, we summarize the results of this internet survey of senior officials responsible for tackling the shadow economy in 31 European countries in labour inspectorates, revenue administrations, social security administrations, trade unions, employer organizations and other relevant agencies (for example, customs, border police, immigration). Of the 499 invitations to participate, 104 responses were received (a 21 per cent response rate). In all 31 countries (including all 27 member states of the European Union as well as Iceland, Liechtenstein, Norway and Switzerland), at least one senior official of the authority that takes the lead on tackling shadow work was surveyed.

Examining the findings, the first important issue to note is that measures associated with the hard compliance approach that seek to detect and punish non-compliance (that is, the negative reinforcement approach) are widely used. Analysing how many of these 31 countries use measures to improve the risk of detection, the finding is that all countries used workplace inspections, 83 per cent data matching and sharing, 74 per cent registration of workers prior to starting work or on first day of work, 65 per cent certification of business and/or payments of social contribution and taxes, 65 per cent coordinated data sharing across government, 65 per cent mandatory identity cards in the workplace, 61 per cent the coordination of operations across government, 57 per cent coordinated strategy across government and 39 per cent peer-to-peer surveillance (for example, telephone hotlines). Similarly, penalty and sanctions were widely used, with 87 per cent of countries using administrative sanctions for purchasers/companies, 83 per cent administrative sanctions for suppliers/employees, 74 per cent penal sanctions for purchasers/companies and 53 per cent penal sanctions for suppliers/employees.

Compared with the use of such 'sticks' to increase the costs and risks of non-compliance, rather fewer European countries use various 'carrots' to incentivize compliance and make it beneficial. On the whole, moreover, where they are used, these tend to focus upon providing incentives to employers to be compliant. Some 87 per cent of countries have simplified compliance procedures, 61 per cent provide training and support to business start-ups, 61 per cent direct tax incentives (for example, exemptions, deductions), 61 per cent provided advice on how to formalize, 52 per cent provided micro-finance to business start-ups, 48 per cent changed the minimum wage upwards, 48 per cent have reduced regulations, 43 per cent restricted the free movement of (foreign) workers, 43 per cent introduced technological innovations (for example, certified cash registers), 35 per cent introduced social security incentives, 30 per cent provided formalization advice to shadow businesses, 22 per cent provided free advice/training on record-keeping, 17 per cent targeted VAT reductions, 17 per cent introduced supply chain responsibility, 13 per cent introduced free record-keeping software to businesses and 9 per cent changed the minimum wage downwards.

Similarly, and on providing incentives for workers to become compliant, 65 per cent of countries have sought to ease the transition from unemployment into self-employment, 61 per cent connected pension schemes to formal labour, 44 per cent eased the transition from employment into self-employment, 35 per cent introduced new categories of work (for example, for small or mini-jobs), 17 per cent used individual-level amnesties for voluntary disclosure, 13 per cent used gradual formalization schemes and 9 per cent used society-wide amnesties. Rather few countries, however, have targeted consumers and sought to introduce incentives for them to use the formal rather than shadow economy and shadow labour. Although 61 per cent of European countries have targeted direct tax incentives at customers who use shadow labour and the shadow economy, just 26 per cent have introduced service vouchers to incentivize the use of the formal economy and merely 17 per cent have targeted indirect taxes at customers of the shadow economy.

Turning to the soft commitment approach and its accompanying measures, meanwhile, an even narrower range have been used. Most initiatives, moreover, have been targeted at changing the norms, values and beliefs of citizens (informal institutions). Some 65 per cent of European countries have used measures to improve tax/social security/labour law knowledge, 61 per cent have used campaigns on the risks and costs of shadow work, 61 per cent have used campaigns to inform users of shadow work of the risks and costs, 57 per cent have used campaigns on the benefits of formalizing their work, 52 per cent have used campaigns to inform users of the benefits of declared work, 52 per cent have used normative appeals to people to declare their activities, 39 per cent have used campaigns

Table 8.3   Policy approaches viewed as most and least important in European Economic Area, stakeholder opinion

% stating:	Most important	2nd most important	Least important
Hard compliance approach: deterrents	57	17	16
Hard compliance approach: supply-side incentives	19	46	23
Hard compliance approach: demand-side incentives	14	19	32
Soft commitment approach	10	18	29
Total	100	100	100

to encourage a culture of commitment to declaration, 30 per cent have used the adoption of the soft commitment rather than hard compliance approach, 26 per cent have used measures to change perceived fairness of the system and 17 per cent have used measures to improve the procedural justice of the system.

This survey on the preponderance of European governments to use different policy measures, however, does not reveal the weight given to each measure or denote which are viewed as the most important means of tackling the shadow economy. To evaluate this, stakeholders were asked to rank the different sets of policy measures from those accorded the most importance to the least importance in their country when tackling the shadow economy. Table 8.3 reports the findings. This displays that just 10 per cent accorded the measures associated with the soft commitment approach the greatest importance in their country when tackling the shadow economy. In other words, very few of these stakeholders viewed the soft commitment approach to be important as a way of tackling the shadow economy and shadow labour. Instead, the vast majority of stakeholders accorded much greater importance to the use of the hard compliance approach as the means of tackling the shadow economy and shadow labour. Breaking this down further, it was the use of 'sticks' to increase the costs of non-compliance that were deemed by the majority (57 per cent) to be the most important approach. As such, and unlike other areas of human activity, those involved in the fight against the shadow economy continue to view negative reinforcement based on detecting and punishing non-compliant behaviour as the most important means of tackling this sphere. Rather fewer deemed positive reinforcement – and the use of 'carrots' to incentivize compliant behaviour – important as an approach. Just 33 per cent overall viewed

Table 8.4 *Policy approaches viewed as most and least effective in European Economic Area, stakeholder opinion*

% stating:	Most effective	2nd most effective	Least effective
Hard compliance approach: deterrents	55	13	12
Hard compliance approach: supply-side incentives	20	41	13
Hard compliance approach: demand-side incentives	15	27	31
Soft commitment approach	10	19	44
Total	100	100	100

this as the most important approach, with 19 per cent stating that providing supply-side incentives was the most important means of tackling the shadow economy and 14 per cent the use of demand-side incentives targeting customers.

Indeed, examining the type of policy measure deemed least important, just 16 per cent cite the hard compliance approach based on the use of negative reinforcement to increase the costs and risks of being non-compliant. The clear intimation is that the majority of countries remain entrenched in a hard compliance approach in general, and more particularly, a hard compliance approach that seeks to increase the costs and risks of non-compliance (that is, a negative reinforcement approach).

Further evidence that this is the case is revealed when stakeholders were asked to highlight what they view as the most effective, second most effective and least effective approach when tackling the shadow economy and shadow labour. As Table 8.4 reveals, the majority (55 per cent) of stakeholders surveyed in 2010 assert that the hard compliance approach that uses sticks to increase the costs and risks of non-compliance is the most effective means of tackling the shadow economy. Despite the widespread shift away from such a negative reinforcement approach in nearly all other areas of human activity, therefore, this is not the case when tackling the shadow economy. Negative reinforcement remains perceived as the most effective means of changing behaviour. Indeed, just 12 per cent believe that this negative reinforcement approach is the least effective means of tackling the shadow economy, despite the evidence to the contrary in most other areas of human behaviour. Turning to the soft commitment approach meanwhile, only a minority (10 per cent) believe that this is the most effective means of tackling the shadow economy and a large proportion believe that this building of the psychological (or social) contract between the state and its citizens is the least effective means of tackling shadow work.

CONCLUSIONS

This chapter has provided an analytical framework for understanding the range of policy approaches and measures available for tackling the shadow economy and shadow labour and then based on this, reviewed the current approaches used in 31 European countries. Learning from those seeking to elicit behaviour change at the organizational level, where there has been a shift from a hard compliance approach to a soft commitment approach, this chapter has charted how a similar range of approaches can be seen to exist at the societal level when tackling the shadow economy.

Examining the very limited literature on which approaches are currently being used and which viewed as most effective, this chapter has reported a study of 31 European countries. This reveals that the approach towards tackling the shadow economy and shadow labour across most European countries remains grounded in a hard compliance approach based on increasing the costs and risks of non-compliance. This is despite the considerable empirical evidence within the literature on the shadow economy that reveals no conclusive evidence that increasing the penalties and risks of detection is an effective approach, and the widespread move away from punishment when seeking to elicit behaviour change in most other spheres of human activity. It has also revealed the lack of importance attached to the soft commitment approach in most countries and also the existence of a widespread unfounded belief among stakeholders that this is an ineffective approach.

In the next chapter, therefore, and based on the assumption that this is in large part due to a lack of understanding of what a soft commitment approach entails, and also a lack of understanding of how the hard compliance and soft commitment approaches can be combined, we outline a possible way forward for tackling the shadow economy and shadow labour. This, as will be shown, recognizes the desire to shift work in the shadow economy into the formal economy, and also the shortcomings of seeking to do this through deterrence measures that merely seek to increase the risks and costs associated with working in the shadow economy.

9.   A way forward

The problem with solely using a 'hard' compliance approach, which seeks to alter the cost/benefit ratio confronting those thinking about or actually participating in the shadow economy, is, on the one hand, that it assumes participants are purely rational economic actors and, on the other hand, that it is expensive and also often ineffective. Rather than 'bribe' somebody to be compliant, for example, a more effective and possibly cost-efficient approach at least in the first instance, is to encourage self-regulation by engendering a willing or voluntary commitment to compliant behaviour (Alm, 2011; Kirchler, 2007; Torgler, 2007, 2011).

To understand this soft commitment approach, it is necessary to appreciate its theoretical underpinnings, which result in a view of participants as social actors rather than purely rational economic actors. This approach can be seen to be grounded in an institutional theoretical approach that argues that activities, including the shadow economy and shadow labour, have to be understood within their institutional context (Baumol, 1990; Baumol and Blinder, 2008; Helmke and Levitsky, 2004; North, 1990). Institutions provide 'the rules of the game' and norms that govern human behaviour (Baumol and Blinder, 2008; Denzau and North 1994; North, 1990). They prescribe the acceptability of human activities (Mathias et al., 2014). All societies have both formal institutions (that is, codified laws and regulations) that define the legal rules of the game (and prescribe what we here term 'state morality') and informal institutions that are the 'socially shared rules, usually unwritten, that are created, communicated and enforced outside of officially sanctioned channels' (Helmke and Levitsky, 2004: 727) and prescribe what we here term 'civic morality'.

Examining this institutional theoretical approach, two contrasting schools of thought can be identified in relation to explaining the shadow economy and shadow labour. In the first school, the tendency of scholars is to identify the relationship between the quality and intensity of formal institutions and the prevalence of the shadow economy and shadow labour (Friedman et al., 2000; Enste, 2010). The focus is upon identifying the influence of formal institutional drivers of the shadow economy and shadow labour, as displayed in Parts II and III of this book. In this school of institutional thought, therefore, there is less emphasis on the impact of informal institutions.

A second school of institutional thought, however, further advances this first school that studies the relationship between formal institutions and the shadow economy and shadow labour. It does this by investigating how the relationship between formal and informal institutions influences the shadow economy and shadow labour (Vu, 2014; Webb et al., 2009, 2013, 2014). Viewing informal institutions as either 'complementary' if they reinforce formal institutions, or 'substitutive' if their rules are incompatible with those of the formal institutions (Helmke and Levitsky, 2004; North, 1990; Williams and Vorley, 2014; Williams and Shahid, 2015), the argument is that the shadow economy and shadow labour arises when they are substitutive. As Webb et al. (2009, p. 495) put it, 'the informal economy exists because of the incongruence between what is defined as legitimate by formal and informal institutions'.

The consequent argument is that when symmetry exists between formal and informal institutions, the shadow economy and shadow labour will be small since the socially shared norms, values and beliefs of informal institutions ('civic morality') are aligned with the codified laws and regulations of formal institutions ('state morality'). However, when asymmetry exists between the formal and informal institutions, such as due to a lack of trust in government, the result is the emergence of the shadow economy and shadow labour, which although socially 'legitimate' in terms of the informal institutions, are deemed 'illegal' in terms of the formal rules (Kistruck et al., 2015; Siqueira et al., 2014; Sutter et al., 2013; Webb et al., 2009).

This institutional theory of the shadow economy and shadow labour, it needs to be stated at the outset, is not stating that the principal causal determinant of the shadow economy and shadow labour is tax morale; that is, the intrinsic motivation to pay taxes (Torgler, 2007). The level of asymmetry between formal and informal institutions in a society can be determined by a whole range of driving forces, such as the level of GDP per capita, the quality of governance, tax burden and social protection spending. As such, we are not proposing in this chapter that tax morale is the principal or main determinant of the shadow economy and shadow labour. Rather, our proposition is that the shadow economy and shadow labour is a result of the existence of institutional asymmetry, and that a whole host of factors lead to the existence of this institutional asymmetry, with many of these conditions already discussed in Parts II and III of this book.

Here, therefore, our intention is to begin to discuss how this institutional asymmetry can be reduced by recognizing that participants are social actors and outlining the measures for facilitating greater psychological and social allegiance to compliant behaviour (Alm et al., 1995; Andreoni et al., 1998; Cullis and Lewis, 1997; Smith and Kinsey, 1987; Torgler, 2003; Weigel et al., 1987; Wenzel, 2002; Williams and Martinez-Perez, 2014d). To tackle the incongruity between the laws, codes and regulations of formal institutions (that is, state morality) and the norms, beliefs and values of informal institutions (that is, civic morality), two broad options exist. On the one hand, one can seek to change the norms, values and beliefs of the population regarding the acceptability of the shadow economy and shadow labour so that these informal institutions align with the laws, regulations and codes of formal institutions. On the other hand, one can also seek to change the formal institutions to align with the norms, values and beliefs of the wider society. These, moreover, are not mutually exclusive. They can be both pursued concurrently in order to align formal and informal institutions.

First, therefore, this chapter reviews the policy measures that seek to change the norms, values and beliefs of the population regarding the acceptability of participating in the shadow economy and shadow labour, so that these informal institutions align with the laws, regulations and codes of formal institutions. This will include a review of tax education initiatives and awareness-raising campaigns. Second, policy measures are reviewed that seek to change the formal institutions so that they align more with the norms, values and beliefs of the wider society. These measures are of two varieties. On the one hand, they include measures that seek to change the processes of formal institutions, namely procedural justice (that is, whether citizens believe the authorities are treating them in a respectful, impartial and responsible manner); procedural fairness (that is, whether citizens believe they are paying their fair share compared with others); and redistributive justice (that is, whether citizens believe they are receiving the goods and services they deserve given the taxes they pay). On the other hand, they include measures that seek to change the wider economic and social conditions in a country in a manner that reduces the shadow economy and shadow labour. Third and finally, how the measures involved in this soft commitment approach might be combined with hard compliance measures is evaluated by discussing, on the one hand, the responsive regulation approach and, on the other hand, the slippery slope framework. The end result will be that this chapter will highlight a potentially new way forward for tackling the shadow economy and shadow labour based on a soft commitment approach that also combines and sequences these soft commitment policy measures with hard compliance measures to elicit behaviour change.

ALTERING INFORMAL INSTITUTIONS

To tackle the shadow economy and shadow labour, one can either reform the laws, regulations and codes of formal institutions to align better with the norms, values and beliefs that comprise the informal institutions of societies, and/or one can alter the norms, values and beliefs of informal institutions to align better with the codified laws and regulations of formal institutions. In this section, an evaluation is undertaken of the policy measures that countries can adopt to alter the norms, values and beliefs to conform to the formal institutions. Here therefore, first, policy measures are evaluated that seek to improve tax knowledge and, second, awareness-raising campaigns are considered.

Educating Citizens About the Tax System

It is perhaps the case that many people do not fully understand why they pay their taxes and/or what these taxes are used for by governments. Put another way, they do not fully make the connection between the public goods and services that they receive (for example, hospitals, schools, transport infrastructure) and the taxes that they pay. Indeed, it might also be asserted that until now, most governments have generally undertaken very little marketing to help citizens make this connection between the taxes they pay and the public goods and services that they receive. However, if the norms, values and beliefs of many in the population are to become better aligned with the codified laws and regulations of formal institutions and a commitment to paying taxes is to ensue, educating citizens about taxation is important. As Erikson and Fallan (1996, p. 399) assert, 'a successful means of preventing tax evasion is to provide more tax knowledge to larger segments of society in order to improve tax ethics and people's conception of the fairness of the tax system'.

To achieve this, two broad forms of tax education are required. On the one hand, and to prevent unintentional tax evasion, citizens need to be educated and informed about what the current tax system requires of them. On the other hand, and more broadly, citizens need to be educated about the benefits and value of paying tax, not least by educating them about what their taxes are used for, in order to develop their intrinsic motivation to do so and facilitate greater self-regulation.

The first type of tax education requires the provision of easily understood information regarding their responsibilities with regard to the tax system. A large body of research is critical of the complexity of tax systems and the problems this poses for achieving high rates of compliance (Andreoni et al., 1998; Natrah, 2013; Tanzi and Shome, 1994). A significant portion of tax non-compliance is unintentional, arising from a lack of knowledge, misunderstanding and ambiguous interpretation of tax law (Hasseldine and Li, 1999; Natrah, 2013). In consequence, one way forward is to provide greater information to taxpayers (Internal Revenue Service, 2007; Vossler et al., 2011). Another way forward is to simplify tax administration in order to make it easier to comply, such as by simplifying tax returns, pre-filling tax returns with information already collected by tax administrations, reducing the complexity of tax law and making it simpler to be fully compliant.

The second and perhaps more important type of tax education is that which seeks to educate citizens about the benefits and value of paying tax. In many developed countries, for instance, some citizens make substantial voluntary donations to private charities but often these same citizens remain steadfastly opposed to paying what they view as high taxes, despite these private charities often having parallel missions to those of government. This is doubtless because they know the activities on which their voluntary donations are being spent when making donations to private charities and are committed to funding the activities in which these charities are engaged. However, they are perhaps not provided with clear information regarding the activities on which their money is being spent when donating to government in the form of taxes (Li et al., 2011) and also perhaps are less committed to some of the activities on which the money is being spent. One potential and partial remedy, therefore, is to educate citizens about the activities on which their taxes are spent. If citizens are informed and knowledgeable about the current and potential public goods and services that they are receiving for their money, they may be more willing to pay their taxes (Bird et al., 2006; Saeed and Shah, 2011). One direct way of doing this, as has occurred in the UK, is to provide information to taxpayers regarding where their taxes are being spent and how much they are contributing to which activities of government. Another simple way of doing this is to display signs such as 'your taxes are paying for this' on public construction projects (for example, new roads), on ambulances, in doctor's waiting rooms, in hospitals and schools, which convey a clear message to the public that the taxes they pay are being used to pay for these public goods and services.

In Canada for example, the Tax System Learning Unit provides information about the tax system as well as how the government spends the tax dollars collected. This unit until now has targeted junior and high school students so as to educate citizens before they start participating in the tax system. While the initiative has enjoyed success in getting participation from education institutions, its impact on compliance has not been measured, since there is no mechanism to track the compliance behaviour of those taking the modules against a control group who have not. Austria has adopted a similar initiative targeted at schools whereby tax officials provide training on future responsibilities for compliance, as have the Internal Revenue Service in the USA (Internal Revenue Service, 2007).

Nevertheless, even if citizens are informed about the public goods and services received for their taxes, they may still disagree with some of the activities on which governments spend their taxes. One option might be to 'hypothecate' taxes in the sense of giving citizens some choices over where their taxes are spent. Another option is to 'earmark' tax revenues stating the precise activities on which it is going to be spent. While little systematic research exists on this issue of whether explicit earmarking (compared with overall transparency of public expenditure) builds stronger self-regulation, a recent study by Jibao and Prichard (2013) found that in Sierra Leone, Bo City Council built support for local tax collection not only by communicating revenue and expenditure information to the public, but also informally linking revenue increases to specific public expenditures. Similarly, Korsun and Meagher (2004) found in Guinea that the collection of market taxes doubled after they were linked explicitly to the construction of new market facilities. Earmarking, however, has the disadvantage of reducing budget flexibility and creating expectations that taxes should function on a fee-for-service basis.

Awareness-raising Campaigns

A related policy measure that can be pursued to change norms, values and beliefs so that there is greater commitment to paying taxes, and thus reduce the shadow economy and shadow labour, is to run awareness-raising campaigns. These campaigns can be of four kinds. They can either: inform those working in the shadow economy of the costs and risks of doing so; inform potential users of shadow labour of the risks and costs; inform those working in the shadow economy of the benefits of being legitimate; and/or inform potential users of shadow labour of the benefits of formal labour.

So far, there has been little evaluation of which approach is most effective. Nevertheless, there is tentative evidence that at least so far as shadow labour is concerned, that emphasizing the benefits of working formally rather than the costs and risks of engaging in shadow labour is more effective. As Thurman et al. (1984) explain, publicizing the adverse consequences of engaging in shadow labour is ineffective because those working in the shadow economy tend to neutralize their guilt about such participation in one or more of the following ways:

- Denial of responsibility: a person working in the shadow economy will tend to interpret any publicity they hear about the negative consequences that result from working in the shadow economy not to be a result of their own actions. Instead, they will view it to result from the actions of others, such as those who they view as engaging on a larger scale than them in the shadow economy.
- Denial of injury: a person working in the shadow economy will tend to disagree that their activity has negative consequences on others and may even rationalize their behaviour by arguing, for example, that all parties involved benefit or that without their activity in the shadow economy, people would have to pay a higher price or even be unable to have such services provided.
- Denial of victim: a person may accept the negative consequences of their actions on the wider community but may believe that the victims deserve it.
- Condemnation of condemners: the person may believe that the formal institutions such as the law, the lawmakers and law enforcers are to blame for the existence of an unjust system that burdens the wider community and that the community should not succumb to these formal institutions and that their activity is therefore socially legitimate.
- Appeal to higher loyalties: the person may justify their action in terms of the wider social order, which they view as different from the codified laws and regulations, and believe that the inappropriate actions of formal institutions justify their actions.
- Metaphor of the ledger: the person engaged in the shadow economy and shadow labour may believe that their actions, although bad, are not reflective of their overall true and good nature, and regard these actions as small temporary deviations from what is otherwise good behaviour on their part.
- Defence of necessity: the person may justify their actions to be the result of personal circumstances that have led to non-compliance, such as the inadequacies of the social support system and their inability to find formal employment, which leads them out of necessity to earn a livelihood in the shadow economy.

In consequence, awareness-raising campaigns targeting those engaged in the shadow economy might perhaps focus upon the benefits of the formal economy, not the risks and costs of engaging in the shadow economy. If awareness-raising campaigns do decide to focus upon the latter, then they will need to ensure that the above rationalizations are not available to participants in the shadow economy. For instance, to prevent any denial of responsibility, the average level of non-compliance might need to be made public in any campaign so that people will not view their own activity as 'minor' compared with others.

Indeed, the limited evidence so far collected suggests that advertising campaigns are effective and cost-efficient relative to 'hard' compliance measures. In the UK, an evaluation of the advertising campaigns run by HMRC reveals that some 8,300 additional people registered to pay tax who would otherwise not have done so, who will pay tax of around £38 million over three years, providing a return of 19:1 on the expenditure of £2 million. This compares with an overall return of 4.5:1 on the £41 million a year spent on 'hard' controls such as improving detection in 2006–7 (National Audit Office, 2008).

For a campaign to be effective, however, it has to use tailored advertisements that will need to vary in form and content depending on the audience targeted. The language, media used, word style and slogans that will be effective for one population group, such as younger people, will not be appropriate for another group, such as the elderly. Similarly, effective media for one target group, such as newspaper adverts for older people, will not be right for the internet-oriented younger generation. As shown in other realms of advertising, harnessing the power of celebrities can also be effective in influencing the target audience. If celebrities and/or opinion leaders are used by tax administrations, then as Lessing and Park (1978) identify, it is necessary to differentiate three types of campaign. These are, first, information campaigns where citizens lacking knowledge refer to opinion leaders for information, such as highly respected economic experts via television commercials, talk shows and newspaper articles; second, utilitarian campaigns when citizens are motivated by hearing about others rewarded or punished, such as when names are published of those who pay taxes and do not; and, third and finally, value-expressive campaigns when citizens are encouraged to associate themselves with positive role models, such as by publicizing the tax payments of famous television and movie stars, athletes, scientists, politicians and business tycoons, holding them up as role models for law-abiding citizens to follow.

Moreover, it does not always have to be governments leading such awareness-raising campaigns. It can also be social partners such as employer or employee representative organizations either independently or in cooperation with the state. In Sweden, for example, employers have led campaigns to tackle the shadow economy and shadow labour in both the construction industry and the taxi-driving sector. The Bulgarian Industrial Association, meanwhile, has run an 'In the Light' (www.nas-vetlo.net) campaign since 2007 and sought to encourage greater awareness of the negative implications of the shadow economy and shadow labour, while in Canada, a national awareness advertising campaign, 'Get it in Writing', to inform purchasers of shadow labour of the risks involved in dealing with home repair and maintenance contractors has been developed in partnership between the tax administration and the Canadian Home Builders' Association. However, few evaluations have been conducted of the effectiveness of these campaigns.

REFORMING FORMAL INSTITUTIONS

Besides changing the norms, values and beliefs in order to synchronize formal and informal institutions, another means of doing this is to change the formal institutions. To achieve this, there are two broad approaches. On the one hand, the processes of formal institutions can be changed so that citizens become more committed to paying their taxes. On the other hand, the products of formal institutions can be changed. Here, each is considered in turn.

Reforming the Processes of Formal Institutions

To reduce the shadow economy and shadow labour and transfer it into the formal economy, the argument of this section is that even if one seeks to change the values, norms and beliefs of citizens using the policy measures above, this will not be effective unless citizens believe there is procedural justice, procedural fairness and redistributive justice. Each is now considered in turn.

Procedural justice
The extent to which citizens perceive government to treat them in a respectful, impartial and responsible manner significantly affects whether citizens engage in compliant behaviour (Hanousek and Palda, 2003; Hartner et al, 2008; Murphy, 2003; Murphy et al., 2009; Torgler and Schneider, 2007; Tyler and Lind, 1992; Wenzel, 2002). Leventhal (1980) formulated the following six rules regarding procedural justice:

1. The consistency rule – procedures should be consistent across people and time; nobody should be favoured or disadvantaged.
2. Bias suppression rule – egoistic intentions and prejudice on the part of the decision-makers should be avoided.
3. Accuracy rule – all relevant sources of information should be exhausted, in order that decisions are based on well-founded information.

4. Correctability rule – the possibility of the adjustment or revision of decisions made.
5. Representativeness rule – the opinions and interests of all parties should be considered.
6. Ethicality rule – procedures should align with the prevailing moral and ethical values.

Leventhal's rules deal primarily with the decision-making process. However, Bies and Moag (1986) argue that it is also important to consider interpersonal interactions and whether there is respectful and fair treatment (that is, interactional fairness). As Wenzel (2006) asserts, compliance is significantly higher when citizens perceive there to be interactional fairness. Being treated politely, in a dignified manner and with respect, being given a say and having genuine respect shown for one's rights and social status all improve compliance (Alm et al., 1993; Feld and Frey, 2002; Gangl et al., 2013; Hartner et al., 2008; Murphy 2005; Tyler, 1997, 2006; Wenzel, 2002).

Conversely, if citizens believe that they are being treated unreasonably, such as by the authorities displaying disrespect, a lack of trust arises and resistance to compliance (Murphy, 2008). When the state adopts a 'cops and robbers' approach viewing citizens as 'robbers' and themselves as 'cops' policing their criminal behaviour, trust is therefore lower and resistance to compliance higher (Murphy, 2003, 2005, 2008). The intrinsic motivation to pay taxes thus declines when audits and sanctions are viewed by citizens as unjust intrusions and as breaking what Feld and Frey (2007) view as the psychological tax contract between tax administrations and their citizens. Indeed, a large body of research has shown that threat and coercion results in greater non-compliance (Alon and Hageman, 2013; Brehm and Brehm, 1981), creative compliance (McBarnett, 2003), criminal behaviour or overt opposition (Fehr and Rokenbach, 2003; Unnever et al., 2004).

Consequently, it is necessary for the state to transcend a 'cops and robbers' approach and move towards a customer-oriented service approach that treats citizens with respect and dignity. This shift from a coercive to cooperative approach is based on allowing citizens to self-regulate in the first instance, which is seen to improve their voluntary compliance (for example, Ayres and Braithwaite, 1992; Sparrow, 2000). This is because self-regulation is important for building and maintaining trust among the regulators and regulated (for example, Alon and Hageman, 2013; Ayres and Braithwaite, 1992; Torgler, 2007, 2012). Indeed, trust appears to be a resource unlike any other; it is depleted not through use, but through a lack of use. Hence, the more regulatory interactions are grounded in trust, the greater is the likelihood of self-regulation or voluntary compliance.

In recent years in consequence, tax administrations have undergone a transition towards a more service-oriented approach in, for instance, Australia (Job and Honaker, 2002), Singapore (Alm et al., 2010) and the USA (Rainey and Bozeman, 2000). In this approach, tax administrations treat taxpayers not as criminals but as clients (Alm et al., 2010; Kirchler, 2007; Rainey and Thompson, 2006). This reflects the broader shifts in approach in the 'new public management' (Lane, 2000; Osbourne, 1993), which advocates customer-friendly services as part of a market-oriented business strategy and 'good governance' (Bovaird and Löffler, 2003; Gemma-Martinez, 2011; Job and Honaker, 2002; Lane, 2000; Osbourne, 1993). This empowers citizens, invites them to participate in public decision processes and more generally aims to improve the quality of citizens' lives. The intention in doing so is to build trust and confidence in public administrations, politicians and governance (Bouckeart and van de Walle, 2003; Heintzman and Marson, 2005).

Procedural fairness
People who receive procedurally fair treatment by an organization will be more likely to trust that organization and will be more inclined to accept its decisions and follow its directions (Murphy, 2005). The fairness of the tax system is one of the most important determinants of compliance (Bobeck and Hatfield, 2003; Hartner et al., 2008, 2011; Kirchgässner, 2010, 2011; McGee, 2005, 2008; McGee et al., 2008; Molero and Pujol, 2012). However, if citizens feel that they are not receiving fair treatment, non-compliance increases (Bird et al., 2006). As Molero and Pujol (2012) find, where grievance exists either in absolute terms (for example, those who feel that taxes are too high, those who feel that public funds are wasted) or in relative terms (for example, the suspected level of others' tax evasion), the result is greater non-compliance. Indeed, and as shown above, citizens can justify their own non-compliance in the perceived non-compliance of others. If the shadow economy and shadow labour are perceived as extensive, then this justifies citizens engaging in non-compliant behaviour themselves. This obviously has implications for tax administrations. If the authorities advertise that the shadow economy and shadow labour is extensive, then they create the conditions for widespread grievance and for greater participation in the shadow economy and shadow labour of those who might not have otherwise done so.

Similarly, if an offender believes that administrations are communicating disapproval to them through disrespect or stigmatizing them, such as by labelling them with negative identities (for example, thief, tax cheat), reoffending results, since the individual externalizes the blame and feels alienated (Ahmed and Braithwaite, 2004, 2005; Braithwaite and Braithwaite, 2001). Murphy and Harris (2007), for example, analysing

652 offenders found that those who deemed their experience stigmatizing were less likely to display remorse and more likely to have once again evaded tax two years later.

Redistributive justice

Whether a citizen adheres to the codified laws and regulations and does not engage in the shadow economy and shadow labour is heavily determined by whether they believe that they receive the goods and services they deserve given the taxes they pay (Richardson and Sawyer, 2001). Taxes, after all, are prices for the public goods and services provided by the government. The question for the moral evaluation of taxes is whether a citizen views the price as equating to the value of these services (that is, whether it is seen as 'just'), namely whether there is a 'just price' (Kirchgässner, 2010). If citizens view their interests as properly represented in formal institutions and they receive what they view as appropriate public goods and services for the taxes they pay, their identification with the state increases and their willingness to contribute is greater.

However, if citizens do not receive the goods and services that they think they deserve given the taxes they pay, non-compliance increases (McGee, 2005). This may occur, for example, when corruption is extensive and the citizen has little trust in formal institutions. In such situations, there will be a low incentive to cooperate. Corruption generally undermines the willingness of citizens to comply, causing them to become frustrated. Taxpayers will feel cheated if they believe that corruption is widespread and their tax burden is not spent well (McGee, 2005; Torgler, 2007, 2012; Uslaner, 2007). Indeed, Tedds (2010) finds that government corruption has the single largest causal effect on under-reporting, resulting in the percentage of sales not reported to the tax authority being 53.4 per cent higher. Similarly, McGee (2005) finds that non-compliance is more morally justified the more unjust and/or corrupt a government. As Kirchgässner (2010, p. 28) puts it: 'If the willingness to pay taxes is to be enforced, a responsible use of tax revenue by the public authorities is necessary as well as a partnership relation (and not a magisterial one) between them.' The result is that governments need to educate citizens about where their taxes are spent. In situations where citizens do not know, or do not fully understand that public goods and services are due to taxes, then compliance will be lower than in situations where citizens are fully aware of the public goods and services they receive for their taxes and agree with how their taxes are spent (Lillemets, 2009). In recent years, therefore, many governments have sought to explain to taxpayers how their money is spent.

Changing the Products of Formal Institutions

Besides reforms in the internal processes of formal institutions, Parts II and III of this book have revealed that macro-level changes in the economic and social conditions also influence the degree of institutional symmetry and participation in the shadow economy and shadow labour. As earlier argued, three competing views have been proposed on what broader economic and social policies need to be pursued in order to enable greater institutional symmetry and to formalize the shadow economy and shadow labour. First, modernization theory has asserted that there is a strong correlation between the shadow economy and economic underdevelopment and thus that the shadow economy can be reduced simply by pursuing economic development and modernization. Second, neo-liberal theory asserts that the shadow economy is significantly associated with high taxes, public sector corruption and state interference in the free market and, therefore, that the way forward is to reduce taxes, deal with public sector corruption and pursue deregulation and minimal state interference in work and welfare arrangements. Third and finally, political economy theory asserts that there is a strong association between the shadow economy and inadequate levels of state intervention to protect workers and, therefore, that greater state intervention in work and welfare arrangements is required. Each is here briefly reviewed in turn in terms of the results of Parts II and III of this book.

Starting with the modernization perspective, support has been found in Parts II and III of this book for the thesis that the size of the shadow economy and institutional asymmetry reduces with economic development and modernization. This is reinforced in other studies (ILO, 2013; Williams, 2014a, 2014b, 2014c). The higher the GDP per capita, the smaller the size of the shadow economy and shadow labour. Evidence has also been found to support the thesis that the quality of formal institutions and level of both institutional symmetry and shadow economy are closely associated. The direction of the association is that the lower the quality of formal institutions the larger the shadow economy. Again, this strong correlation between governance quality and the shadow economy is supported in many other studies (Chong and Gradstein, 2007; Friedman et al., 2000; Frey and Torgler, 2007; Hanousek and Palda, 2003; Kuehn, 2014; Slemrod, 2007). The greater the quality of governance, the lower is the shadow economy. As Kuehn (2014) reveals in relation to OECD nations, tax rates alone explain just 23 per cent of the variation in the shadow economy, but when governance quality is included, the two combined explain 72 per cent of the variance. Indeed, if governance quality in Greece, Italy, Spain and Portugal was improved to Finnish standards, this would reduce the shadow economy by 13 percentage points.

Shadow economies are larger not only where there are unmodern state institutions but also higher levels of public sector corruption. Indeed, many studies reveal a strong significant correlation between cross-national variations in perceptions of public sector corruption, as measured by Transparency International's perceptions of public sector corruption index, and cross-national variations in the size of the shadow economy (Buehn and Schneider, 2012b; Friedman et al., 2000; Hibbs and Piculescu, 2005; Hindriks et al., 1999; Johnson et al. 1997, 1998a; Wallace and Latcheva, 2006; Williams and Gurtoo, 2012). The direction of the relationship is that the higher the perceived level of public sector corruption, the larger the size of the shadow economy. Others, however, argue that corruption and informality are substitutes; as more enter the shadow economy, this reduces the ability of officials to secure bribes (Choi and Thum, 2005; Dreher et al., 2009; Katsios, 2006; Rose-Ackerman, 1997). Yet others have adopted a more nuanced approach, arguing either that they are complements in low-income countries, but no relationship exists between corruption and the shadow economy in high income countries (Dreher and Schneider, 2010), or that corruption and the shadow economy are only significantly associated in the tropics, where they are substitutes, but are not significantly associated elsewhere (Virta, 2010).

Akin to corruption, the findings on the relationship between taxation and the shadow economy and shadow labour are by no means clear-cut. In Parts II and III, we began to see this in the sense that there appeared to be a positive relationship between the size of the shadow economy and tax rates but a negative relationship between participation in shadow labour and tax rates. Indeed, this is similarly the case when examining the wider literature. Some studies do not find that the greater is the tax burden on labour, the smaller is the shadow economy (Eurofound, 2013; Kleven et al., 2011; Vanderseypen et al., 2013). For example, Vanderseypen et al (2013), using the implicit tax rate on labour, the share of labour wages in total taxes and the tax wedge on labour, find no statistically significant correlations. Similarly, Leth-Petersen and Ebbesen Skow (2014) measure the effect of changing the marginal tax rate on earned income on shadow labour by examining the effect of a Danish 2010 tax reform that changed the marginal rate of taxation of earned income from 63 per cent to 56 per cent. Examining longitudinal data over the period 2009–12, they find no connection between the marginal tax rate and shadow labour. They also investigate the effect of the introduction of a tax deduction for the purchase of selected services on shadow labour and again detect no significant effect. This is perhaps because, as Friedman et al. (2000) find, the relationship between taxes and shadow labour ceases to be significant once per capita income levels are considered, suggesting that enforcement and the quality of governance play a crucial role (Ihrig and Moe, 2000; Kuehn, 2007). This is similarly argued by Johnson et al. (1998a), who come to the conclusion that what increases the size of the shadow economy is not higher tax rates but the ineffective and discretionary application of the tax system and regulations by governments (Schneider, 2002).

Is it the case, however, that higher levels of state interference in the free market leads to larger shadow economies or, alternatively, does the shadow economy reduce with greater intervention in work and welfare regimes? Examining the relationship between the shadow economy and social protection expenditure, studies find a statistically significant association between the cross-national variations in the size of the shadow economy and total social expenditure per head of the population at current prices and taking into account personal purchasing power standards (Eurofound, 2013; Vanderseypen et al., 2013; Williams, 2013a, 2014b). The greater the level of social expenditure, the smaller the shadow economy. This supports the argument that the introduction of social protection reduces the size of the shadow economy. Globally, more than two billion (about one-third) of people are not covered by any form of social protection; that is, neither by a contribution-based social insurance scheme nor by tax-financed social assistance (Mehrotra and Biggeri, 2007). As such, they turn to the shadow economy as a survival practice. It is similarly the case that when the state reduces the proportion of the population at risk of poverty using social transfers, shadow labour is lower (Eurofound, 2013; Gaviria, 2002; Lago Peñas and Lago Peñas, 2010; Vanderseypen et al., 2013; Williams, 2013a, 2014a, 2014b, 2014c). The result is that societies characterized by greater equality have smaller shadow economies (Chong and Gradstein, 2007; Eurofound, 2013; Vanderseypen et al., 2013; Williams, 2013a, 2014b).

The outcome is that larger shadow economies are associated with underdevelopment, the institutional strength and quality of the bureaucracy and higher levels of perceived public sector corruption, lower levels of taxation and expenditure on social protection and effective social transfer systems. This suggests that tackling the shadow economy and shadow labour also requires changes in the macro-level economic and social conditions in countries if it is to be reduced. Unless these macro-level conditions are introduced, there will continue to be an asymmetry between the informal and formal institutions in a country.

COMBINING HARD AND SOFT POLICY APPROACHES

If these soft commitment policy measures are used to tackle the shadow economy and shadow labour, this does not mean that hard compliance policy measures cannot be used. Indeed, there has been growing recognition that a soft commitment approach that seeks to change formal and informal institutions, although necessary, is insufficient on its own as a means of formalizing the shadow economy and shadow labour (Williams, 2014a; Williams and Renooy, 2013). For example, governments may pursue culture changes in government departments towards a more customer-oriented approach and introduce public campaigns to elicit greater commitment to compliance, but may also simplify regulatory compliance and introduce incentives (for example, amnesties, tax deductions) to enable shadow labour to move into the formal realm. At the same time, and in relation to those failing to comply, they may also pursue improvements in the probability of detection and tougher sanctions for those subsequently caught.

Put another way, there is recognition that a soft commitment and hard compliance approach can be combined. The debate, therefore, is not over whether to use either a soft commitment or hard compliance approach. The emergent consensus is that both are required. Instead, the current debate is over how to combine and sequence such policy measures. For instance, measures to improve detection through inspections are currently often combined with campaigns aimed at raising awareness or warning customers that inspections are about to occur. Tougher sanctions, furthermore, follow amnesties and voluntary disclosure schemes. However, whether these combinations are more effective than other sequences and combinations requires evaluation. In recent years, nevertheless, two ways of combining these policy approaches in particular sequences have come to the fore, namely the responsive regulation approach and the slippery slope framework. Here, each is reviewed in turn.

Responsive Regulation

Braithwaite (2002) distinguishes between 'regulatory formalism' and 'responsive regulation'. In regulatory formalism, akin to Weber's ideal-type bureaucracy discussed earlier, an agency lists its problems in advance, specifies the appropriate response and generates manuals of rules to achieve these responses. This arguably enables process efficiency and outcome consistency. In recent years, the nature of regulatory formalism has shifted away from reliance mostly on deterrents and towards the use of incentives to engage in formal work. There has also been a greater consideration of the fair and respectful treatment of taxpayers. Such a 'humanizing' of regulatory formalism, nevertheless, is not the same as responsive regulation.

In responsive regulation, taxpayers are openly engaged to think about their obligations and accept responsibility for regulating themselves in a manner consistent with the codified laws and regulations of formal institutions. This approach is about winning their 'hearts and minds' so that there is a culture of commitment to compliance and people regulate themselves rather than need to be regulated by external rules. However, responsive regulation does not exclusively confine itself to the use of such soft measures. For Braithwaite (2009), responsive regulation means influencing the community's commitment to paying tax through respectful treatment, through dealing with resistance and reforming faulty processes, through fairly directed and fully explained disapproval of non-compliant behaviour, through preparedness to administer sanctions and to follow through to escalate regulatory intervention in the face of continuing non-compliance.

Indeed, since responsive regulation was first proposed, it has enjoyed widespread acceptance by many scholars (Abbott and Snidal, 2013; Braithwaite, 2007, 2010; Dwenger et al., 2014; Grabosky, 2013; Hashimzade et al., 2013; Parker, 2013; Wood et al., 2010) as well as tax administrations (see Job et al., 2007). The Australian government, for example, has adopted this 'responsive regulation' approach. In the first instance, indirect controls facilitate voluntary self-regulated compliance, followed by persuasion and only then punitive measures to tackle tax non-compliance (Braithwaite, 2009; Job et al., 2007). In other words, the responsive regulation approach envisages a regulatory pyramid with various options that a tax authority can use to engender compliance, sequenced from the least intrusive soft commitment measures at the bottom and used first to the most intrusive hard compliance measures at the top. The idea is that a tax authority does not need in most cases to pursue the coercion option at the top of the pyramid to win compliance. Instead, it can start with the soft commitment measures at the bottom of the pyramid and if these fail to elicit behaviour change with some groups, then the level of intrusiveness escalates up the pyramid until it reaches the intervention that elicits the desired response. The outcome is recognition of a continuum of attitudes towards compliance and different policy responses that can be temporally sequenced, starting with commitment measures and moving through to sanctions.

Whether this combination and temporal sequencing of measures is the most appropriate is debatable. Until now, there has been no evaluation of whether this sequencing is the most appropriate and/or effective. Neither has there been any evaluation of whether this sequencing is appropriate everywhere or only in particular contexts. In other words, although it seems to be appropriate and effective as an approach for tackling the shadow economy and shadow labour, no evidence-base currently exists that this is the case.

Moreover, and as Grabosky (2013) highlights, responsive regulation is largely state-centric and little attention is given to the role of non-state actors in the regulatory process. Perhaps their involvement could best occur at the bottom of the pyramid when engendering commitment. How this might occur, however, remains open for discussion. Further thought is also required to how shifting towards such an approach represents a challenge to the cultures of state organizations such as tax administrations. As Job et al. (2007) find, in Australia, New Zealand and East Timor, administrations face major challenges in bringing about culture change among their staff, with resistance to change, problems in meeting the legal principles of consistency and equity, allowing staff discretion while avoiding corruption, recognizing the different occupational skillsets required of staff and changing the language and discourse used.

Finally, little discussion has taken place regarding the implementation of responsive regulation at the supra-national level. As Abbott and Snidal (2013) argue, intergovernmental organizations can take responsive regulation transnational. The European Commission, especially in its proposal for a European platform for tackling undeclared work, and the International Labour Organization, are two potential institutions for taking this forward.

Slippery Slope Framework

Another way of combining soft commitment and hard compliance measures is the 'slippery slope framework' (Kirchler et al., 2008), which has started to be widely discussed (Alm and Torgler, 2011; Alm et al., 2012; Alm and McClennan 2012; Bazart and Pickhardt 2011; Durham et al. 2014; Kastlunger et al., 2013; Khurana and Diwan, 2014; Kogler et al., 2015; Lisi, 2012; Muehlbacher et al., 2011a, 2011b; Prinz et al., 2013). This distinguishes between voluntary compliance and enforced compliance, which depend in turn on the trust that individuals have in the authorities and on the power of authorities respectively. If both trust and power are low, the shadow economy and shadow labour will be prevalent. When trust and/or power increases, compliance increases. The slippery slope framework posits that citizens' compliance therefore depends on the power of the authorities to enforce compliance, and/or the level of trust in the authorities that engenders voluntary cooperation.

The slippery slope framework integrates both the rational economic actor and social actor perspectives by assuming that taxpayers abide by the law either because they fear detection and fines (enforced compliance) or because they feel an obligation to honestly contribute their share (voluntary cooperation). The slippery slope framework thus assumes two routes to tax compliance: deterrence of tax evasion by audits and fines on the one hand; and building a trusting relationship with taxpayers by services and support on the other.

To empirically test the basic assumptions of the slippery slope framework, Wahl et al. (2010a) randomly presented participants with one of four different descriptions of a fictitious country, in which the authorities were characterized as either trustworthy or untrustworthy on the one hand and as either powerful or powerless on the other hand. Their results showed that participants paid significantly more taxes when power and trust were high, as suggested by the framework. They also found that voluntary compliance was highest when the authorities were trustworthy and powerful, while enforced compliance was highest when authorities were portrayed as powerful, but not trustworthy. This has been further reinforced by two surveys of real-world taxpayers (Muehlbacher et al., 2011a, 2011b). Kogler et al (2013), meanwhile, conducted an experiment to manipulate the power of authorities and taxpayers' trust in authorities using scenario techniques, and to assess intentions to declare taxes honestly in four European countries: Austria, Hungary, Romania and Russia. The aim was to test the impact of power and trust on compliance in countries with different institutional, political, and societal characteristics. In a 2×2 design, scenarios described tax authorities as trustworthy or untrustworthy and as either powerful or powerless. The finding is that intentions to declare taxes honestly were highest in all countries if the authorities were described as powerful and trustworthy; conversely, evasion was high if both power and trust were at a minimum. In addition, perceptions of high power boosted enforced compliance, whereas high trust was related to strong voluntary cooperation. As in many studies on tax evasion, women were found to be more honest than men.

Kogler et al. (2015), based on a survey of 476 self-employed taxpayers, show that perceptions of procedural and distributive justice predict voluntary compliance, and trust in authorities mediates this observed relation. In addition, the relation between retributive justice (that is, the perceived fairness with regard to the sanctioning of tax evaders) and enforced compliance was mediated by power, just as the relation between perceived deterrence of authorities' enforcement strategies and enforced compliance. With regard to both retributive justice and deterrence also a mediational effect of trust on the relation to voluntary compliance was identified. Furthermore, voluntary and enforced compliance were related to perceived social norms, but these relations were neither mediated by trust nor power.

In a further extension of the slippery slope framework, Gangl et al. (2012) distinguish three climates: a service climate, an antagonistic climate and a confidence climate. They argue that a service climate requires legitimate power of tax authorities and that this leads to reason-based trust on the part of taxpayers and increases voluntary tax compliance. An antagonistic climate, meanwhile, occurs when the coercive power of tax authorities prevails, leading to enforced compliance and an atmosphere where tax authorities and citizens work against each other. A confidence climate, finally, is characterized by an implicit trust between tax authorities and taxpayers (an unintentional and automatic form of trust), which results in the perception of tax compliance as a moral obligation and, again, voluntary cooperation of taxpayers.

That power and trust are essential for good tax governance is being seriously considered by authorities in various countries (OECD, 2013). For instance, to improve interactions with their clientele, tax administrators in the Netherlands and Austria have started pilot projects for young entrepreneurs. Duties and service facilities are explained to these inexperienced taxpayers, and cooperation – rather than control – is fostered right from the start of a business. In the 'fair-play' initiative, Austrian tax authorities emphasize differences between taxpayers in their willingness to pay and the importance of reacting with adequate regulation strategies ranging from deterrence to support (Müller, 2012). In 2005, the Dutch Tax and Customs Administration introduced a pioneering supervisory approach, 'horizontal monitoring', as an alternative to the traditional 'vertical monitoring'. This approach is based on the firm conviction that a positive relationship, based on mutual trust, between taxpayers, tax practitioners and tax authorities reduces unnecessary supervisory costs and burdens, complex discussions about tax designs on the edge of legality and aggressive tax planning with retrospective adjustments (Committee Horizontal Monitoring Tax and Customs Administration, 2012).

CONCLUSIONS

This chapter has introduced a way forward for tackling the shadow economy and shadow labour that goes beyond the current reliance on a hard compliance approach in general, and the use of 'sticks' to ensure that the costs and risks of engaging in the shadow economy and shadow labour outweigh the benefits of doing so. It has proposed that greater emphasis should be put on a soft commitment approach that encourages a social contract to be forged between the state and its citizens. In many societies, there is an incongruity between the laws, codes and regulations of formal institutions and the norms, beliefs and values of informal institutions. Work in the shadow economy takes place when the norms, values and beliefs differ to the laws, codes and regulations, resulting in what formal institutions deem to be illegal activities to be legitimate in terms of the norms, values and beliefs of the society or particular population groups. To tackle the shadow economy and shadow labour, therefore, a reduction in this institutional incongruence is required.

On the one hand, this can be achieved by altering the norms, values and beliefs of the population regarding the acceptability of working in the shadow economy so that these informal institutions align with the laws, regulations and codes of formal institutions. The measures reviewed that can achieve this include awareness-raising campaigns about the costs of shadow work and benefits of declared work, as well as tax education initiatives. On the other hand, one can reform the formal institutions to align with the norms, values and beliefs of the wider society. This can be achieved by reforming the processes of government to ensure that citizens believe that they are paying their fair share of taxes compared with others, receive the goods and services they believe that they deserve given the taxes that they pay, and believe that the tax authority has treated then in a respectful, impartial and responsible manner. It can also be achieved, as shown, by developing the broader economic and social conditions in a manner that has been shown to be correlated with reductions in the size of the shadow economy. In practice, however, these are not mutually exclusive approaches. Changes in formal institutions shape, and are shaped by, changes in informal institutions, and changes in both are required in order to reduce the level of institutional incongruence.

It is also the case that the soft commitment and hard compliance approaches are not mutually exclusive. Both can be combined and sequenced in various ways. This chapter has outlined two such ways of doing so, namely the responsive regulation approach and slippery slope framework. However, to obtain a fuller understanding of how to combine and sequence the soft commitment and hard compliance approach when tackling the shadow economy, evaluations will need to be conducted of which combinations of measures ordered in what sequence are most effective. Before this can be done, however, evaluations will be required of which individual policy measures work and which do not, albeit perhaps in conjunction with other measures. Currently, few evaluations exist of the effectiveness of even individual policy measures, never mind their effectiveness when used in conjunction with other measures. Only when such evaluations have been conducted in consequence, will one be able to determine which policy measures can be used and in what sequence in different contexts. There is thus much research required before solutions can be concretely stated. Hopefully, nevertheless, this chapter has begun to outline the breadth of approaches and measures required. What is for sure, however, is that a hard compliance approach that solely focuses upon increasing the penalties and risks of detection is not going to solve the problem.

10. Conclusions

In this concluding chapter, we synthesize the lessons learned so as to draw some conclusions on the way forward for the study of the shadow economy and shadow labour. These lessons relate to not only how the shadow economy and shadow labour is measured but also the size and character of this realm as well as how it can be explained and tackled.

To synthesize what has been found, first, we review the findings regarding the measurement methods used to evaluate the extent and nature of the shadow economy and shadow labour. With this understanding in hand, the second section then turns to drawing some concluding comments about the size and character of the shadow economy when the indirect MIMIC method is used, followed in the third section by some conclusions about the size and nature of the global shadow labour force using the survey method. Revealing that both the direct and indirect measurement methods highlight how there is a close relationship between the size and character of the shadow economy and shadow labour force, and various country-level economic and social conditions, we then turn our attention in the fourth section to how to tackle the shadow economy and shadow labour force. Our argument, it will be shown, is that the conventional deterrence approach needs to be complemented with not only a range of incentives to make formalization more attractive but also macro-level 'soft' approaches in order to engender a culture of commitment to compliance. The net outcome, as will be revealed, is a call for the longstanding division between those using indirect and direct measurement methods to be transcended and for both to be used, and also for the currently dominant approach that uses deterrence measures to eradicate the shadow economy to be moved beyond and for greater use to be made of other macro-level policy approaches and measures to deal with the determinants of the shadow economy and shadow labour force rather than continue with the current approach of seeking to mop up the effects.

MEASUREMENT METHODS

When measuring the shadow economy and shadow labour force, the conventional debate has been over whether direct or indirect measurement methods should be used. In Part I of this book, we reviewed these contrasting measurement methods. Chapter 2 evaluated critically the range of indirect methods. Starting with the discrepancy method, we revealed that the difficulty is that often a combination of 'rough' estimations and unclear assumptions are made, and the calculation method is often not clear with the documentation and procedure often not made public. The monetary and/or electricity methods, meanwhile, result in some very high estimates and only macro-estimates are available. Moreover, a breakdown by sector or industry is not possible, and there are difficulties when converting millions of kWh into a value-added figure when using the electricity method (see Schneider and Williams, 2013; Thomas, 1992). The MIMIC (latent) method, furthermore, has several critical issues associated with it. These include the fact that: only relative coefficients, not absolute values, are obtained; the estimations are quite often highly sensitive with respect to changes in the data and specifications; there are difficulties in differentiating between the selection of causes and indicators, and the calibration procedure and starting values used have a significant influence on the results obtained.

Chapter 3, meanwhile, reviewed the survey method and reviewed the issues that need to be addressed when designing a survey of the shadow labour force. This revealed that decisions are required on, first, the unit of analysis to be examined; second, the data collection methodology used; third, a multifarious variety of questionnaire design issues; fourth, the sample size; fifth, the sampled populations; and sixth and finally, the sampling method used. To reveal the results of using different types of survey method, we have then reported evidence from the Netherlands on the different results produced when using different mediums of communication between the researcher and respondent (face-to-face, mail and telephone). This displayed that face-to-face interviews not only yield a higher response rate but also a higher incidence of shadow work being conducted than the mixed mode approach using the internet, paper and telephone interviews.

Examining the lessons from four decades of shadow economy research, four summary points are made. First, there is no ideal or dominant method to estimate the size and development of the shadow economy. All methods have serious methodological problems and weaknesses. Second, and if possible, we conclude that researchers should use several methods to come somewhat closer to the 'true' value of the size and development of the shadow economy. Third, we find that much more research is needed, not only with respect to the estimation methodology so far as modelling methods are concerned, but also a wider range of data collection using survey methods for different countries and periods. And fourth and finally, we conclude that the focus should be now on micro-shadow economy research, and to undertake more primary data collection in order to reach two goals: a better micro-foundation, and a better knowledge of the nature of the work in the shadow economy, the character of the labour force, what their motivations are and what they earn.

If this research is to be effectively used, moreover, three further issues will need to be resolved. First, a common and internationally accepted definition of the shadow economy remains absent. Such a definition or convention is perhaps needed in order to make comparisons between the shadow economies of different countries more reliable. Second, the link between theory and empirical estimation of the shadow economy remains unsatisfactory; in the best case theory provides us with derived signs of the causal factors, but which are the 'core' causal factors is still open to question. And third and finally, a satisfactory validation of the empirical results should be developed so that it is easier to judge the empirical results with respect to their plausibility and validity. How to achieve this, nevertheless, is very much open to discussion since little thought has so far been given to how this can be achieved. This, therefore, provides an agenda for the issues that need to be resolved in order to develop methodology in relation to estimating the shadow economy and shadow labour force.

THE SHADOW ECONOMY IN GLOBAL PERSPECTIVE

To report what is so far known about the shadow economy, Part II reported the results obtained by applying the MIMIC method. The headline finding is that the unweighted mean size of the shadow economy across the world during the period 1999–2007 was 33 per cent of GDP. However, when we examine the weighted mean size of the shadow economy across the world during this period, taking into account the population size of each country, the finding is that it was 17.1 per cent of GDP. Unless the shadow economy is taken into account in economic studies, therefore, just over one-sixth of all economic activity across the world will be omitted from analyses.

Comparing OECD (developed) nations, developing countries and transition economies, the finding is that in 2007, the weighted mean size of the shadow economy was 13 per cent in OECD nations, 26.2 per cent in developing countries and 33.7 per cent in transition economies. Transition economies, therefore, have larger shadow economies than developing countries. However, across all three of these broad groupings of economies, there has been a decrease in the size of the shadow economy between 1999 and 2007. In the OECD nations, the size of the shadow economy decreased from 14.1 per cent of GDP in 1999 to 13 per cent of GDP in 2007 (that is, a 7.8 per cent decrease in size), while in developing countries, the shadow economy decreased in size from 29.6 per cent to 26.2 per cent (that is, an 11.5 per cent decrease in size) and in the transition economies the shadow economy decreased from 37.9 per cent to 33.7 per cent of GDP (that is, a decrease of 11.1 per cent). The result is that the shadow economy declined slowest in the OECD nations where it was smallest to start with and quickest in the developing and transition economies where the shadow economy was larger. The very tentative intimation is, therefore, that there is a partial convergence of these three broad groupings of economies over this time period in terms of the size of their shadow economies.

In Chapter 4, attention focused on the results of using the MIMIC method to examine the size of the shadow economy in 116 developing countries and 25 transition economies. The finding was that the shadow economy is not evenly distributed. Examining the weighted mean, the finding is that the global region with the largest shadow economy is sub-Saharan Africa where the equivalent of 37.6 per cent of GDP is in the shadow economy, followed by 36.4 per cent of GDP in Europe and Central Asia, 34.7 per cent in Latin America and the Caribbean, 27.3 per cent in the Middle East and North Africa, 25.1 per cent in South Asia, 20.8 per cent in other high-income countries, 17.5 per cent in East Asia and the Pacific, and 13.4 per cent in high-income OECD nations. There are also significant cross-national variations both within each of these global regions and across these regions. Although the weighted mean is 17.1 per cent of GDP globally, the standard deviation is 9.9 per cent, displaying the highly uneven distribution of the shadow economy globally across countries. Moreover, in some nations it is growing, in others it is static and in yet others declining.

In Chapter 5, meanwhile, the focus of attention turned to the cross-national variations in the magnitude of the shadow economy across developed nations as well as the causal determinants of the shadow economy and how the relative weighting attached to these causal determinants change both across countries and over time. The finding was that although the shadow economy is overall smaller in the developed world than in the developing world, there are nevertheless marked variations. In countries such as Bulgaria, Romania and Turkey the shadow economy is the equivalent of 34.6 per cent, 32.2 per cent and 30.6 per cent of GDP respectively, while countries in which the shadow economy is smallest are Luxembourg, Switzerland and the United States whose shadow economies are the equivalent of 9.6 per cent, 8.3 per cent and 8.7 per cent of official GDP respectively.

To explain the shadow economy, Chapter 5 then investigated the average relative influence (in percentage terms) of various causal variables for all OECD countries between 1999 and 2010. This revealed that tax morale, unemployment and self-employment are the most influential determinants of the shadow economy. Examining the average values for all developed OECD nations, unemployment and self-employment have the highest influence (14.6 per cent) across countries. This is followed by tax morale with an average relative impact of 14.5 per cent, then GDP growth (14.3 per cent), business freedom (14.2 per cent), indirect taxes (14.1 per cent) and finally the personal income tax with an average relative impact of 13.8 per cent.

However, the relative importance of these causal variables changes both across countries and over time within countries. In Australia, for example, unemployment is a far more important determinant of the shadow economy than in developed countries in general and the level of personal income tax a less important determinant, suggesting that relative to other developed world governments, Australia should place more emphasis on resolving the level of unemployment than reducing personal income tax rates if it wishes to reduce the size of its shadow economy. Indeed, Chapter 5 provided a detailed review of both the relative importance of these causal variables in France, Germany, Austria, Spain and Italy, as well as how the importance of each of these causal variables has changed over time in each of these countries. The result is that it was clearly revealed that it is not possible to adopt a universally similar approach to tackling the shadow economy across all countries and neither is the approach that needs to be adopted static over time. The emphasis given to tackling particular macro-level determinants needs to vary across countries. Moreover, as the relative weighting attached to different causal variables shifts over time, there is a need for the focus of the policy approach adopted by national governments to also change to reflect these shifts. The important point, nevertheless, is that tackling the shadow economy requires macro-level determinants of the shadow economy to be addressed. It cannot be tackled simply by increasing the probability of detection which deals only with the effects rather than causes of the problem.

THE SHADOW LABOUR FORCE IN GLOBAL PERSPECTIVE

Having examined the results of using the MIMIC method to evaluate the size of the shadow economy across the world, Part III then analysed the results of using survey methods to measure the size and nature of the shadow labour force across the globe. Chapter 6 reviewed the findings regarding the extent and character of the shadow labour force in developing and transition economies using the International Labour Organization estimates and in doing so, also revealed the country-level determinants that influence the size and nature of the shadow labour force. To do this, a typology of economies was developed, positioning countries on continua in terms of the scale and intensity of employment in the shadow economy. Analysing the results of the ILO surveys, the finding is that in the 36 countries covered, three in five (59.8 per cent) of the non-agricultural workforce have their main employment in the shadow economy and just under three in four (74 per cent) of those who have their main employment in the shadow economy are in shadow employment in shadow enterprises.

Nevertheless, there are cross-national variations. Not only does the scale of the shadow labour force range from 86.6 per cent of the non-agricultural workforce in Pakistan to 6.5 per cent in Serbia, but there are similar variations in the intensity of shadow employment. The share of those employed in the shadow sector who engage in shadow employment in shadow enterprises ranges from 85.2 per cent in Mali to 18.8 per cent in Lesotho. In two-thirds (67 per cent) of the 36 countries surveyed nevertheless, more than half of the non-agricultural workforce have their main job in the shadow economy and in 32 (89 per cent) countries more than half of this employment in the shadow sector is in the form of shadow employment in shadow enterprises. Employment in the shadow sector, in consequence, is not some small segment of the labour market in developing and transition economies and of marginal importance. Rather, the majority of the workforce has their main job in the shadow labour force.

Exploring the reasons for these cross-national variations in the scale and intensity of the shadow labour force, three competing perspectives have been critically evaluated. These have variously argued that the degree and intensity of the shadow economy is associated with economic underdevelopment (modernization perspective), higher taxes, corruption and state interference (neo-liberal perspective) and/or inadequate state intervention to protect workers from poverty (political economy perspective). Evidence was found to support the modernization and political economy perspectives that associate the shadow labour force with underdevelopment and inadequate state protection of workers from poverty respectively and the neo-liberal corruption thesis that the scale of shadow employment is higher in countries where the perception of public sector corruption is greater. However, no evidence has been found to support the validity of the neo-liberal theses that shadow employment is associated with higher taxes and more state interference. Instead, quite the opposite was identified. Higher taxes and more state intervention reduce the scale and intensity of shadow employment, presumably due to the ability of governments to have efficient enforcement systems, make social transfers and reduce the need of the population to resort to employment in the shadow economy to survive.

These findings now require further evaluation across a wider range of developing and transition economies as well as using time-series data for individual countries and, if possible, using multivariate regression analysis on a larger sample size to determine how important each characteristic is to the final outcome while controlling for the other characteristics. The major barrier to doing this, nevertheless, is the lack of availability of cross-national comparative data on employment in the shadow sector.

Chapter 7 then examined the results regarding the extent and character of the shadow labour force in developed countries using the 2007 Eurobarometer survey of 27 European countries and also the country-level determinants of the size of the shadow labour force. This revealed that the majority (90.8 per cent) of employment in the EU-27 is formal employment, and that the EU-27 is therefore a 'quasi-formal' employment relations system. The majority of shadow employment, moreover, results from a desire to voluntarily exit, rather than exclusion from, the formal economy. However, major variations exist across the EU-27 in both the extent and nature of employment in the shadow economy.

First, variations in the extent of employment in the shadow economy were identified. Western Europe and the Nordic nations have 'quasi-formal' employment relations systems (4.6 per cent and 8.4 per cent of employment respectively is in the shadow economy), while Southern Europe has a 'largely formal' employment relations system (10.3 per cent of employment is in the shadow economy) and East-Central Europe has a 'mostly formal' employment relations system with 20.1 per cent of employment in the shadow economy. Consequently, there is a divide from east to west and south to north in the EU-27 with greater levels of employment in the shadow economy on the eastern/southern side than on the western/Nordic side, although the east-to-west divide is more marked than the south-to-north divide. Second, there are also differences in the nature of employment in the shadow economy. Although shadow employment in the EU-27 as a whole is largely driven by a desire to voluntarily exit, rather than exclusion from, the formal economy, a clear east-to-west and north-to-south divide was identified. While East-Central Europe and

Southern Europe are 'semi-driven' by exclusion rationales, Western Europe and Nordic nations are 'mostly driven' by exit rationales.

To tentatively explain these variations in employment relations systems, the competing modernization, neo-liberal and political economy perspectives have again been evaluated. The finding, using bivariate regression analysis, is that these competing perspectives need to be combined. In short, wealthier, more equal societies with less public sector corruption that pursue higher levels of taxation, social protection and more effective redistribution via social transfers are significantly correlated with lower levels of employment in the shadow economy that are driven largely by exit rather than exclusion rationales. Indeed, this explains the higher levels of shadow employment and preponderance of exclusion rationales in East-Central and Southern European countries, which are generally less wealthy and less equal societies with higher rates of public sector corruption and lower levels of taxation, social protection and state redistribution via social transfers compared with West European and Nordic nations.

This finding regarding the relationship between employment in the shadow economy and different regulatory environments has clear policy implications. In stark contrast to previous literature on tackling employment in the shadow economy, which has focused on whether deterrence measures need to be introduced or more enabling measures that smooth the transition to formality and provide incentives (OECD, 2012; Williams, 2006a, 2006b), Parts II and III revealed that the wider regulatory environment is also important. How this can be incorporated into policy approaches was then addressed in Part IV.

TACKLING THE SHADOW ECONOMY AND SHADOW LABOUR FORCE

Having reviewed how both indirect and direct methods measure the extent and character of the size of the shadow economy and shadow labour force in Part I, along with their respective findings in Parts II and III in relation to both developing and developed countries, Part IV turned attention to what needs to be done to tackle the shadow economy and shadow labour force. Chapter 8 reviewed the current policy approaches and measures used. To do this, a classificatory schema was presented of the different policy approaches and measures available. Learning from those eliciting behaviour changes at the organizational level, where there has been a shift from a hard compliance approach to a soft commitment approach, a similar range of possible approaches were shown to exist at the societal level when tackling the shadow economy.

Examining the very limited literature on which approaches are currently being used and viewed as most effective, a study of 31 European countries was reported, which reveals that the approach in these countries remains largely grounded in a hard compliance approach based on increasing the costs and risks of non-compliance, despite the existence of no conclusive evidence that increasing the penalties and risks of detection and therefore punishing 'bad' behaviour is an effective approach, and the widespread move away from such an approach when seeking to elicit behaviour change in most other spheres of human activity. It also revealed the lack of importance attached to the soft commitment approach and the persistence of a widespread but unfounded belief among stakeholders that this is an ineffective approach.

In Chapter 9, therefore, a way forward for tackling the shadow economy and shadow labour was proposed that puts greater emphasis on a soft commitment approach that encourages a social contract to be forged between the state and its citizens. In many societies, there is an incongruity between the laws, codes and regulations of formal institutions and the norms, beliefs and values of informal institutions. Work in the shadow economy takes place when the norms, values and beliefs differ to the laws, codes and regulations, resulting in what formal institutions deem to be illegal activities to be legitimate in terms of the norms, values and beliefs of the society or particular population groups. To tackle the shadow economy and shadow labour, therefore, a reduction in this institutional incongruence is required.

On the one hand, it was shown that this can be achieved by altering the norms, values and beliefs of the population regarding the acceptability of working in the shadow economy so that these informal institutions align with the laws, regulations and codes of formal institutions. The measures reviewed that can achieve this include awareness-raising campaigns about the costs of shadow work and benefits of declared work, as well as tax education initiatives. On the other hand, it was shown that this can also be achieved by reforming the formal institutions to align with the norms, values and beliefs of the wider society. This necessitates changing the processes of government institutions to ensure that citizens believe that they are paying their fair share of taxes compared with others, receive the goods and services they believe that they deserve given the taxes that they pay, and believe that the tax authority has treated then in a respectful, impartial and responsible manner. It also necessitates, as shown, changing those broader economic and social conditions shown to be correlated with reductions in the size of the shadow economy. In practice, however, these are not mutually exclusive approaches. Changes in formal institutions shape, and are shaped by, changes in informal institutions, and changes in both are required in order to reduce the level of institutional incongruence.

It has also been shown that the soft commitment and hard compliance approaches are not mutually exclusive. It is wholly feasible and appropriate to combine and sequence these soft and hard approaches and their measures in various ways. This chapter has outlined two such ways of doing so, namely the responsive regulation approach and slippery slope framework. However, a fuller understanding of the most effective ways of combining and sequencing the soft commitment and hard compliance approach when tackling the shadow economy is required. Before doing so, however, evaluations will be required of what works so far as individual policy measures are concerned, albeit perhaps in conjunction with other measures. Currently, few such evaluations have been conducted of the effectiveness of individual policy measures, never mind their effectiveness when used in various sequences with other measures. Until such evaluations are conducted in consequence, little will be known about which policy measures to use in which combinations and in what sequence in different contexts. Much research is therefore required before solutions can be concretely stated. Hopefully, this book will encourage such research.

Given the large size of the shadow economy and shadow labour force across the world, along with the major deleterious consequences that result from its existence, it is therefore to be hoped that this book will stimulate both researchers and governments to seek better understandings of this phenomenon and what can be done about it. What can be stated with certainty, however, is that far more research is required if the extent and nature of the shadow economy and shadow labour force, and its causes, is to be more fully understood, and that a hard compliance approach that solely focuses upon increasing the penalties and risks of detection is extremely unlikely on its own to be capable of shifting work in the shadow economy into the formal economy.

References

Abbott, K.W. and D. Snidal (2013), 'Taking responsive regulation transnational: strategies for international organisation', *Regulation and Governance*, **7**(1), 95–113.

Ahmad, A.N. (2008), 'Dead men working: time and space in London's ("illegal") migrant economy', *Work, Employment and Society*, **22**(2), 301–18.

Ahmed, E. and V. Braithwaite (2004), 'When tax collectors become collectors for child support and student loans: jeopardising or protecting the revenue base?', *Kyklos*, **3**, 303–26.

Ahmed, E. and V. Braithwaite (2005), 'Understanding small business taxpayers: issues of deterrence, tax morale, fairness and work practice', *International Small Business Journal*, **23**(5), 539–68.

Ahumada, H., A. Facundo, A. Canavese and P. Canavese (2004), *The Demand for Currency Approach and the Size of the Shadow Economy: A Critical Assessment*, Paris: Discussion Paper, Delta Ecole Normale Superieure.

Aigner, D., F. Schneider and D. Ghosh (1988), 'Me and my shadow: estimating the size of the US hidden economy from time series data', in W.A. Barnett, E.R. Berndt and H. White (eds.), *Dynamic Econometric Modelling*, Cambridge: Cambridge University Press, pp. 224–43.

Allingham, M. and A. Sandmo (1972), 'Income tax evasion: a theoretical analysis', *Journal of Public Economics*, **1**(2), 323–38.

Alm, J. (2011), 'Designing alternative strategies to reduce tax evasion', in M. Pickhardt and A. Prinz (eds.), *Tax Evasion and the Shadow Economy*, Cheltenham: Edward Elgar Publishing, pp. 13–32.

Alm, J. and C. McClennan (2012), 'Tax morale and tax compliance from the firm's perspective', *Kyklos*, **65**, 1–17.

Alm, J. and B. Torgler (2011), 'Do ethics matter? Tax compliance and morality', *Journal of Business Ethics*, **101**, 635–51.

Alm, J., G. McClelland and W. Schulze (1992), 'Why do people pay taxes?', *Journal of Public Economics*, **1**, 323–38.

Alm, J., B. Jackson and M. McKee (1993), 'Fiscal exchange, collective decision institutions and tax compliance', *Journal of Economic Behaviour and Organization*, **22**, 285–303.

Alm, J., I. Sanchez and A. De Juan (1995), 'Economic and non-economic factors in tax compliance', *Kyklos*, **48**, 3–18.

Alm, J., T. Cherry, M. Jones and M. McKee (2010), 'Taxpayer information assistance services and tax compliance behaviour', *Journal of Economic Psychology*, **31**, 577–86.

Alm, J., E. Kirchler, S. Muehlbacher, K. Gangl, E. Hofmann, C. Kogler and M. Pollai (2012), 'Rethinking the research paradigms for analysing tax compliance behaviour', *CESifo Forum*, **13**(2), 33–40.

Alon, A. and A.M. Hageman (2013), 'The impact of corruption on firm tax compliance in transition economies: whom do you trust?', *Journal of Business Ethics*, **116**, 479–94.

Alvesson, M. and H. Willmott (1996), *Making Sense of Management: A Critical Introduction*, London: Sage.

Amin, A., A. Cameron and R. Hudson (2002), *Placing the Social Economy*, London: Routledge.

Andreoni, J., B. Erard and J. Fainstein (1998), 'Tax compliance', *Journal of Economic Literature*, **36**(2), 818–60.

Andrews, D., A. Caldera Sanchez and A. Johansson (2011), *Towards a Better Understanding of the Informal Economy*, Paris: OECD Economics Department Working Paper No. 873.

Apel, M. (1994), *An Expenditure-based Estimate of Tax Evasion in Sweden*, Stockholm: RSV Tax Reform Evaluation Report No. 1.

Arnold, R.A. (1996), *Economics*, St Paul, MN: West Publishing.

Autio, E. and K. Fu (2015), 'Economic and political institutions and entry into formal and informal entrepreneurship', *Asia-Pacific Journal of Management*, **32**(1), 67–94.

Ayres, I. and J. Braithwaite (1992), *Responsive Regulation: Transcending the Deregulation Debate*, New York: Oxford University Press.

Bàculo, L. (2001), *The Shadow Economy in Italy: Results from Field Studies*, paper presented at the European Scientific Workshop on 'The Shadow Economy: Empirical Evidence and New Policy Issues at the European Level', Ragusa, Sicily, 20–21 September.

Bajada, C. (2011), 'The shadow economy in the residential construction sector', in F. Schneider (ed.), *Handbook on the Shadow Economy*, Cheltenham: Edward Elgar Publishing, pp. 293–323.

Bajada, C. and F. Schneider (2005), 'Introduction', in C. Bajada and F. Schneider (eds.), *Size, Causes and Consequences of the Underground Economy: An International Perspective*, Aldershot: Ashgate, pp. 1–14.

Bajada, C. and F. Schneider (2009), 'Unemployment and the shadow economy in the OECD', *Review Economique*, **60**(4), 1011–33.

Baldry, J.C. (1986), 'Tax evasion is not a gamble: a report on two experiments', *Economics Letters*, **22**(1), 22–25.

Barbour, A. and M. Llanes (2013), *Supporting People to Legitimise their Informal Businesses*, York: Joseph Rowntree Foundation.

Bardasi, E., K. Beegle, A. Dillon and P. Serneels (2010), *Do Labor Statistics Depend On How and to Whom the Questions Are Asked?* Washington, DC: World Bank Policy Research Working Paper No. 5192.

Baumol, W.J. (1990), 'Entrepreneurship: productive, unproductive and destructive', *Journal of Political Economy*, **98**, 893–921.

Baumol, W.J. and A. Blinder (2008), *Macroeconomics: Principles and Policy*, Cincinnati, OH: South-Western Publishing.

Bazart. C. and M. Pickhardt (2011), 'Fighting income tax evasion with positive rewards', *Public Finance Review*, **31**, 124–49.

Beaman, R. and K. Wheldall (2000), 'Teachers' use of approval and disapproval in the classroom', *Educational Psychology*, **20**(4), 431–46.

Beccaria, C. ([1797] 1986), *On Crimes and Punishment*, Indianapolis: Hackett Publishers.

Becker, G.S. (1968), 'Crime and punishment: an econometric approach', *Journal of Political Economy*, **76**(1), 169–217.

Becker, K.F. (2004), *The Informal Economy*, Stockholm: Swedish International Development Agency.

Bell, D. (1960), *The End of Ideology*, London: Collier Macmillan.

Bentham, J. ([1788] 1983), 'Principles of penal law', in J.H. Burton (ed.), *The Works of Jeremy Bentham*, Philadelphia: Lea and Blanchard.

Bernasconi, M. (1998), 'Tax evasion and orders of risk aversion', *Journal of Public Economics*, **67**(1), 123–34.

Beron, K.J., H.V. Tauchen and A.D. Witte (1992), 'The effect of audits and socio-economic variables on compliance', in J. Slemerod (ed.), *Why People Pay Taxes*, Ann Arbor: University of Michigan Press, pp. 67–89.

Bethlehem, J. (2009), *Applied Survey Methods; A Statistical Perspective*, London: Wiley.

Bhattacharya, S. (2014), 'Is labour still a relevant category for praxis? Critical reflections on some contemporary discourses on work and labour in capitalism', *Development and Change*, **45**(5), 941–62.

Bhattacharyya, D.K. (1999), 'On the economic rationale of estimating the hidden economy', *Economic Journal*, **109**, 348–59.

Bies, R.J. and J.S. Moag (1986), 'Interactional fairness', in R.J. Lewicki, B.M. Sheppard and M.H. Bazerman (eds.), *Research on Negotiations in Organizations*, Greenwich, CT: Jai, pp. 43–55.

Bird, R., J. Martinez-Vazquez and B. Torgler (2006), 'Societal institutions and tax effort in developing countries', in J. Alm, J. Martinez-Vazquez and M. Rider (eds.), *The Challenges of Tax Reform in the Global Economy*, New York: Springer, pp. 283–338.

Blades, D. (1982), *The Hidden Economy and the National Accounts*, Paris: OECD Occasional Studies.

Blau, P. and W.R. Scott (1963), *Formal Organisations: A Comparative Approach*, London: Routledge and Kegan Paul.

Blumenthal, M., C. Christian and J. Slemrod (1998), *The Determinants of Income Tax Compliance: Evidence From a Controlled Experiment in Minnesota*, Massachusetts: National Bureau of Economic Research Working Paper No. 6575.

Bobeck, D.D. and R.C. Hatfield (2003), 'An investigation of the theory of planned behaviour and the role of moral obligation in tax compliance', *Behavioural Research in Accounting*, **52**(1), 13–38.

Boeschoten, W.C. and M.M.G. Fase (1984), *The Volume of Payments and the Informal Economy in the Netherlands 1965–1982*, Dordrecht: M. Nijhoff.

Bollen, K.A. (1989), *Structural Equations with Latent Variables*, New York: Wiley.

Bouckeart, G. and S. van de Walle (2003), 'Comparing measures of citizen trust and user satisfaction as indicators of "good governance": difficulties in linking trust and satisfaction indicators', *International Review of Administrative Science*, **69**(2), 329–43.

Bovaird, T. and E. Löffler (2003), 'Evaluating the quality of public governance: indicators, models and methodologies', *International Review of Administrative Science*, **69**, 313–28.

Braithwaite, J. (2002), *Restorative Justice and Responsive Regulation*, New York: Oxford University Press.

Braithwaite, J. and V. Braithwaite (2001), 'Shame, shame management and regulation', in E. Ahmed, N. Harris. J. Braithwaite and V. Braithwaite (eds.), *Shame Management through Reintegration*, Cambridge: Cambridge University Press, pp. 101–19.

Braithwaite, V. (2007), 'Responsive regulation and taxation: an introduction', *Law and Policy*, **29**(1), 121–39.

Braithwaite, V. (2009), *Defiance in Taxation and Governance: Resisting and Dismissing Authority in a Democracy*, Cheltenham: Edward Elgar Publishing.

Braithwaite, V. (2010), 'Criminal prosecution within responsive regulatory practice', *Criminology and Public Policy*, **9**(3), 85–99.

Braithwaite, V. and M. Reinhart (2000), *The Taxpayers' Charter: Does the Australian Tax Office Comply and Who Benefits?* Canberra: Centre for Tax System Integrity Working Paper No.1, Australian National University.

Brehm, S.S. and J.W. Brehm (1981), *Psychological Reactance: A Theory of Freedom and Control*, New York: Academic Press.

Breusch, T. (2005a), 'The Canadian underground economy: an examination of Giles and Tedds', *Canadian Tax Journal*, **53**(2), 367–91.

Breusch, T. (2005b), *Estimating the Underground Economy Using MIMIC Models*, Working Paper, http://econwpa.wustl.edu/eps/em/papers/0507/0507003.pdf.

Brill, L. (2011), *Women's Participation in the Informal Economy: What Can We Learn from Oxfam's Work?* Manchester: Oxfam.

Bromley, R. (2007), 'Foreword', in J. Cross and A. Morales (eds.), *Street Entrepreneurs: People, Place and Politics in Local and Global Perspective*, London: Routledge, pp. xv–xvii.

Buehn, A. (2012), 'The shadow economy in German regions: an empirical assessment', *German Economic Review*, **13**(3), 275–90.

Buehn, A. and F. Schneider (2012a), 'Corruption and the shadow economy: like oil and vinegar, like water and fire?', *International Tax and Public Finance*, **19**, 172–94.

Buehn, A. and F. Schneider (2012b), 'Shadow economies around the world: novel insights, accepted knowledge, and new estimates', *International Tax and Public Finance*, **19**, 139–71.

Bunting, M. (2004), *Willing Slaves: How the Overwork Culture is Ruling Our Lives*, London: HarperCollins.

Cagan, P. (1958), 'The demand for currency relative to the total money supply', *Journal of Political Economy*, **66**(2), 302–28.

Cassar, A. (2001), 'An index of the underground economy in Malta', *Bank of Valletta Review*, **23**, 44–62.

Castells, M. and A. Portes (1989), 'World underneath: the origins, dynamics and effects of the informal economy', in A. Portes, M. Castells and L.A. Benton (eds.), *The Informal Economy: Studies in Advanced and Less Developing Countries*, Baltimore: Johns Hopkins University Press, pp. 11–39.

Centre for the Study of Democracy (2008), *Levelling the Playing Field in Bulgaria: How Public and Private Institutions Can Partner for Effective Policies Targeting Grey Economy and Corruption*, Sofia: Centre for the Study of Democracy.

Chavdarova, T. (2002), 'The informal economy in Bulgaria: historical background and present situation', in R. Neef and M. Stănculescu (eds.), *The Social Impact of Informal Economies in Eastern Europe*, Aldershot: Ashgate, pp. 56–76.

Chen, M. (2012), *The Informal Economy: Definitions, Theories and Policies*, Manchester: Women in Informal Employment Global and Organising.

Chen, M. (2014), 'Informal employment and development: patterns of inclusion and exclusion', *European Journal of Development Research*, **26**(4), 397–418.

Choi, J. and M. Thum (2004), 'Corruption and the shadow economy', *International Economic Review*, **12**(4), 308–42.

Chong, A. and M. Gradstein (2007), 'Inequality and informality', *Journal of Public Economics*, **91**, 159–79.

Cicero, F.R. and A. Pfadt (2002), 'Investigation of a reinforcement-based toilet training procedure for children with autism', *Research in Developmental Disabilities*, **23**(5), 319–31.

Ciulla, J. (2000), *The Working Life: The Promise and Betrayal of Modern Work*, London: Random House.

Committee Horizontal Monitoring Tax and Customs Administration (2012), *Tax Supervision – Made to Measure: Flexible When Possible, Strict Where Necessary*, www.ifa.nl/Document/Publicaties/ Enhanced% 20Relationship%20Project/tax_supervision_made_to_measure_tz0151z 1fdeng.pdf.

Commonwealth Association of Tax Administrators (2006), *Tax Evasion and Avoidance: Strategies and Initiatives for Tax Administrators*, London: Commonwealth Association of Tax Administrators.

Contini, B. (1981), 'Labor market segmentation and the development of the parallel economy: the Italian experience', *Oxford Economic Papers*, **33**, 401–12.

Cornuel, D. and B. Duriez (1985), 'Local exchange and state intervention', in N. Redclift and E. Mingione (eds.), *Beyond Employment: Household, Gender and Subsistence*, Oxford: Basil Blackwell, pp. 101–35.

Couper, M. (2001), 'Web surveys: a review of issues and approaches', *Public Opinion Quarterly*, **64**, 464–94.

Couper, M. (2008), *Designing Effective Web Surveys*, Cambridge: Cambridge University Press.

Crnkovic-Pozaic, S. (1999), 'Measuring employment in the unofficial economy by using labor market data', in E.L. Feige and K. Ott (eds.), *Underground Economies in Transition: Unrecorded Activity, Tax Evasion, Corruption and Organized Crime*, Aldershot: Ashgate, pp. 120–32.

Cross, J. (2000), 'Street vendors, modernity and postmodernity: conflict and compromise in the global economy', *International Journal of Sociology and Social Policy*, **20**, 29–51.

Cross, J. and A. Morales (2007), 'Introduction: locating street markets in the modern/postmodern world', in J. Cross and A. Morales (eds.), *Street Entrepreneurs: People, Place and Politics in Local and Global Perspective*, London: Routledge, pp. 1–13.

Cullis, J.G. and A. Lewis (1997), 'Why do people pay taxes? From a conventional economic model to a model of social convention', *Journal of Economic Psychology*, **18**(2/3), 305–21.

Cziraky, D. (2004), 'LISREL 8.54: A program for structural equation modelling with latent variables', *Journal of Applied Econometrics*, **19**, 135–41.

Dallago, B. (1990), *The Irregular Economy: The Underground Economy and the Black Labour Market*, Aldershot: Dartmouth.

Davis, M. (2006), *Planet of Slums*, London: Verso.

De Beer, J., K. Fu and S. Wunsch-Vincent (2013), *The Informal Economy, Innovation and Intellectual Property: Concepts, Metrics and Policy Considerations*, Geneva: Economic Research Working Paper No. 10, World Intellectual Property Organization.

De Juan, A., M.A. Lasheras and R. Mayo (1994), 'Voluntary tax compliant behavior of Spanish income taxpayers', *Public Finance*, **49**, 90–105.

De Mel, S., D. McKenzie and C. Woodruff (2012), *The Demand For, and Consequences of, Formalization among Informal Firms in Sri Lanka*, Washington, DC: World Bank Policy Research Working Paper 5991.

De Soto, H. (1989), *The Other Path: The Economic Answer to Terrorism*, London: Harper and Row.

De Soto, H. (2001), *The Mystery of Capital: Why Capitalism Triumphs in the West and Fails Everywhere Else*, London: Black Swan.

Dekker, H., E. Oranje, P. Renooy, F. Rosing and C.C. Williams (2010), *Joining Up the Fight against Undeclared Work in the European Union*, Brussels: DG Employment, Social Affairs and Equal Opportunities.

Del Boca, D. (1981), 'Parallel economy and allocation of time', *Micros (Quarterly Journal of Microeconomics)*, **4**(1), 13–18.

Del Boca, D. and F. Forte (1982), 'Recent empirical surveys and theoretical interpretations of the parallel economy in Italy', in V. Tanzi (ed.), *The Underground Economy in the United States and Abroad*, Lexington MA: Lexington Books, pp. 160–78.

Dell'Anno, R. (2003), *Estimating the Shadow Economy in Italy: A Structural Equation Approach*, Aarhus: Working Paper 2003-7, Department of Economics, University of Aarhus.

Dell'Anno, R. and F. Schneider (2003), 'The shadow economy of Italy and other OECD countries: what do we know?', *Journal of Public Finance and Public Choice*, **21**, 223–45.

Dell'Anno, R. and F. Schneider (2004), *The Shadow Economy of Italy and Other OECD Countries: What Do We Know?* Linz: Discussion Paper, Department of Economics, University of Linz.

Dell'Anno, R. and F. Schneider (2009), 'A complex approach to estimate shadow economy: the structural equation modelling', in M. Faggnini and T. Looks (eds.), *Coping with the Complexity of Economics*, Berlin: Springer, pp. 110–30.

Dellot, B. (2012), *Untapped Enterprise: Learning to Live with the Informal Economy*, London: Royal Society of the Arts.

Denzau, A.T. and D. North (1994), 'Shared mental models: ideologies and institutions', *Kyklos*, **47**, 3–30.

Devas, N. and R. Kelly (2001), 'Regulation or revenue? An analysis of local business licenses, with a case study of the single business permit reform in Kenya', *Public Administration and Development*, **21**, 381–91.

Dibben, P. and C.C. Williams (2012), 'Varieties of capitalism and employment relations: informally dominated market economies', *Industrial Relations: A Review of Economy and Society*, **51**(S1), 563–82.

Dillman, D., J. Smith and L.M. Christian (2009), *Internet, Mail and Mixed-Mode Surveys*, London: Wiley.

Dilnot, A. and C.N. Morris (1981), 'What do we know about the black economy?', *Fiscal Studies*, **2**(1), 58–73.

Dong, B., U. Dulleck and B. Torgler (2012), 'Conditional corruption', *Journal of Economic Psychology*, **33**, 609–27.

Dreher, A. and F. Schneider (2010), 'Corruption and the shadow economy: an empirical analysis', *Public Choice*, **144**, 215–38.

Dreher, A., C. Kotsogiannis and S. McCorriston (2009), 'How do institutions affect corruption and the shadow economy?', *International Tax and Public Finance*, **16**, 773–96.

du Gay, P. (2000), *In Praise of Bureaucracy*, London: Sage.

du Gay, P. (2005), 'The values of bureaucracy: an introduction', in P. du Gay (ed.), *The Values of Bureaucracy*, Oxford: Oxford University Press, pp. 1–19.

Dubin, J. and L. Wilde (1988), 'An empirical analysis of federal income tax auditing and compliance', *National Tax Journal*, **16**, 61–74.

Dubin, J., M. Graetz and L. Wilde (1987), 'Are we a nation of tax cheaters? New econometric evidence on tax compliance', *The America Economic Review*, **77**, 240–45.

Durham, Y., T.S. Manly and C. Ritsema (2014), 'The effects of income source, context, and income level on tax compliance decisions in a dynamic experiment', *Journal of Economic Psychology*, **40**, 220–32.

Dwenger, N., H. Kleven, I. Rasul and J. Rincke (2014), 'Extrinsic and intrinsic motivations for tax compliance: evidence from a field experiment in Germany', www2.warwick.ac.uk/fac/soc/economics/news_events/calendar/henrik_kleven.pdf.

Elffers, H., R.H. Weigel and D.J. Hessing (1987), 'The consequences of different strategies for measuring tax evasion behaviour', *Journal of Economic Psychology*, **8**, 311–37.

Enste, D. (2010), 'Who is working illicitly and why? Insights from representative survey data in Germany', in F. Schneider (ed.), *Handbook on the Shadow Economy*, Cheltenham: Edward Elgar Publishing, pp. 324–45.

Enste, D. and F. Schneider (2006), 'Umfang und Entwicklung der

Schattenwirtschaft in 145 Ländern', in F. Schneider and D. Enste (eds.), *Jahrbuch Schattenwirtschaft 2006/07. Zum Spannungsfeld von Poltik und Ökonomie*, Berlin: LIT Verlag, pp. 55–80.

Erard, B. and J.S. Feinstein (1994), 'Honesty and evasion in the tax compliance game', *Rand Journal of Economics*, **25**(1), 1–20.

Eriksen, K. and L. Fallan (1996), 'Tax knowledge and attitudes towards taxation: a report on a quasi-experiment', *Journal of Economic Psychology*, **17**, 387–402.

Estonian Institute of Economic Research (2012), *Varimajandus Eestis 2011: elanike hinnangute alusel*, Tallinn: Estonian Institute of Economic Research.

Etzioni, A. (1961), *A Comparative Analysis of Complex Organisations*, New York: Free Press.

Eurofound (2013), *Tackling Undeclared Work in 27 European Union Member States and Norway: Approaches and Measures since 2008*, Dublin: Eurofound.

European Commission (1998), *Communication of the Commission on Undeclared Work*, http://europa.eu.int/comm/employment_social/empl_esf/docs/com98-219_en.pdf.

European Commission (2007a), *Special Eurobarometer 284: Undeclared Work in the European Union*, Brussels: European Commission.

European Commission (2007b), *Stepping up the Fight against Undeclared Work*, Brussels: European Commission.

European Commission (2011), *Employment and Social Developments in Europe 2011*, Brussels: European Commission.

European Commission (2013), *Employment and Social Developments in Europe 2013*, Brussels: European Commission.

European Commission (2014), *Special Eurobarometer 402: Undeclared Work*, Brussels: European Commission.

Eurostat (2007), *Taxation Trends in the European Union: Data for the EU Member States and Norway*, Brussels: Eurostat.

Eurostat (2010), *Taxation Trends in the European Union: Main Results*, Brussels: Eurostat.

Eurostat (2013a), 'GDP per capita in PPS', http://epp.eurostat.ec.europa.eu/tgm/table.do?tab=table&init=1&plugin=1&language=en&pcode=tec00114.

Eurostat (2013b), 'At risk of poverty rate by sex', http://epp.eurostat.ec.europa.eu/tgm/table.do?tab=table&init=1&plugin=1&language=en&pcode=tsdsc260.

Eurostat (2013c), 'Inequality of income distribution', http://epp.eurostat.ec.europa.eu/tgm/table.do?tab=table&init=1&plugin=1&language=en&pcode=tessi010.

Evans, M., S. Syrett and C.C. Williams (2006), *Informal Economic Activities and Deprived Neighbourhoods*, London: Department of Communities and Local Government.

Fehr, E. and B. Rokenbach (2003), 'Detrimental effects of sanctions on human altruism', *Nature*, **422**, 137–40.

Feige, E.L. (1986), 'A re-examination of the underground economy in the United States', *IMF Staff Papers*, **33**(4), 768–81.

Feige, E.L. (1996), 'Overseas holdings of US currency and the underground economy', in S. Pozo (ed.), *Exploring the Underground Economy*, Kalamazoo, MI: W.E. Upjohn Institute for Employment Research, Kalamazoo, pp. 5–62.

Feld, L.P. and B. Frey (2002), 'Trust breeds trust: how taxpayers are treated', *Economics of Government*, **3**(2), 87–99.

Feld, L.P. and B.S. Frey (2007), 'Tax compliance as the result of a psychological tax contract: the role of incentives and responsive regulation', *Law and Policy*, **29**, 102–20.

Feld, L.P. and C. Larsen (2005), *Black Activities in Germany in 2001 and 2004: A Comparison Based on Survey Data*, Copenhagen: Study No. 12, Rockwool Foundation Research Unit.

Feld, L.P. and C. Larsen (2008), 'Black activities low in Germany in 2006', *News from the Rockwool Foundation Research Unit*, March, 1–12.

Feld, L.P. and C. Larsen (2009), *Undeclared Work in Germany 2001–2007: Impact of Deterrence, Tax Policy, and Social Norms: An Analysis Based on Survey Data*, Berlin: Springer.

Feld, L.P. and C. Larsen (2012), *Undeclared Work, Deterrence and Social Norms: The Case of Germany*, Berlin: Springer Verlag.

Feld, L.P. and F. Schneider (2010), 'Survey on the shadow economy and undeclared earnings in OECD countries', *German Economic Review*, **11**(2), 109–49.

Feld, L.P., A. Schmidt and F. Schneider (2007), *Tax Evasion, Black Activities and Deterrence in Germany: An Institutional and Empirical Perspective*, Heidelberg: Department of Economics Discussion Paper, University of Heidelberg.

Fernandez-Kelly, P. (2006), 'Introduction', in P. Fernandez-Kelly and J. Shefner (eds.), *Out of the Shadows: Political Action and the Informal Economy in Latin America*, Pennsylvania: Pennsylvania State University Press, pp. 1–18.

Flaming, D., B. Haydamack and P. Joassart (2005), *Hopeful Workers, Marginal Jobs: LA's Off-the-Books Labor Force*, Los Angeles: Economic Roundtable.

Folmer, H. and A. Karmann (1992), 'The permanent income

hypothesis revisited – a dynamic LISREL approach', *Methods of Operations Research*, **64**(3), 355–9.

Fortin, B., G. Garneau, G. Lacroix, T. Lemieux and C. Montmarquette (1996), *L'Economie Souterraine au Quebec: mythes et realites*, Laval: Presses de l'Universite Laval.

Franck, A.K. (2012), 'Factors motivating women's informal micro-entrepreneurship: experiences from Penang, Malaysia', *International Journal of Gender and Entrepreneurship*, **4**(1), 65–78.

Franck, A.K. and J. Olsson (2014), 'Missing women? The under-recording and under-reporting of women's work in Malaysia', *International Labour Review*, **153**(2), 209–21.

Franz, A. (1983), 'Wie groß ist die "schwarze" Wirtschaft?', *Mitteilungsblatt der Österreichischen Statistischen Gesellschaft*, **49**, 1–6.

Frey, B.S. and W. Pommerehne (1984), 'The hidden economy: state and prospect for measurement', *Review of Income and Wealth*, **30**(1), 1–23.

Frey, B.S. and B. Torgler (2007), 'Tax morale and conditional cooperation', *Journal of Comparative Economics*, **35**, 136–59.

Frey, B.S. and H. Weck (1983a), 'Bureaucracy and the shadow economy: a macro-approach', in H. Hanusch (ed.), *Anatomy of Government Deficiencies*, Berlin: Springer, pp. 89–109.

Frey, B.S. and H. Weck (1983b), 'Estimating the shadow economy: a "naïve" approach', *Oxford Economic Papers*, **35**(1), 23–44.

Frey, B.S. and H. Weck-Hannemann (1984), 'The hidden economy as an "unobserved" variable', *European Economic Review*, **26**, 33–53.

Frey, B.S., H. Weck and W.W. Pommerehne (1982), 'Has the shadow economy grown in Germany? An exploratory study', *Weltwirtschaftliches Archiv*, **118**, 499–524.

Friedland, N. (1982), 'A note on tax evasion as a function of the quality of information about the magnitude and credibility of threatened fines: some preliminary research', *Journal of Applied Social Psychology*, **12**, 54–9.

Friedland, N., Maital, S. and Rutenberg, A. (1978), 'A simulation study of income tax evasion', *Journal of Public Economics*, **10**, 107–16.

Friedman, E., S. Johnson, D. Kaufmann and P. Zoido (2000), 'Dodging the grabbing hand: the determinants of unofficial activity in 69 countries', *Journal of Public Economics*, **76**(3), 459–93.

Fries, S., T. Lysenko and S. Polanec (2003), *The 2002 Business Environment and Enterprise Performance Survey: Results from a Survey of 6,100 Firms*, EBRD Working Paper No. 84, www.ebrd.com/pubs/find/index.html.

Gallin, D. (2001), 'Propositions on trade unions and informal employment in a time of globalisation', *Antipode*, **19**(4), 531–49.

Gangl, K., E. Hofmann, M. Pollai and E. Kirchler (2012), *The Dynamics of Power and Trust in the 'Slippery Slope Framework' and its Impact on the Tax Climate*, http://papers/.ssrn.com/sol3/papers.cfm?abstract_id=2024946.

Gangl, K., S. Muehlbacher, M. de Groot, S. Goslinga, E. Hofmann, C. Kogler, G. Antonides and E. Kirchler (2013), '"How can I help you?" Perceived service orientation of tax authorities and tax compliance', *Public Finance Analysis*, **69**(4), 487–510.

Garcia, G. (1978), 'The currency ratio and the subterranean economy', *Financial Analysts Journal*, **69**, 64–6.

Garcia-Bolivar, O. (2006), *Informal Economy: Is it a Problem, a Solution or Both? The Perspective of the Informal Business*, Berkeley, CA: Paper 1065, Bepress Legal Series.

Gaviria, A. (2002), 'Assessing the effects of corruption and crime on firm performance: evidence from Latin America', *Emerging Markets Review*, **3**, 245–68.

Geertz, C. (1963), *Old Societies and New States: The Quest for Modernity in Asia and Africa*, Glencoe, IL: Free Press.

Gemma-Martinez, B. (2011), 'The role of good governance in the tax systems of the European Union', *Bulletin for International Taxation*, **63**, 370–79.

Gerxhani, K. (2004), 'The informal sector in developed and less developed countries: a literature survey', *Public Choice*, **120**, 267–300.

Ghinararu, C. (2007), *Undeclared Work in Romania*, www.eu-employment-observatory.net/resources/reports/RomaniaUDW2007.pdf.

Gilbert, A. (1998), *The Latin American City*, London: Latin American Bureau.

Giles, D.E.A. (1997a), 'Causality between the measured and underground economies in New Zealand', *Applied Economics Letters*, **4**, 63–7.

Giles, D.E.A. (1997b), 'Testing the asymmetry in the measured and underground business cycles in New Zealand', *Economic Record*, **71**, 225–32.

Giles, D.E.A. (1999a), 'Measuring the hidden economy: implications for econometric modelling', *Economic Journal*, **109**(3), 370–80.

Giles, D.E.A. (1999b), 'Modeling the hidden economy in the tax-gap in New Zealand', *Empirical Economics*, **24**(3), 621–40.

Giles, D.E.A. (1999c), 'The rise and fall of the New Zealand underground economy: are the reasons symmetric?', *Applied Economics Letters*, **6**(2), 185–9.

Giles, D.E.A. and L.M. Tedds (2002), *Taxes and the Canadian Underground Economy*, Toronto: Canadian Tax Paper 106, Canadian Tax Foundation.

Giles, D.E.A., L.M. Tedds and W. Gugsa (2002), 'The Canadian underground and measured economies', *Applied Economics*, **34**, 2347–52.

Glautier, S. (2004), 'Measures and models of nicotine dependence: positive reinforcement', *Addiction*, **99**(1), 30–50.

Gouweneel, J. and P. Knottnerus (2008), *Steekproeftheorie; Deelthema: Herhaald wegen. Statistische Methoden (08006)*, The Hague: Statistics Netherlands.

Grabiner, Lord (2000), *The Informal Economy*, London: HM Treasury.

Grabosky, P. (2013), 'Beyond responsive regulation: the expanding role of non-state actors in the regulatory process', *Regulation and Governance*, **7**, 114–23.

Gramsick, H. and R. Bursik (1990), 'Conscience, significant others and rational choice: extending the deterrence model', *Law and Society Review*, **24**, 837–61.

Grant, R. (2013), 'Gendered spaces of informal entrepreneurship in Soweto, South Africa', *Urban Geography*, **34**(1), 86–108.

Grey, C. (2005), *A Very Short, Fairly Interesting and Reasonably Cheap Book about Studying Organizations*, London: Sage.

Guest, D. (1987), 'Human resource management and industrial relations', *Journal of Management Studies*, **27**(4), 377–97.

Gurtoo, A. and C.C. Williams (2009), 'Entrepreneurship and the informal sector: some lessons from India', *International Journal of Entrepreneurship and Innovation*, **10**(1), 55–62.

Gutmann, P.M. (1977), 'The subterranean economy', *Financial Analysts Journal*, **34**(1), 24–7.

Hall, P. and D. Soskice (eds.) (2001), *Varieties of Capitalism: The Institutional Foundations of Comparative Advantage*, Oxford: Oxford University Press.

Hanousek, J. and F. Palda (2003), 'Why people evade taxes in the Czech and Slovak Republics: a tale of twins', in B. Belev (ed.), *The Informal Economy in the EU Accession Countries*, Sofia: Center for the Study of Democracy, pp. 19–42.

Harriss-White, B. (2014), 'Labour and petty production', *Development and Change*, **45**(5), 981–1000.

Hartner, M., S. Rechberger, E. Kirchler and A. Schabmann (2008), 'Procedural justice and tax compliance', *Economic Analysis and Policy*, **38**(1), 137–52.

Hartner, M., S. Rechberger, E. Kirchler and M. Wenzel (2011), 'Perceived distributive fairness of EU transfer payments, outcome favourability, identity and EU-tax compliance', *Law and Policy*, **33**(1), 22–31.

Hashimzade, N., G.D. Myles and B. Tran-Nam (2013), 'Applications of behavioural economics to tax evasion', *Journal of Economic Surveys*, **27**(5), 941–77.

Hasseldine, J. and Z. Li (1999), 'More tax evasion research required in new millennium', *Crime, Law and Social Change*, **31**(1), 91–104.

Heintzman, R. and B. Marson (2005), 'People, service and trust: is there a public service chain?', *International Review of Administrative Science*, **71**, 549–75.

Helberger, C. and H. Knepel (1988), 'How big is the shadow economy? A re-analysis of the unobserved-variable approach of B.S. Frey and H. Weck-Hannemann', *European Economic Review*, **32**(4), 965–76.

Helberger, C. and J. Schwarze (1986), *Umfang und struktur der nebenerwerbstatigkeit in der Bundesrepublik Deutschland*, Berlin: Mitteilungen aus der Arbeits-market- und Berufsforschung.

Helmke, G. and S. Levitsky (2004), 'Informal institutions and comparative politics: a research agenda', *Perspectives on Politics*, **2**(6), 725–40.

Hibbs, D.A. and V. Piculescu (2005), *Institutions, Corruption and Tax Evasion in the Unofficial Economy*, Göteborg: Department of Economics.

Hill, R. and M. Kabir (1996), 'Tax rates, the tax mix, and the growth of the underground economy in Canada: what can we infer?', *Canadian Tax Journal/Revue Fiscale Canadienne*, **44**, 1552–83.

Hindriks, J., A. Muthoo and M. Keen (1999), 'Corruption, extortion and evasion', *Journal of Public Economics*, **74**, 395–430.

Hite, P. (1989), 'A positive approach to taxpayer compliance', *Public Finance/Finances Publiques*, **44**, 249–67.

Houbiers, M., P. Knottnerus, A.H. Kroese, R.H. Renssen and V. Snijders (2003), *Estimating Consistent Table Sets: Position Paper on Repeated Weighting*, Hague: Discussion Paper 03005, Statistics Netherlands.

Howe, L. (1988), 'Unemployment, doing the double and local labour markets in Belfast', in C. Cartin and T. Wilson (eds.), *Ireland from Below: Social Change and Local Communities in Modern Ireland*, Dublin: Gill and Macmillan, pp. 41–59.

Howe, L. (1990), *Being Unemployed in Northern Ireland: An Ethnographic Study*, Cambridge: Cambridge University Press.

Hudson, R. (2005), *Economic Geographies: Circuits, Flows and Spaces*, London: Sage.

Hussmanns, R. (2005), *Measuring the Informal Economy: From Employment in the Informal Sector to Informal Employment*, Geneva: ILO Policy Integration Department/Bureau of Statistics, Working Paper No. 53.

IfD Allensbach (1975), *Studie im Auftrag der Kommission für Wirtschaftlichen und Sozialen Wandel*, Bodensee: Allensbach.

Ignjatović, M. (2007), *Undeclared Work in Slovenia*, www.eu-employment-observatory.net/resources/reports/SloveniaUDW2007.pdf.

Ihrig, J. and K.S. Moe (2000), 'The influence of government policies on informal labor: implications for long-run growth', *De Economist*, **148**(3), 3.

ILO (2002a), *Decent Work and the Informal Economy*, Geneva: International Labour Office.

ILO (2002b), *Women and Men in the Informal Economy: A Statistical Picture*, Geneva: International Labour Office.

ILO (2011), *Statistical Update on Employment in the Informal Economy*, Geneva: International Labour Office Department of Statistics.

ILO (2012), *Statistical Update on Employment in the Informal Economy*, Geneva: International Labour Office Department of Statistics.

ILO (2013), *Women and Men in the Informal Economy: Statistical Picture*, http://laborsta.ilo.org/informal_economy_E.html.

ILO (2014), *Transitioning from the Informal to the Formal Economy*, Report V(1), International Labour Conference, 103rd Session, Geneva: International Labour Office.

ILO (2015), *Transitioning from the Informal to the Formal Economy*. Report V(1), International Labour Conference, 104th Session, Geneva: International Labour Office.

Internal Revenue Service (2007), 'Understanding taxes', www.irs.gov/app/understandingTaxes/jsp.

Isachsen, A.J. and S. Strom (1985), 'The size and growth of the hidden economy in Norway', *Review of Income and Wealth*, **31**(1), 21–38.

Isachsen, A.J. and S. Strom (1989), 'The underground economy in Norway with special emphasis on the hidden labor market', in E.L. Feige (ed.), *The Underground Economies: Tax Evasion and Information Distortion*, Cambridge: Cambridge University Press, pp. 141–59.

Isachsen, A.J., J. Klovland and S. Strom (1982), 'The hidden economy in Norway', in V. Tanzi (ed.), *The Underground Economy in the United States and Abroad*, Lexington, MA: DC Heath Lexington Books, pp. 209–31.

Jaramillo, M. (2009), *Is There Demand for Formality Among Informal Firms? Evidence from Microfirms in Downtown Lima*, German Development Institute Discussion Paper 12/2009, Bonn: German Development Institute.

Jensen, L., G.T. Cornwell and J.L. Findeis (1995), 'Informal work in non-metropolitan Pennsylvania', *Rural Sociology*, **60**(1), 91–107.

Jibao, S., and W. Prichard (2013), *Rebuilding Local Government Finances After Conflict: The Political Economy of Property Taxation in Post-Conflict Sierra Leone*, Brighton: Institute of Development Studies, ICTD Working Paper 12.

Job, J. and D. Honaker (2002), 'Short term experience with responsive regulation in the Australian Tax Office', in V. Braithwaite (ed.), *Taxing*

Democracy: Understanding Tax Avoidance and Tax Evasion, Aldershot: Ashgate, pp. 111–30.

Job, J., A. Stout and R. Smith (2007), 'Culture change in three taxation administrations: from command and control to responsive regulation', *Law and Policy*, **29**(1), 84–101.

Johnson, S., D. Kaufmann and A. Shleifer (1997), 'The unofficial economy in transition', *Brookings Papers on Economic Activity*, **2**, 159–239.

Johnson, S., D. Kaufmann and P. Zoido-Lobatón (1998a), 'Regulatory discretion and the unofficial economy', *The American Economic Review*, **88**(2), 387–92.

Johnson, S., D. Kaufmann and P. Zoido-Lobatón (1998b), *Corruption, Public Finances and the Unofficial Economy*, Washington, DC: World Bank Policy Research Working Paper Series No. 2169.

Jones, T., M. Ram and P. Edwards (2004), 'Illegal immigrants and the informal economy: worker and employer experiences in the Asian underground economy', *International Journal of Economic Development*, **6**(1), 92–106.

Jönsson, H. (2001), *Undeclared Work in Sweden: Results and Recommendations*, paper presented at the European Scientific Workshop on 'The Shadow Economy: Empirical Evidence and New Policy Issues at the European Level', Ragusa, Sicily, 20–21 September.

Jöreskog, K.G. and D. Sörbom (2001), *LISREL 8: User's Reference Guide*, Lincolnwood: Scientific Software International.

Jütting, J.P. and J.R. Laiglesia (2009), 'Employment, poverty reduction and development: what's new?', in J.P. Jütting and J.R. Laiglesia (eds.), *Is Informal Normal? Towards More and Better Jobs in Developing Countries*, Paris, OECD, pp. 142–65.

Kagan, R.A. and J.T. Scholz (1984), 'The criminology of the corporation and regulatory enforcement strategies', in K. Hawkins and J.M. Thomas (eds.), *Enforcing Regulation*, Boston: Klewer-Nijhoff, pp. 62–84.

Karjanen, D. (2014), 'When is an illicit taxi driver more than a taxi driver? Case studies from transit and trucking in post-socialist Slovakia', in J. Morris and A. Polese (eds.), *The Informal Post-Socialist Economy: Embedded Practices and Livelihoods*, London: Routledge, pp. 102–17.

Karlinger, L. (2013), 'The "dark side" of deregulation: how competition affects the size of the shadow economy', *Journal of Public Economic Theory*, **16**(2), 283–321.

Karmann, A. (1986), 'Monetäre Ansätze zur Erfassung der Schattenwirtschaft: Ein Vergleich verschiedener Messansätze', *Kredit und Kapitel*, **19**, 233–47.

Karmann, A. (1990), 'Schattenwirtschaft und ihre Ursachen: Eine empirische Analyse zur Schwarzwirtschaft und Selbstversorgung in der Bundesrepublik Deutschland', *Zeitschrift für Wirtschafts- und Sozialwissenschaften*, **110**, 185–206.

Karpuskiene, V. (2007), *Undeclared Work, Tax Evasion and Avoidance in Lithuania*, paper presented at colloquium of the Belgian Federal Service for Social Security on 'Undeclared Work, Tax Evasion and Avoidance', Brussels, June.

Kastlunger, B., E. Lozza, E. Kirchler and A. Schabmann (2013), 'Powerful authorities and trusting citizens: the slippery slope framework and tax compliance in Italy', *Journal of Economic Psychology*, **34**(1), 36–45.

Katsios, S. (2006), 'The shadow economy and corruption in Greece, South-Eastern Europe', *Journal of Economics*, **1**, 61–80.

Katungi, D., E. Neale and A. Barbour (2006), *People in Low-Paid Informal Work*, York: Joseph Rowntree Foundation.

Kaufmann, D. and A. Kaliberda (1996), 'Integrating the unofficial economy into the dynamics of post socialist economies: a framework of analyses and evidence', in B. Kaminski (ed.), *Economic Transition in Russia and the New States of Eurasia*, London: M.E. Sharpe, pp. 81–120.

Kazemier, B. (2006), 'Monitoring the underground economy: a survey of methods and estimates', in F. Schneider and D. Enste (eds.), *Jahrbuch Schattenwirtschaft 2006/07. Zum Spannungsfeld von Politik und Ökonomie*, Berlin: LIT Verlag, pp. 11–53.

Kazemier, B. (2014), 'Hidden workers and the hidden worker potential in the Netherlands', *Economic Analysis and Policy*, **44**(1), pp. 39–50.

Kazemier, B. and R. van Eck (1992), 'Survey investigations of the hidden economy: some methodological results', *Journal of Economic Psychology*, **13**, 569–87.

Kempson, E. (1996), *Life on a Low Income*, York: York Publishing Services.

Kerr, C., J. Dunlop, F. Harbison and C. Meyers (1973), *Industrialism and Industrial Man*, Harmondsworth: Penguin.

Kesteloot, C. and H. Meert (1999), 'Informal spaces: the geography of informal economic activities in Brussels', *International Journal of Urban and Regional Research*, **23**(2), 232–51.

Ketchen, D.J., R.D. Ireland and J.W. Webb (2014), 'Towards a research agenda for the informal economy: a survey of the *Strategic Entrepreneurship Journal*'s editorial board', *Strategic Entrepreneurship Journal*, **8**(1), 95–100.

Khurana, P. and U. Diwan (2014), 'A comparison of psychological factors for tax compliance: self-employed versus salaried people', *International Journal in Management and Social Science*, **2**(3), 107–24.

Kim, B.-Y. (2005), 'Poverty and informal economy participation: evidence from Romania', *Economics of Transition*, **13**(1), 163–85.

Kinsey, K. and H. Gramsick (1993), 'Did the tax reform act of 1986 improve compliance? Three studies of pre- and post-TRA compliance attitudes', *Law and Policy*, **15**, 239–325.

Kirchgässner, G. (1983), 'Size and development of the West German shadow economy, 1955–1980', *Zeitschrift für die Gesamte Staatswissenschaft*, **139**, 197–214.

Kirchgässner, G. (1984), 'Verfahren zur Erfassung des in der Schattenwirtschaft erarbeiteten Sozialprodukts', *Allgemeines Statistisches Archiv*, **68**, 378–405.

Kirchgässner, G. (2010), *Tax Morale, Tax Evasion and the Shadow Economy*, St Gallen: Discussion Paper No. 2010-17, Department of Economics, University of St Gallen.

Kirchgässner, G. (2011), 'Tax morale, tax evasion and the shadow economy', in F. Schneider (ed.), *Handbook of the Shadow Economy*, Cheltenham: Edward Elgar Publishing, pp. 347–74.

Kirchler, E. (1997), 'The burden of new taxes: acceptance of taxes as a function of affectedness and egoistic versus altruistic orientation', *Journal of Socio-Economics*, **26**, 421–36.

Kirchler, E. (1998), 'Differential representations of taxes: analysis of free associations and judgments of five employment groups', *Journal of Socio-Economics*, **27**, 117–31.

Kirchler, E. (1999), 'Reactance to taxation: employers' attitudes towards taxes', *Journal of Socio-Economics*, **28**, 131–8.

Kirchler, E. (2007), *The Economic Psychology of Tax Behaviour*, Cambridge: Cambridge University Press.

Kirchler, E., E. Hoelzl and I. Wahl (2008), 'Enforced versus voluntary tax compliance: the "slippery slope" framework', *Journal of Economic Psychology*, **29**(2), 210–25.

Kistruck, G.M., J.W. Webb, C.J. Sutter and A.V.G. Bailey (2015), 'The double-edged sword of legitimacy in base-of-the-pyramid markets', *Journal of Business Venturing*, **30**(3), 436–51.

Klepper, S. and D. Nagin (1989), 'Tax compliance and perceptions of the risks of detection and criminal prosecution', *Law and Society Review*, **23**, 209–40.

Kleven, H.J., M.B. Knudsen, C.T. Kreiner, S. Pedersen and E. Saez (2011), 'Unwilling or unable to cheat? Evidence from a tax audit experiment in Denmark', *Econometrica*, **79**, 651–92.

Klovland, J. (1984), 'Tax evasion and the demand for currency in Norway and Sweden: is there a hidden relationship?', *Scandinavian Journal of Economics*, **86**(3), 423–39.

Knottnerus, P. and C. van Duin (2006), 'Variances in repeated weighting with an application to the Dutch Labour Force Survey', *Journal of Official Statistics*, **22**, 565–84.

Kogler, C., L. Batrancea, A. Nichita, J, Pantya, A. Belianin and E. Kirchler, E. (2013), 'Trust and power as determinants of tax compliance: testing the assumptions of the slippery slope framework in Austria, Hungary, Romania and Russia', *Journal of Economic Psychology*, **34**, 169–80.

Kogler, C., S. Muelbacher and E. Kirchler (2015), 'Testing the "slippery slope framework" among self-employed taxpayers', *Economics of Governance*, **16**(2), 125–42.

Korsun, G. and P. Meagher (2004), 'Failure by design? Fiscal decentralization in West Africa', in M. Kimenyi and P. Meagher (eds.), *Devolution and Development: Governance Prospects in Decentralizing States*, Aldershot: Ashgate, pp. 137–55.

Kovács, B. (2014), 'Nannies and informality in Romanian local childcare markets', in J. Morris and A. Polese (eds.), *The Informal Post-Socialist Economy: Embedded Practices and Livelihoods*, London: Routledge, pp. 67–84.

Krumplyte, J. (2010), *Analysis of Undeclared Work: The Lithuanian Case*, proceedings of the 6th International Scientific Conference on Business and Management, 13–14 May, Vilnius, www.vgtu.lt/en/editions/ proceedings.

Kuehn, Z. (2007), *Tax Rates, Governance and the Informal Economy in High-Income Countries*, Madrid: Universidad Carolos III de Madrid, Economic Series Working Paper No. 07-85.

Kuehn, Z. (2014), 'Tax rates, governance and the informal economy in high-income countries', *Economic Inquiry*, **52**(1), 405–30.

Kuznets, S. (1962), 'How to judge quality', *The New Republic*, 20 October, 13–15.

La Porta, R. and A. Shleifer (2008), 'The unofficial economy and economic development', *Brookings Papers on Economic Activity*, **47**(1), 123–35.

La Porta, R. and A. Shleifer (2014), 'Informality and development', *Journal of Economic Perspectives*, **28**(3), 109–26.

Lackó, M. (1996), *Hidden Economy in East-European Countries in International Comparison*, Luxembourg: Working Paper, International Institute for Applied Systems Analysis.

Lackó, M. (1998), 'The hidden economies of Visegrad countries in international comparison: a household electricity approach', in L. Halpern and Ch. Wyplosz (Eds.), *Hungary: Towards a Market Economy*, Cambridge: Cambridge University Press, pp. 128–48.

Lackó, M. (1999), 'Electricity intensity and the unrecorded economy in post-socialist countries', in E. Feige and K. Ott (eds.), *Underground Economies in Transition*, Aldershot: Ashgate, pp. 102–42.

Lackó, M. (2000a), 'Do power consumption data tell the story? Electricity intensity and hidden economy in post-socialist countries', in E. Maskin and A. Simonovits (eds.), *Planning, Shortage and Transformation: Essays in Honor of Janos Kornai*, Cambridge, MA: MIT Press, pp. 43–60.

Lackó, M. (2000b), 'Hidden economy – an unknown quantity? Comparative analysis of hidden economies in transition economies, 1989–95', *Economics of Transition*, **8**(1), 117–49.

Lago Peñas, I. and S. Lago Peñas (2010), 'The determinants of tax morale in comparative perspective: evidence from European countries', *European Journal of Political Economy*, **26**(4), 441–53.

Lane, J.-E. (2000), *New Public Management*, London: Routledge.

Langfeldt, E. (1984), 'The unobserved economy in the Federal Republic of Germany', in E.L. Feige (ed.), *The Unobserved Economy*, Cambridge: Cambridge University Press, pp. 236–60.

Langsten, R. and R. Salen (2008), 'Two approaches to measuring women's work in developing countries: a comparison of survey data from Egypt', *Population and Development Review*, **34**(2), pp. 283–305.

Lazaridis, G. and M. Koumandraki (2003), 'Survival ethnic entrepreneurs in Greece: a mosaic of informal and formal business activities', *Sociological Research On-Line*, www.socresonline.org.uk/8/2/lazaridis.html.

Legge, K. (1989), 'Human resource management: a critical analysis', in J. Storey (ed.), *New Perspectives in Human Resource Management*, London: Routledge, pp. 29–52.

Legge, K. (1995), *Human Resource Management: Rhetorics and Realities*, Basingstoke: Macmillan.

Lemieux, T., B. Fortin and P. Frechette (1994), 'The effect of taxes on labor supply in the underground economy', *American Economic Review*, **84**(1), 231–54.

Leonard, M. (1994), *Informal Economic Activity in Belfast*, Aldershot: Avebury.

Leonard, M. (1998), *Invisible Work, Invisible Workers: The Informal Economy in Europe and the US*, London: Macmillan.

Lessing, V.P. and C.W. Park (1978), 'Promotional perspectives of reference group influence: advertising implications', *Journal of Advertising*, **7**(2), 41–7.

Leth-Petersen, S. and P. Ebbesen Skow (2014), *Does the Marginal Tax Rate Affect Activity in the Informal Sector?* Copenhagen: Rockwool Foundation Research Unit Study Paper No. 64.

Leventhal, G.S. (1980), 'What should be done with equity theory? New approaches to the study of fairness in social relationships', in K. Gergen, M. Greenberg and R. Willis (eds.), *Social Exchange: Advances in Theory and Research*, New York: Plenum Press, pp. 27–55.

Lewis, A. (1959), *The Theory of Economic Growth*, London: Allen and Unwin.

Lewis, A. (1982), *The Psychology of Taxation*, Oxford: Martin Robertson.

Li, S.X., C.C. Eckel, P.J. Grossman and T.L. Brown (2011), 'Giving to government: voluntary taxation in the lab', *Journal of Public Economics*, **95**, 1190–201.

Lillemets, K. (2009), 'Maksumoraal maksukäitumise kujundajana ja selle peamised isikupõhised mõjutegurid', www.riigikogu.ee/rito/index. php?id=14002&op=archive2.

Lin, J. (1995), 'Polarized development and urban change in New York's Chinatown', *Urban Affairs Review*, **30**(3), 332–54.

Lippert, O. and M. Walker (eds.) (1997), *The Underground Economy: Global Evidence of its Size and Impact*, Vancouver, BC: The Frazer Institute.

Lisi, G. (2012), 'Testing the slippery slope framework', *Economic Bulletin*, **32**, 1369–77.

Lizzeri, C. (1979), *Mezzogiorno in Controluce*, Naples: Enel.

Llanes, M. and A. Barbour (2007), *Self-Employed and Micro-Entrepreneurs: Informal Trading and the Journey Towards Formalization*, London: Community Links.

Lobo, F.M. (1990), 'Irregular work in Spain', in *Underground Economy and Irregular Forms of Employment*, *Final Synthesis Report*, Brussels: Office for Official Publications of the European Communities.

London, T. and S.L. Hart (2004), 'Reinventing strategies for emerging markets: beyond the transnational model', *Journal of International Business Studies*, **35**(5), 350–70.

London, T., H. Esper, A. Grogan-Taylor and G.M. Kistruck (2014), 'Connecting poverty to purchase in informal markets', *Strategic Entrepreneurship Journal*, **8**(1), 37–55.

Long, J.S. (1983a), *Confirmatory Factor Analysis*, London: Sage.

Long, J.S. (1983b), *Covariance Structure Models: An Introduction to LISREL*, London: Sage.

Loukanova, P. and T. Bezlov (2007), 'Bulgaria', www.eu-employment-observatory.net/resources/reports/BulgariaUDW2007.pdf.

Luiselli, J., R.F. Putnam and M. Sunderland (2002), 'Longitudinal evaluation of behaviour support intervention in a public middle school', *Journal of Positive Behaviour Interventions*, **4**(3), 184–91.

MacAfee, K. (1980), 'A glimpse of the hidden economy in the national accounts', *Economic Trends*, **136**, 81–7.

MacDonald, R. (1994), 'Fiddly jobs, undeclared working and the something for nothing society', *Work, Employment and Society*, **8**(4), 507–30.

Maloney, W.F. (2004), 'Informality revisited', *World Development*, **32**, 1159–78.

Mason, C., S. Carter and S. Tagg (2008), *Invisible Businesses: The*

Characteristics of Home-Based Businesses in the United Kingdom, Glasgow: Working Paper No.1, Hunter Centre for Entrepreneurship, University of Strathclyde.

Massey, D. (2005), *For Space*, London: Sage.

Mateman, S. and P. Renooy (2001), *Undeclared Labour in Europe: Towards an Integrated Approach of Combating Undeclared Labour*, Amsterdam: Regioplan.

Mathias, B.D., S. Lux, T.R. Crook, C. Autry and R. Zaretzki (2014), 'Competing against the unknown: the impact of enabling and constraining institutions on the informal economy', *Journal of Business Ethics*, **127**, 251–64.

Mattera, P. (1985), *Off the Books: The Rise of the Underground Economy*, New York: St Martin's Press.

Mayo, E. (1933), *The Human Problems of Industrial Civilisation*, New York: Macmillan.

McBarnett, D. (2003), 'When compliance is not the solution but the problem: from changes in law to changes in attitudes', in V. Braithwaite (ed.), *Taxing Democracy: Understanding Tax Avoidance and Evasion*, Aldershot: Ashgate.

McCrohan, K., J.D. Smith and T.K. Adams (1991), 'Consumer purchases in informal markets: estimates for the 1980s, prospects for the 1990s', *Journal of Retailing*, **67**(1), 22–50.

McGee, R.W. (2005), *The Ethics of Tax Evasion: A Survey of International Business Academics*, paper presented at the 60th International Atlantic Economic Conference, New York, 6–9 October.

McGee, R.W. (2008), *Taxation and Public Finance in Transition and Developing Countries*, New York: Springer.

McGee, R.W., J. Alver and L. Alver (2008), 'The ethics of tax evasion: a survey of Estonian Opinion' in R.W. McGee (ed.), *Taxation and Public Finance in Transition and Developing Countries*, Berlin: Springer, pp. 119–36.

Meagher, K. (2010), *Identity Economics: Social Networks and the Informal Economy in Nigeria*, New York: James Currey.

Mehrotra, S. and M. Biggeri (2007), 'Extending social insurance to informal wage workers', in S. Mehrotra and M. Biggeri (eds.), *Asian Informal Workers: Global Risks, Local Protection*, London: Routledge, pp. 400–52.

Meriküll, J. and K. Staehr (2010), 'Unreported employment and envelope wages in mid-transition: comparing developments and causes in the Baltic countries', *Comparative Economic Studies*, **52**(3), 637–70.

Meriküll, J., T. Rõõm and K. Staehr (2013), 'Perceptions of unreported economic activities in Baltic firms: individualistic and non-individualistic motives', in T. Vissak and M. Vadi (eds.), *(Dis)Honesty in Management*, Bingley: Emerald, pp. 85–125.

Merton, R. (1949), *Social Theory and Social Structure*, New York: Collier Macmillan.

Milliron, V. and D. Toy (1988), 'Tax compliance: an investigation of key features', *Journal of the American Tax Association*, **9**(1), 84–104.

Mogensen, G.V. (1985), *Sort Arbejde i Danmark*, Copenhagen: Institut for Nationalokonomi.

Mogensen, G.V., H.K. Kvist, E. Kfrmendi and S. Pedersen (1995), *The Shadow Economy in Denmark 1994: Measurement and Results*, Copenhagen: Study No. 3, Rockwool Foundation Research Unit.

Molero, J.C. and F. Pujol (2012), 'Walking inside the potential tax evader's mind: tax morale does matter', *Journal of Business Ethics*, **105**, 151–62.

Morissette, C. (2014), *The Underground Economy in Canada, 1992 to 2011*, Vancouver: Statistics Canada.

Morris, B. (1993), 'Editorial statement', *International Economic Insides*, vol. IV, Budapest: International Statistical Yearbook.

Morris, J. and A. Polese (2014), 'Introduction: informality – enduring practices, entwined livelihoods', in J. Morris and A. Polese (eds.), *The Informal Post-Socialist Economy: Embedded Practices and Livelihoods*, London: Routledge, pp. 1–18.

Muehlbacher, S., E. Kirchler and H. Schwarzenberger (2011a), 'Voluntary versus enforced tax compliance: empirical evidence for the "slippery slope" framework', *European Journal of Law and Economics*, **32**, 89–97.

Muehlbacher, S., C. Kogler and E. Kirchler (2011b), *An Empirical Testing of the Slippery Slope Framework: The Role of Trust and Power in Explaining Tax Compliance*, Vienna: University of Vienna Department of Economics Working Paper.

Müller, E. (2012), *Fair Play: Fairness zahlt sich aus*, lecture presented at the meeting of the Austrian Science Fund, Vienna, June.

Müller, K. and Miggelbrink, J. (2014), 'The glove compartment half full of letters: informality and cross-border trade at the edge of the Schengen area', in J. Morris and A. Polese (eds.), *The Informal Post-Socialist Economy: Embedded Practices and Livelihoods*, London: Routledge, pp. 151–64.

Murphy, K. (2003), 'Procedural fairness and tax compliance', *Australian Journal of Social Issues*, **38**(3), 379–408.

Murphy, K. (2005), 'Regulating more effectively: the relationship between procedural justice, legitimacy and tax non-compliance', *Journal of Law and Society*, **32**(4), 562–89.

Murphy, K. (2008), 'Enforcing tax compliance: to punish or persuade?', *Economic Analysis and Policy*, **38**(1), 113–35.

Murphy, K. and N. Harris (2007), 'Shaming, shame and recidivism: a test of re-integrative shaming theory in the white-collar crime context', *British Journal of Criminology*, **47**, 900–17.

Murphy, K., T. Tyler and A. Curtis (2009), 'Nurturing regulatory compliance: is procedural fairness effective when people question the legitimacy of the law?', *Regulation and Governance*, **3**, 1–26.

National Audit Office (2008), *Tackling the Hidden Economy*, London: National Audit Office.

Natrah, S. (2013), 'Tax knowledge, tax complexity and tax compliance: taxpayers' view', *Procedia: Social and Behavioural Sciences*, **109**, 1069–76.

Neef, R. (2002), 'Aspects of the informal economy in a transforming country: the case of Romania', *International Journal of Urban and Regional Research*, **26**(2), 299–322.

Nelson, M.K. and J. Smith (1999), *Working Hard and Making Do: Surviving in Small Town America*, Los Angeles: University of California Press.

Neuwirth, R. (2011), *Stealth of Nations: The Global Rise of the Informal Economy*, New York: Pantheon.

North, D.C. (1990), *Institutions, Institutional Change and Economic Performance*, Cambridge: Cambridge University Press.

Nwabuzor, A. (2005), 'Corruption and development: new initiatives in economic openness and strengthened rule of law', *Journal of Business Ethics*, **59**(1/2), 121–38.

O'Higgins, M. (1989), 'Assessing the underground economy in the United Kingdom', in E.L. Feige (ed.), *The Underground Economies: Tax Evasion and Information Distortion*, Cambridge: Cambridge University Press, pp. 175–95.

O'Neill, D.M. (1983), *Growth of the Underground Economy 1950–81: Some Evidence from the Current Population Survey*, Washington, DC: Study for the Joint Economic Committee, US Congress Joint Committee Print, US Government Printing Office.

OECD (2002), *Measuring the Non-Observed Economy*, Paris: Organisation for Economic Co-operation and Development.

OECD (2008), *OECD Employment Outlook*, Paris: Organisation for Economic Co-operation and Development.

OECD (2012), *Reducing Opportunities for Tax Non-Compliance in the Underground Economy*, Paris: Organisation for Economic Co-operation and Development.

OECD (2013), *Co-operative Compliance: A Framework from Enhanced Relationship to Co-operative Compliance*, www.oecd.org/ctp/administration/co-operativecompliance.htm.

Ofcom (2012), *The Communications Market 2012: Telecoms and Networks*, http://stakeholders.ofcom.org.uk/binaries/research/cmr/cmr12/UK_5. pdf.

Ojo, S., S. Nwankwo and A. Gbadamosi (2013), 'Ethnic entrepreneurship: the myths of informal and illegal enterprise in the UK', *Entrepreneurship and Regional Development*, **25**(7–8), 587–611.

Olssen, U.H., S.V. Troye and R.D. Howell (1999), 'Theoretic fit and empirical fit: the performance of maximum likelihood versus generalized least squares estimation in structural equations models', *Multivariate Behavioral Research*, **34**(1), 31–58.

Olssen, U.H., T. Foss, S.V. Troye and R.D. Howell (2000), 'The performance of ML, GLS, and WLS estimation in structural equation modeling under conditions of misspecification and non-normality', *Structural Equation Modeling*, **7**, 557–95.

Osbourne, D. (1993), 'Reinventing government', *Public Productivity and Management Review*, **16**, 349–56.

Oviedo, A-M., M.R. Thomas and K. Karakurum-Özdemir (2009), *Economic Informality: Causes, Costs and Policies – a Literature Survey*, Washington, DC: World Bank Working Paper No. 167.

Packard, T.G. (2007), *Do Workers in Chile Choose Informal Employment? A Dynamic Analysis of Sector Choice*, Washington, DC: World Bank Policy Research Paper No. 4232.

Paglin, M. (1994), 'The underground economy: new estimates from household income and expenditure surveys', *The Yale Law Journal*, **103**(8), 2239–57.

Pahl, R.E. (1984), *Divisions of Labour*, Oxford: Blackwell.

Park, T. (1979), *Reconciliation Between Personal Income and Taxable Income*, Washington, DC: Bureau of Economic Analysis.

Parker, C. (2013), 'Twenty years of responsive regulation: an appreciation and appraisal', *Regulation and Governance*, **7**(1), 2–13.

Parker, M. (2002), *Against Management*, Cambridge: Polity.

Parra-Medina, D., A. D'Antonio, S.M. Smith, S. Levin, G. Kirkner and E. Mayer-Davis (2004), 'Successful recruitment and retention strategies for a randomized weight management trial for people with diabetes living in rural, medically underserved counties of South Carolina: the POWER study', *Journal of the American Dietetic Association*, **104**(1), 7–75.

Pedersen, S. (1998), *The Shadow Economy in Western Europe: Measurement and Results for Selected Countries*, Copenhagen: Rockwool Foundation Research Unit.

Pedersen, S. (2003), *The Shadow Economy in Germany, Great Britain and Scandinavia: A Measurement Based on Questionnaire Surveys*, Copenhagen: Rockwool Foundation Research Unit.

Perry, G.E. and W.F. Maloney (2007), 'Overview: informality – exit and exclusion', in G.E. Perry, W.F. Maloney, O.S. Arias, P. Fajnzylber, A.D. Mason and J. Saavedra-Chanduvi (eds.), *Informality: Exit and Exclusion*, Washington, DC: World Bank, 1–20.

Persson, A. and H. Malmer (2006), *Purchasing and Performing Undeclared Work in Sweden: Part 1: Results from Various Studies*, Stockholm: Skatteverket.

Petersen, H.G. (1982), 'Size of the public sector, economic growth and the informal economy: development trends in the federal republic of Germany', *Review of Income and Wealth*, **28**, 191–215.

Pfau-Effinger, B. (2009), 'Varieties of undeclared work in European societies', *British Journal of Industrial Relations*, **47**(1), 79–99.

Phizacklea, A. and C. Wolkowitz (1995), *Homeworking Women: Gender, Racism and Class at Work*, London: Sage.

Pickhardt, M. and J. Sardà Pons (2006), 'Size and scope of the underground economy in Germany', *Applied Economics*, **38**(4), 1707–13.

Polese, A. (2014), 'Drinking with Vova: an individual entrepreneur between illegality and informality', in J. Morris and A. Polese (eds.), *The Informal Post-Socialist Economy: Embedded Practices and Livelihoods*, London: Routledge, pp. 85–101.

Pommerehne, W.W. and F. Schneider (1985), *The Decline of Productivity Growth and the Rise of the Shadow Economy in the US*, Aarhus: Working Paper 85-9, University of Aarhus.

Portes, A. (1994), 'The informal economy and its paradoxes', in N.J. Smelser and R. Swedberg (eds.), *The Handbook of Economic Sociology*, Princeton: Princeton University Press, pp. 142–65.

Portes, A. (1996), 'The informal economy', in S. Pozo (ed.), *Exploring the Underground Economy*, Kalamazoo: W.E. Upjohn Institute for Employment Research, pp. 147–165.

Pozo, S. (ed.) (1996), *Exploring the Underground Economy: Studies of Illegal and Unreported Activity*, Michigan: W.E. Upjohn Institute for Employment Research.

Prewitt, V. (2003), 'Leadership development of learning organisations', *Leadership and Organization Development Journal*, **24**(2), 58–61.

Prinz, A., S. Muehlbacher and E. Kirchler (2013), 'The slippery slope framework on tax compliance: an attempt to formalization', *Journal of Economic Psychology*, **40**(1), 20–34.

Putniņš, T. and A. Sauka (2015), 'Measuring the shadow economy using company managers', *Journal of Comparative Economics*, **43**(2), 471–90.

Rainey, H.G. and B. Bozeman (2000), 'Comparing public and private organizations: empirical research and the power of the a priori', *Journal of Public Administration Research and Theory*, **10**, 447–70.

Rainey, H.G. and J. Thompson (2006), 'Leadership and the transformation of a major institution: Charles Rossotti and the Internal Revenue Service', *Public Administration Review*, **66**, 596–604.

Ram, M., P. Edwards, M. Gilman and J. Arrowsmith (2001), 'The dynamics of informality: employment relations in small firms and the effects of regulatory change', *Work, Employment and Society*, **15**(4), 845–61.

Ram, M., P. Edwards and T. Jones (2002a), *Employers and Illegal Migrant Workers in the Clothing and Restaurant Sectors*, London: DTI Central Unit Research.

Ram, M., T. Jones, T. Abbas and B. Sanghera (2002b), 'Ethnic minority enterprise in its urban context: South Asian restaurants in Birmingham', *International Journal of Urban and Regional Research*, **26**(1), 24–40.

Ram, M., M. Gilman, J. Arrowsmith and P. Edwards (2003), 'Once more into the sunset? Asian clothing firms after the national minimum wage', *Environment and Planning C: Government and Policy*, **71**(3), 238–61.

Ram, M., P. Edwards and T. Jones (2007), 'Staying underground: informal work, small firms and employment regulation in the United Kingdom', *Work and Occupations*, **34**(3), 318–44.

Rani, U., P. Belser, M. Oelz and S. Ranjbar (2013), 'Minimum wage coverage and compliance in developing countries', *International Labour Review*, **152**(3–4), 381–410.

Reed, M. (1992), *The Sociology of Organisations: Themes, Perspectives and Prospects*, Hemel Hempstead: Harvester Wheatsheaf.

Renooy, P. (1990), *The Informal Economy: Meaning, Measurement and Social Significance*, Amsterdam: Netherlands Geographical Studies No. 115.

Renooy, P., S. Ivarsson, O. van der Wusten-Gritsai and R. Meijer (2004), *Undeclared Work in an Enlarged Union: An Analysis of Shadow Work – an In-Depth Study of Specific Items*, Brussels: European Commission.

Richardson, M. and A. Sawyer (2001), 'A taxonomy of the tax compliance literature: further findings, problems and prospects', *Australian Tax Forum*, **16**(2), 137–320.

Roberts, C. (2007), *Mixing Modes of Data Collection in Surveys: A Methodological Review*, Swindon: ESRC National Centre for Research Methods Briefing Paper.

Rodgers, P. and C.C. Williams (2009), 'The informal economy in the former Soviet Union and in central and eastern Europe', *International Journal of Sociology*, **39**(1), 3–11.

Rodgers, P. and C.C. Williams (2012), 'From market hegemony to diverse economies: evaluating the plurality of labour practices in Ukraine', *Journal of Economy and its Applications*, **2**(1), 66–84.

Roethlisberger, F.J. and W.J. Dickson (1939), *Management and the Worker*, Cambridge, MA: Harvard University Press.

Rogoff, K. (1998), 'Blessing or curse? Foreign and underground demand for euro notes', *Economic Policy: The European Forum*, **26**, 261–304.

Rohlf, W.D. (1998), *Introduction to Economic Reasoning*, London: Addison-Wesley.

Romero, J. and B.H. Kleiner (2000), 'Global trends in motivating employees', *Management Research News*, **23**(78), 14–17.

Rose-Ackerman, S. (1997), *Corruption and Development*, presented at Annual Bank Conference on Development Economics, World Bank, Washington, DC, June.

Round, J., C.C. Williams and P. Rodgers (2008), 'Corruption in the post-Soviet workplace: the experiences of recent graduates in contemporary Ukraine', *Work, Employment and Society*, **22**(1), 149–66.

Saeed, A. and A. Shah (2011), 'Enhancing tax morale with marketing tactics: a review of the literature', *African Journal of Business Management*, **5**(35), 13659–65.

Sander, C. (2003), *Less is More: Better Compliance and Increased Revenues by Streamlining Business Registration in Uganda*, a contribution to WDR 2005 on Investment Climate, Growth and Poverty, London: Department for International Development.

Sandford, C. (1999), 'Policies dealing with tax evasion', in E. Feige and K. Ott (eds.), *Underground Economies in Transition: Unrecorded Activity, Tax Evasion, Corruption and Organized Crime*, Aldershot: Ashgate, pp. 169–82.

Sassen, S. (1996), 'Service employment regimes and the new inequality', in E. Mingione (ed.), *Urban Poverty and the Underclass*, Oxford: Basil Blackwell, pp. 142–59.

Sasunkevich, O. (2014), 'Business as casual: shuttle trade on the Belarus–Lithuania border', in J. Morris and A. Polese (eds.), *The Informal Post-Socialist Economy: Embedded Practices and Livelihoods*, London: Routledge, pp. 135–51.

Sauka, A. and T. Putniņš (2011), *Shadow Economy Index for the Baltic countries 2009 and 2010*, Riga: Stockholm School of Economics in Riga.

Sauvy, A. (1984), *Le Travail Noir et l'Economie de Demain*, Paris: Calmann-Levy.

Schmölders, G. (1951/2), 'Finanzpsychologie', *Finanzarchiv*, **13**, 1–36.

Schmölders, G. (1960), *Das Irrationale in der öffentlichen Finanzwissenschaft*, Hamburg: Rowolt.

Schmölders, G. (1962), *Volkswirtschaftslehre und Psychologie*, Berlin: Reinbek.

Schneider, F. (1986), 'Estimating the size of the Danish shadow economy using the currency demand approach: an attempt', *The Scandinavian Journal of Economics*, **88**, 643–68.

Schneider, F. (1997), 'The shadow economies of Western Europe', *Journal of the Institute of Economic Affairs*, **17**(3), 42–8.

Schneider, F. (1998), *Further Empirical Results of the Size of the Shadow Economy of 17 OECD Countries Over Time*, Linz: Discussion Paper, Department of Economics, University of Linz.

Schneider, F. (2002), *Size and Measurement of the Informal Economy in 110 Countries Around the World*, paper presented at an Workshop of Australian National Tax Centre, ANU, Canberra, July.

Schneider, F. (2003), 'The shadow economy', in C.K. Rowley and F. Schneider (eds.), *Encyclopedia of Public Choice*, Dordrecht: Kluwer.

Schneider, F. (2005), 'Shadow economies around the world: what do we really know?', *European Journal of Political Economy*, **21**(4), 598–642.

Schneider, F. (2007), 'Shadow economies and corruption all over the world: new estimates for 145 countries', *Economics*, **9**, 1–45.

Schneider, F. (2009), 'Size and development of the shadow economy in Germany, Austria and other OECD countries: some preliminary findings', *Revue Economique*, **60**, 1079–116.

Schneider, F. (ed.) (2011), *Handbook on the Shadow Economy*, Cheltenham: Edward Elgar Publishing.

Schneider, F. (2013), *Size and Development of the Shadow Economy of 31 European and 5 Other OECD Countries from 2003 to 2013: A Further Decline*, www.econ.jku.at/members/Schneider/files/publications/2013/ShadEcEurope31_Jan2013.pdf.

Schneider, F. and D. Enste (2000a), *Schattenwirtschaft und Schwarzarbeit – Umfang, Ursachen, Wirkungen und wirtschaftspolitische Empfehlungen*, Munich: Oldenbourg.

Schneider, F. and D. Enste (2000b), 'Shadow economies: size, causes and consequences', *Journal of Economic Literature*, **38**(1), 73–110.

Schneider, F. and D. Enste (2002), *The Shadow Economy: Theoretical Approaches, Empirical Studies, and Political Implications*, Cambridge: Cambridge University Press.

Schneider, F. and C.C. Williams (2013), *The Shadow Economy*, London: Institute of Economic Affairs.

Schneider, F., A. Buehn and A. Montenegro (2010), 'New estimates for the shadow economies all over the world', *International Economic Journal*, **24**(4), 443–61.

Schwartz, R.D. and S. Orleans (1967), 'On legal sanctions', *University of Chicago Law Review*, **34**, 282–300.

Sedlenieks, K. (2003), 'Cash in an envelope: corruption and tax avoidance as an economic strategy in Contemporary Riga', in K-O. Arnstberg and T. Boren (eds.), *Everyday Economy in Russia, Poland and Latvia*, Stockholm: Almqvist and Wiksell, pp. 42–62.

Sepulveda, L. and S. Syrett (2007), 'Out of the shadows? Formalisation approaches to informal economic activity', *Policy and Politics*, **35**(1), 87–104.

Shaw, J., J. Slemrod and J. Whiting (2008), *Administration and Compliance*, London; Institute for Fiscal Studies.

Siqueira, A.C.O., J.W. Webb, and G.D. Bruton (2014), 'Informal entrepreneurship and industry conditions,' *Entrepreneurship Theory and Practice*.

Skatteverket (2006), *Purchasing and Performing Undeclared Work in Sweden*, Stockholm: Skatteverket.

Skatteverket (2012), *Medborganas synpunkter på skattesystemet, skattefusket och Skatteverkets kontroll: resultat från en riksomfattande undersökning våren 2012*, Stockholm: Skatteverket.

Slavnic, Z. (2010), 'Political economy of informalization', *European Societies*, **12**(1), 3–23.

Slemrod, J. (1992), 'Why people pay taxes: introduction', in J. Slemrod (ed.), *Why People Pay Taxes*, Ann Arbor, MI: University of Michigan Press, pp. 1–19.

Slemrod, J. (2007), 'Cheating ourselves: the economics of tax evasion', *Journal of Economic Perspectives*, **21**, 25–48.

Slemrod, J., M. Blumenthal and C.W. Christian (2001), 'Taxpayer response to an increased probability of audit: evidence from a controlled experiment in Minnesota', *Journal of Public Economics*, **79**, 455–83.

Small Business Council (2004), *Small Business in the Informal Economy: Making the Transition to the Formal Economy*, London: Small Business Council.

Smith, J.D. (1985), 'Market motives in the informal economy', in W. Gaertner and A. Wenig (eds.), *The Economics of the Shadow Economy*, Heidelberg: Springer, pp. 161–77.

Smith, K. and K. Kinsey (1987), 'Understanding taxpayer behaviour: a conceptual framework with implications for research', *Law and Society Review*, **21**, 639–63.

Smith, S. (1986), *Britain's Shadow Economy*, Oxford: Clarendon.

Snyder, K.A. (2004), 'Routes to the informal economy in New York's East village: crisis, economics and identity', *Sociological Perspectives*, **47**(2), 215–40.

Social Progress Imperative (2014), *Social Progress Index*, www.socialprogressimperative.org.

Sparrow, M. (2000), *The Regulatory Craft: Controlling Risks, Solving Problems, and Managing Compliance*, Washington, DC: Brookings Institution Press.

Spicer, M.W. and S.B. Lunstedt (1976), 'Understanding tax evasion', *Public Finance*, **31**, 295–305.

Stănculescu, M. (2002), 'Romania: households between state, market and informal economies', in R. Neef and M. Stănculescu (eds.), *The Social Impact of Informal Economies in Eastern Europe*, Aldershot: Ashgate, pp. 120–42.

Stapleton, D.C. (1978), 'Analyzing political participation data with a MIMIC model', *Sociological Methodology*, **15**(1), 52–74.

Strümpel, B. (1969), 'The contribution of survey research to public finance', in A.T. Peacock (ed.), *Quantitative Analysis in Public Finance*, New York: Praeger Press, pp. 12–32.

Sue, V. and L. Ritter (2007), *Conducting Online Surveys*, London: Sage.

Sutter, C.J., J.W. Webb, G.M. Kistruck, and A.V.G. Bailey (2013), 'Entrepreneurs' responses to semi-formal illegitimate institutional arrangements', *Journal of Business Venturing*, **28**(5), 743–58.

Swaminathan, H. and J. Algina (1978), 'Scale freeness in factor analysis', *Psychometrika*, **43**, 581–3.

Tafenau, E., H. Herwartz and F. Schneider (2010), 'Regional estimates for the shadow economy in Europe', *International Economic Journal*, **24**(4), 629–36.

Taiwo, O. (2013), 'Employment choice and mobility in multi-sector labour markets: theoretical model and evidence from Ghana', *International Labour Review*, **152**(3–4), 469–92.

Tanzi, V. (1980), 'The underground economy in the United States: estimates and implications', *Banca Nazionale del Lavoro*, **135**, 427–53.

Tanzi, V. (ed.) (1982a), *The Underground Economy in the United States and Abroad*, Lexington, MA: Lexington Books.

Tanzi, V. (1982b), 'A second (and more skeptical) look at the underground economy in the United States', in V. Tanzi (ed.), *The Underground Economy in the United States and Abroad*, Lexington MA: Lexington Books, pp. 38–56.

Tanzi, V. (1983), 'The underground economy in the United States: annual estimates, 1930–1980', *IMF Staff Papers*, **30**, 283–305.

Tanzi, V. (1986), 'The underground economy in the United States: reply to comments by Feige, Thomas, and Zilberfarb', *IMF Staff Papers*, **33**, 799–811.

Tanzi, V. and P. Shome (1994), 'A primer on tax evasion', *International Bureau of Fiscal Documentation*, June/July, 328–37.

Tedds, L.M. (2010), 'Keeping it off the books: an empirical investigation of firms that engage in tax evasion', *Applied Economics*, **42**(19), 2459–73.

Thomas, J.J. (1986), 'The underground economy in the United States: comment on Tanzi', *IMF Staff Papers*, **33**, 782–9.

Thomas, J.J. (1988), 'The politics of the black economy', *Work, Employment and Society*, **2**(2), 169–90.

Thomas, J.J. (1992), *Informal Economic Activity*, Hemel Hempstead: Harvester Wheatsheaf.

Thomas, J.J. (1999), 'Quantifying the black economy: "measurement without theory" yet again?', *Economic Journal*, **109**, 381–9.

Thompson, P. (1993), 'Fatal distraction: postmodernism and organization theory', in J. Hassard and M. Parker (eds.), *Postmodernism and Organizations*, London: Sage, pp. 27–49.

Thompson, P. and M. Alvesson (2005), 'Bureaucracy at work: misunderstandings and mixed blessings', in P. du Gay (ed.), *The Values of Bureaucracy*, Oxford: Oxford University Press, pp. 121–42.

Thurman, Q.C., C. St John and L. Riggs (1984), 'Neutralisation and tax evasion: how effective would a moral appeal be in improving compliance to tax laws?', *Law and Policy*, **6**(3), 309–27.

Tonoyan, V., R. Strohmeyer, M. Habib and M. Perlitz (2010), 'Corruption and entrepreneurship: how formal and informal institutions shape small firm behaviour in transition and mature market economies', *Entrepreneurship Theory and Practice*, **34**(5), 803–31.

Torgler, B. (2003), 'To evade taxes or not: that is the question', *Journal of Socio-Economics*, **32**, 283–302.

Torgler, B. (2005a), 'Tax morale in Latin America', *Public Choice*, **122**, 133–57.

Torgler, B. (2005b), 'Tax morale and direct democracy', *European Journal of Political Economy*, **21**, 525–31.

Torgler, B. (2006a), *Tax Compliance and Tax Morale: A Theoretical and Empirical Analysis*, Cheltenham: Edward Elgar Publishing.

Torgler, B. (2006b), 'The importance of faith: tax morale and religiosity', *Journal of Economic Behavior and Organization*, **61**(1), 81–109.

Torgler, B. (2007), 'Tax morale in Central and Eastern European countries', in N. Hayoz and S. Hug (eds.), *Tax Evasion, Trust and State Capacities: How Good is Tax Morale in Central and Eastern Europe?* Bern: Peter Lang, pp. 155–86.

Torgler, B. (2011), *Tax Morale and Compliance: Review of Evidence and Case Studies for Europe*, Washington, DC: World Bank Policy Research Working Paper 5922.

Torgler, B. (2012), 'Tax morale, Eastern Europe and European enlargement', *Communist and Post-Communist Studies*, **45**(1), 11–25.

Torgler, B. and F. Schneider (2007), *Shadow Economy, Tax Morale, Governance and Institutional Quality: A Panel Analysis*, Bonn: IZA Discussion Paper No. 2563, IZA.

Transparency International (2013), *Corruption Perceptions Index (CPI)*, www.transparency.org/research/cpi/cpi_2007.

TUC (2008), *Hard Work, Hidden Lives: The Short Report of the Commission on Vulnerable Employment*, London: TUC.

Tyler, T. (1997), 'The psychology of legitimacy: a relational perspective on voluntary deference to authorities', *Personality and Social Psychology Review*, **1**(4), 323–45.

Tyler, T. (2006), *Why People Obey the Law*, Princeton: Princeton University Press.

Tyler, T. and E. Lind (1992), 'A relational model of authority in groups', in M.P. Zanna (ed.), *Advances in Experimental Social Psychology*, Vol. XXV, San Diego, CA: Academic Press, pp. 115–91.

Tyler, T., L. Sherman, H. Strang, G. Barnes and D. Woods (2007), 'Reintegrative shaming, procedural justice and recidivism: the engagement of offenders' psychological mechanisms in the Canberra RISE drinking and driving experiment', *Law and Society Review*, **41**, 533–86.

United Nations Development Programme (2014), *Human Development Index and its Components*, http://hdr.undp.org/en/data.

Unnever, J., M. Colvin and F. Cullen (2004), 'Crime and coercion: a test of core theoretical propositions', *Journal of Research in Crime and Delinquency*, **41**, 2190–243.

US Congress Joint Economic Committee (1983), *Growth of the Underground Economy 1950–81*, Washington, DC: Government Printing Office.

Uslaner, E. (2007), 'Tax evasion, trust, and the strong arm of the law', in N. Hayoz and S. Hug (eds.), *Tax Evasion, Trust and State Capacities: How Good is Tax Morale in Central and Eastern Europe?* Bern: Peter Lang, pp. 187–225.

Vainio, A. (2012), *Market-Based and Rights-Based Approaches to the Informal Economy: A Comparative Analysis of the Policy Implications*, Oslo: Nordiska Afrijainstitutet.

van Eck, R. and B. Kazemeier (1985), *Swarte Inkomsten uit Arbeid: resultaten van in 1983 gehouden experimentele*, The Hague: CBS-Statistische Katernen No. 3, Central Bureau of Statistics.

Vanderseypen, G., T. Tchipeva, J. Peschner, P. Rennoy and C.C. Williams (2013), 'Undeclared work: recent developments', in European Commission (ed.), *Employment and Social Developments in Europe 2013*, Brussels: European Commission, pp. 231–74.

Varma, K. and A. Doob (1998), 'Deterring economic crimes: the case of tax evasion', *Canadian Journal of Criminology*, **40**, 165–84.

Venkatesh, S.A. (2006), *Off the Books: The Underground Economy of the Urban Poor*, Cambridge, MA: Harvard University Press.

Virta, H. (2010), 'The linkage between corruption and shadow economy size: does geography matter?', *International Journal of Development Issues*, **9**(1), 4–24.

von Schanz, G. (1890), *Die Steuern der Schweiz in ihrer Entwicklung seit Beginn des 19 Jahrhunderts, Vol I to V*, Stuttgart.

Vossler, C.A., M. McKee and M. Jones (2011), 'Some effects of tax information services reliability and availability on tax reporting behaviour', http://mpra.ub.uni-muenchen.de/38870.

Vu, T.T. (2014), *Institutional Incongruence and the Informal Economy: an Empirical Analysis*, paper presented at the European Public Choice Society meeting, Cambridge.

Wahl, I., B. Kastlunger and E. Kirchler (2010a), 'Trust in authorities and power to enforce tax compliance: an empirical analysis of the slippery slope framework', *Law Policy*, **32**(4), 383–406.

Wahl, I., S. Muehlbacher and E. Kirchler (2010b), 'The impact of voting on tax payments', *Kyklos*, **63**(1), 144–58.

Wallace, C. and R. Latcheva (2006), 'Economic transformation outside the law: corruption, trust in public institutions and the informal economy in transition countries of Central and Eastern Europe', *Europe-Asia Studies*, **58**(1), 81–102,

Warde, A. (1990), 'Household work strategies and forms of labour: conceptual and empirical issues', *Work, Employment and Society*, **4**(4), 495–515.

Watson, T.J. (2003), *Sociology, Work and Industry*, 4th edn, London: Routledge.

Webb, J.W., L. Tihanyi, R.D. Ireland and D.G. Sirmon (2009), 'You say illegal, I say legitimate: entrepreneurship in the informal economy', *Academy of Management Review*, **34**(3), 492–510.

Webb, J.W., G.D. Bruton, L. Tihanyi and R.D. Ireland (2013), 'Research on entrepreneurship in the informal economy: framing a research agenda', *Journal of Business Venturing*, **28**, 598–614.

Webb, J.W., R.D. Ireland and D.J. Ketchen (2014), 'Towards a greater understanding of entrepreneurship and strategy in the informal economy', *Strategic Entrepreneurship Journal*, **8**(1), 1–15.

Weber, M. (1978), *Economy and Society: An Outline of Interpretive Sociology*, Berkeley, CA: University of California Press.

Webley, P. and S. Halstead (1986), 'Tax evasion on the micro: significant stimulations per expedient experiments', *Journal of Interdisciplinary Economics*, **1**, 87–100.

Weck-Hannemann, H. (1983), *Schattenwirtschaft: Eine Möglichkeit zur Einschränkung der öffentlichen Verwaltung? Eine ökonomische Analyse*, Frankfurt: Bern.

Weck-Hanneman, H. and B.S. Frey (1985), 'Measuring the shadow economy: the case of Switzerland', in W. Gaertner and A. Wenig (eds.), *The Economics of the Shadow Economy*, Berlin: Springer-Verlag, pp. 142–65.

Weigel, R., D. Hessin and H. Elffers (1987), 'Tax evasion research: a critical appraisal and theoretical model', *Journal of Economic Psychology*, **8**(2), 215–35.

Wenzel, M. (2002), 'The impact of outcome orientation and justice concerns on tax compliance: the role of taxpayers' identity', *Journal of Applied Psychology*, **87**, 639–45.

Wenzel, M. (2004a), 'An analysis of norm processes in tax compliance', *Journal of Economic Psychology*, **25**(2), 213–28.

Wenzel, M. (2004b), 'The social side of sanction: personal and social norms as moderators of deterrence', *Law and Human Behaviour*, **28**, 547–67.

Wenzel, M. (2006), 'A letter from the tax office: compliance effects of informational and interpersonal fairness', *Social Fairness Research*, **19**, 345–64.

Wilkinson, A. and H. Willmott (1994), 'Introduction', in A. Wilkinson and H. Wilmott (eds.), *Making Quality Critical: New Perspectives on Organisational Change*, London: Routledge and Kegan Paul, pp. 140–65.

Williams, C.C. (2001), 'Tackling the participation of the unemployed in paid informal work: a critical evaluation of the deterrence approach', *Environment and Planning C*, **19**(5), 729–49.

Williams, C.C. (2004a), *Cash-in-Hand Work: The Underground Sector and the Hidden Economy of Favours*, Basingstoke: Palgrave Macmillan.

Williams, C.C. (2004b), 'Tackling the underground economy in deprived populations: a critical evaluation of the deterrence approach', *Public Administration and Management*, **9**(3), 224–39.

Williams, C.C. (2004c), 'Beyond deterrence: rethinking the UK public policy approach towards undeclared work', *Public Policy and Administration*, **19**(1), 15–30.

Williams, C.C. (2006a), *The Hidden Enterprise Culture: Entrepreneurship in the Underground Economy*, Cheltenham: Edward Elgar Publishing.

Williams, C.C. (2006b), 'What is to be done about undeclared work? An evaluation of the policy options', *Policy and Politics*, **34**(1), 91–113.

Williams, C.C. (2006c), 'Beyond the sweatshop: off-the-books work in contemporary England', *Journal of Small Business and Enterprise Development*, **13**(1), 89–99.

Williams, C.C. (2006d), 'Evaluating the magnitude of the shadow economy: a direct survey approach', *Journal of Economic Studies*, **33**(5), 369–85.

Williams, C.C. (2007a), *Rethinking the Future of Work: Directions and Visions*, Basingstoke: Palgrave Macmillan.

Williams, C.C. (2007b), 'Tackling undeclared work in Europe: lessons from a study of Ukraine', *European Journal of Industrial Relations*, **13**(2), 219–37.

Williams, C.C. (2008a), 'A critical evaluation of public policy towards undeclared work in the European Union', *Journal of European Integration*, **30**(2), 273–90.

Williams, C.C. (2008b), 'Evaluating public sector management approaches towards undeclared work in the European Union', *International Journal of Public Sector Management*, **21**(3), 285–94.

Williams, C.C. (2009a), 'Explaining participation in off-the-books entrepreneurship in Ukraine: a gendered evaluation', *International Entrepreneurship and Management Journal*, **5**(4), 497–513.

Williams, C.C. (2009b), 'Entrepreneurship and the off-the-books economy: some lessons from England', *International Journal of Management and Enterprise Development*, **7**(4), 429–44.

Williams, C.C. (2009c), 'Formal and informal employment in Europe: beyond dualistic representations', *European Urban and Regional Studies*, **16**(2), 147–59.

Williams, C.C. (2009d), 'Informal entrepreneurs and their motives: a gender perspective', *International Journal of Gender and Entrepreneurship*, **1**(3), 219–25.

Williams, C.C. (2010a), 'Beyond the formal/informal jobs divide: evaluating the prevalence of hybrid "under-declared" employment in South-Eastern Europe', *International Journal of Human Resource Management*, **21**(14), 2529–46.

Williams, C.C. (2010b), 'Spatial variations in the hidden enterprise culture: some lessons from England', *Entrepreneurship and Regional Development*, **22**(5), 403–23.

Williams, C.C. (2011), 'Reconceptualising men's and women's undeclared work: evidence from Europe', *Gender, Work and Organisation*, **18**(4), 415–37.

Williams, C.C. (2012a), 'Cross-national variations in the under-reporting of wages in South-East Europe: a result of over-regulation or under-regulation?', *The South East European Journal of Economics and Business*, **7**(1), 53–61.

Williams, C.C. (2012b), 'Explaining undeclared wage payments by employers in Central and Eastern Europe: a critique of the neo-liberal de-regulatory theory', *Debatte: Journal of Contemporary Central and Eastern Europe*, **20**(1), 3–20.

Williams, C.C. (2013a), 'Beyond the formal economy: evaluating the level of employment in informal sector enterprises in global perspective', *Journal of Developmental Entrepreneurship*, **18**(4), 1–18.

Williams, C.C. (2013b), 'Evaluating cross-national variations in the extent and nature of informal employment in the European Union', *Industrial Relations Journal*, **44**(5–6), 479–94.

Williams, C.C. (2013c), 'Evaluating the cross-national variations in under-declared wages in the European Union: an exploratory study', *The Open Area Studies Journal*, **5**, 12–21.

Williams, C.C. (2013d), 'Explaining employers' illicit envelope wage payments in the EU-27: a product of over- or under-regulation?', *Business Ethics: A European Review*, **22**(3), 325–40.

Williams, C.C. (2014a) *Confronting the Shadow Economy: Evaluating Tax Behaviour and Policies*, Cheltenham: Edward Elgar Publishing.

Williams, C.C. (2014b), 'Evaluating cross-national variations in envelope wage payments in East-Central Europe', *Economic and Industrial Democracy: An International Journal*, **36**(2), 283–303.

Williams, C.C. (2014c), 'Out of the shadows: a classification of economies by the size and character of their informal sector', *Work, Employment and Society*, **28**(5), 735–53.

Williams, C.C. (2014d), 'Explaining cross-national variations in the commonality of informal sector entrepreneurship: an exploratory analysis of 38 emerging economies', *Journal of Small Business and Entrepreneurship*, **27**(2), 191–212.

Williams, C.C. (2014e), 'Explaining cross-national variations in the size of the shadow economy in Central and Eastern Europe', *Debatte: Journal of Contemporary Central and Eastern Europe*, **22**(2), 241–58.

Williams, C.C. (2015a), 'Explaining cross-national variations in the scale of informal employment: an exploratory analysis of 41 less developed economies', *International Journal of Manpower*, **36**(2), 118–35.

Williams, C.C. (2015b), 'Out of the margins: classifying economies by the prevalence and character of employment in the informal economy', *International Labour Review*, **154**(3).

Williams, C.C. (2015c), 'Explaining cross-national variations in the informalisation of employment: some lessons from Central and Eastern Europe', *European Societies*, **17**(4), 492–512.

Williams, C.C. and A. Gurtoo (2012), 'Evaluating competing theories of street entrepreneurship: some lessons from Bangalore, India', *International Entrepreneurship and Management Journal*, **8**(4), 391–409.

Williams, C.C. and M. Lansky (2013), 'Informal employment in developed and emerging economies: perspectives and policy responses', *International Labour Review*, **152**(3–4), 355–80.

Williams, C.C. and A. Martinez-Perez (2014a), 'Is the informal economy an incubator for new enterprise creation? A gender perspective', *International Journal of Entrepreneurial Behaviour and Research*, **20**(1), 4–19.

Williams, C.C. and A. Martinez-Perez (2014b), 'Why do consumers purchase goods and services in the informal economy?', *Journal of Business Research*, **67**(5), 802–6.

Williams, C.C. and A. Martinez-Perez (2014c), 'Do small business start-ups test-trade in the informal economy? Evidence from a UK small business survey', *International Journal of Entrepreneurship and Small Business*, **22**(1), 1–16.

Williams, C.C. and A. Martinez-Perez (2014d), 'Explaining cross-national variations in tax morality in the European Union: an exploratory analysis', *Studies in Transition States and Societies*, **6**(2), 5–18.

Williams, C.C. and S. Nadin (2012a), 'Entrepreneurship in the informal economy: commercial or social entrepreneurs?', *International Entrepreneurship and Management Journal*, **8**(3), 309–24.

Williams, C.C. and S. Nadin (2012b), 'Joining-up the fight against undeclared work in Europe', *Management Decision*, **50**(10), 1758–71.

Williams, C.C. and S. Nadin (2013), 'Harnessing the hidden enterprise culture: supporting the formalization of off-the-books business start-ups', *Journal of Small Business and Enterprise Development*, **20**(2), 434–47.

Williams, C.C. and S. Nadin (2014), 'Facilitating the formalisation of entrepreneurs in the informal economy: towards a variegated policy approach', *Journal of Entrepreneurship and Public Policy*, **3**(1), 33–48.

Williams, C.C. and P. Renooy (2013), *Tackling Undeclared Work in 27 European Union Member States and Norway: Approaches and Measures Since 2008*, Dublin: European Foundation for the Improvement of Living and Working Conditions.

Williams, C.C. and J. Round (2009), 'Evaluating informal entrepreneurs' motives: some lessons from Moscow', *International Journal of Entrepreneurial Behaviour and Research*, **15**(1), 94–107.

Williams, C.C. and M. Shahid, M. (2015), 'Informal entrepreneurship and institutional theory: explaining the varying degrees of (in)formalisation of entrepreneurs in Pakistan', *Entrepreneurship and Regional Development*.

Williams, C.C. and J. Windebank (1995), 'Black market work in the European Community: peripheral work for peripheral localities?', *International Journal of Urban and Regional Research*, **19**, 23–39.

Williams, C.C. and J. Windebank (1998), *Informal Employment in the Advanced Economies: Implications for Work and Welfare*, London: Routledge.

Williams, C.C. and J. Windebank (1999), 'The formalisation of work thesis: a critical evaluation', *Futures*, **31**(6), 547–58.

Williams, C.C. and J. Windebank (2001), 'Reconceptualising paid informal exchange: some lessons from English cities', *Environment and Planning A*, **33**(1), 121–40.

Williams, C.C. and J. Windebank (2003), 'The slow advance and uneven penetration of commodification', *International Journal of Urban and Regional Research*, **27**(2), 250–64.

Williams, C.C. and Y. Youssef (2013), 'Evaluating the gender variations in informal sector entrepreneurship: some lessons from Brazil', *Journal of Developmental Entrepreneurship*, **18**(1), 1–16.

Williams, C.C. and Y. Youssef (2014), 'Classifying Latin American economies: a degrees of informalisation approach', *International Journal of Business Administration*, **5**(3), 73–85.

Williams, C.C., S. Nadin, A. Barbour and M. Llanes (2012a), *Enabling Enterprise: Tackling the Barriers to Formalisation*, London: Community Links.

Williams, C.C., S. Nadin and P. Rodgers (2012b), 'Evaluating competing theories of informal entrepreneurship: some lessons from Ukraine', *International Journal of Entrepreneurial Behaviour and Research*, **18**(5), 528–43.

Williams, C.C., S. Nadin and J. Windebank (2012c), 'How much for cash? Tackling the cash-in-hand culture in the European property and construction sector', *Journal of Financial Management of Property and Construction*, **17**(2), 123–34.

Williams, C.C., J. Round and P. Rodgers (2013a), *The Role of Informal Economies in the Post-Soviet World: The End of Transition?* London: Routledge.

Williams, C.C., J. Windebank, M. Baric and S. Nadin (2013b), 'Public policy innovations: the case of undeclared work', *Management Decision*, **51**(6), 1161–75.

Williams, N. and T. Vorley (2014), 'Institutional asymmetry: how formal and informal institutions affect entrepreneurship in Bulgaria', *International Small Business Journal*.

Witte, A.D. and D.F. Woodbury (1985), 'The effect of tax laws and tax administration on tax compliance: the case of US individual income tax', *National Tax Journal*, **38**, 1–15.

Wood, C., M. Ivec, J. Job and V. Braithwaite (2010), *Applications of Responsive Regulatory Theory in Australia and Overseas*, Canberra: Occasional Paper No. 15, Regulatory Institutions Network, Australian National University.

Woolfson, C. (2007), 'Pushing the envelope: the "informalization" of labour in post-communist new EU member states', *Work, Employment and Society*, **21**, 551–64.

World Bank (2013), *World Development Indicators*, Washington, DC: World Bank, http://data.worldbank.org/data-catalog/world-development-indicators.

World Bank (2014), *World Bank Enterprise Surveys*, www.enterprise-surveys.org.

Yamada, G. (1996), 'Urban informal employment and self-employment in developing countries: theory and evidence', *Economic Development and Cultural Change*, **44**(2), 244–66.

Žabko, O. and F. Rajevska (2007), *Undeclared Work and Tax Evasion: Case of Latvia*, paper presented at colloquium of the Belgian Federal Service for Social Security on 'Undeclared Work, Tax Evasion and Avoidance', Brussels, June.

Zilberfarb, B.-Z. (1986), 'Estimates of the underground economy in the United States, 1930–80', *IMF Staff Papers*, **33**, 790–98.

Zohar, D. and I. Marshall (2001), *Spiritual Intelligence: The Ultimate Intelligence*, London: Bloomsbury.

Zohar, D. and I. Marshall (2005), *Spiritual Capital: Wealth We Can Live By*, London: Bloomsbury.

Index

Abbott, K. 173, 174
accuracy, expenditure declaration,
    reliance on in indirect
    measurement methods 18–19
activity-based shadow economy
    definitions 5–6
    see also definitions
advertising
    awareness-raising campaigns 162–5,
        167
    restrictions for workers 8
Africa *see* individual countries
Ahmad, A. 120
Ahmed, E. 144, 167
Ahumada, H. 22, 23
Aigner, D. 26
Albania 70
Algeria 68
Allingham, M. 146
Alm, J. 147, 149, 157, 159, 166, 167, 174
Alon, A. 166
Alvesson, M. 141, 142
Amin, A. 120
Andreoni, J. 149, 159, 160
Andrews, D. 7, 11
Angola 67
anonymity reassurances 47
    see also direct survey methods
Apel, M. 18
Argentina 69, 111
Armenia 70, 111
Arnold, R. 97, 99, 119
Australia
    relative impact of shadow economy
        84, 85, 92
    responsive regulation approach 167,
        174
    shadow economy size 64, 66, 75
Austria
    extent and nature of shadow
        economy 124, 125

relative impact of shadow economy
    83, 84, 85, 87–8
shadow economy size 18, 64, 66, 74,
    75
tax education 162, 175, 176
Autio, E. 7–8, 139
awareness-raising campaigns 162–5,
    167
    see also policy approaches, future
Ayres, I. 147, 166
Azerbaijan 70

Bàculo, L. 39, 40, 41
Bahamas 68
Bahrain 69
Bajada, C. 7, 11, 41, 74
Baldry, J. 147–8
Bangladesh 68
Barbour, A. 8, 9, 10
Bardasi, E. 105
Baumol, W. 157
Bazart, C. 174
Becker, G. 146
Becker, K. 102, 121
Belarus 70
Belgium
    employment relations system 126
    extent and nature of shadow
        employment 124, 125
    relative impact of shadow economy
        83, 84, 85
    shadow economy size 40, 66, 75
Belize 67
Bell, D. 142
benefits of working formally, raising
    awareness of 162–4
    see also policy approaches, future
Benin 67
Bernasconi, M. 146
Beron, K. 147
Bethlehem, J. 50, 53